W9-DHG-902

Library of Shakespearean Biography and Criticism

Library of Shakespearean Biography and Criticism

Series III, Part A

More Talking of Shakespeare

Library of Shakespearean Biography and Criticism

More Talking of Shakespeare

EDITED BY JOHN GARRETT

 BOOKS FOR LIBRARIES PRESS
FREEPORT, NEW YORK

INTERNATIONAL STANDARD BOOK NUMBER:
0-8369-5507-2

LIBRARY OF CONGRESS CATALOG CARD NUMBER:
73-128887

PRINTED IN THE UNITED STATES OF AMERICA

CONTENTS

FOREWORD

THE twelve lectures brought together in this volume have nothing more in common than the fact that they were delivered at the Shakespeare Memorial Theatre's Summer Schools on Shakespeare between the years 1954 and 1958. These courses are designed primarily to serve as stimulus and refreshment for teachers whose responsibility it is to introduce young people in schools, colleges and other places of learning to Shakespeare, and to make available to them some of the fruits of contemporary scholarship in their particular field of study. If by becoming themselves excited by the performances of the plays in the theatre, they can make their pupils enthusiastic to see the plays on the stage as opposed only to studying them as texts in the classroom, so much the better. As no particular theme is imposed on any course, it follows that no pattern or continuity is apparent in this volume. Each lecture stands on its own merit and has been selected for no better reason than that it made immediate impact when it was delivered, provoked discussion, and seemed to merit a more permanent form than the ephemeral life of the spoken word. A first volume of these Stratford lectures was published in 1954, under the title *Talking of Shakespeare*. Here is more talking of Shakespeare. It is hoped that it will give pleasure and profit.

JOHN GARRETT

I

WAGS, CLOWNS AND JESTERS

by NEVILL COGHILL

AMONG the less exalted orders of the Shakespearian populace there are three that tend to shade off into a kind of class, whose main functions, mannerisms and idiosyncrasies are easy to recognize, though they tend to merge and mingle, or at least to overlap: they are the Wags, the Clowns and the Jesters.

Mainly they are meant to be funny, whether as wits or butts or both: but they have other functions and qualities too. Time has dealt unkindly with many of their jokes, and some have not survived the footnotes that expound them. Not their jokes only, but their very being, in some cases, may call for explanation. We still meet with rustics in the modern world, with clown-policemen and bull-calf recruits; a yokel needs no footnote. But where are now the pert boys whom Shakespeare shows us paging their young masters from Verona to Milan, from Pisa to Padua, and throwing out a barrage of waggery in choplogic, cross-purpose, paronomasia and arch comment upon the love-affairs of their betters? And where are the professional fools, those privileged jesters, men like Will Sommers, who called Henry VIII 'Harry' to his face, and could make him roar with laughter on damp days?

Some pictures of the Jesters remain. Richard Tarlton was a snub-nosed smiler, with wide-set eyes, a curly moustache and a little chin-beard; he could play tabor and pipe together, a difficult art. Watteau has left us the melancholy face of Gilles, Court Jester to the King of France, and there is, I learn from Professor Davis, an epitaph in Beckley Church, to the last of all the Jesters, Dicky Pearce, the Earl of Suffolk's Fool, who died in 1728. It is ascribed, for what good reason I do not know, to Jonathan Swift:

> Here lies the Earl of Suffolk's Fool
> Men call'd him Dicky Pearce:
> His folly served to make men laugh
> When wit and mirth were scarce.

I

> Poor Dick, alas! is dead and gone,
> What signifies to cry?
> Dickys enough are left behind
> To laugh at by and by.[1]

Wags and Jesters are now denizens of a museum world and there they lead their fancy-dress existence; it may well be that this is a factor which helps us to achieve that never-never-landish state of mind suited to a comedy of Shakespeare's golden world, a state in which it is easy to cross the frontiers of Illyria or Arden, and bid lullaby to our social consciences for an hour or two, for the refreshment of their foolery.

What a fantastic foolery it is! It has an extravagance in which, for once, Ben Jonson has outdone Shakespeare, who has nothing to match the macabre trinity of twisted creatures or grotesques, Nano the dwarf, Castrone the Eunuch, and Androgyno the Man-Woman, who are Volpone's household monsters, his kept Fools. Each of them is a museum piece, a creature of great rarity, quaintness and cost: their collective function in the play is more than that of entertaining their master: it is to appear as further items in, and emblems of, his inordinate wealth and connoisseurship. They are the *trouvailles* of a collector.

When we first meet with them, whether in the text or on the stage, we have to open our mouths wide to swallow them; we teach ourselves to accept them as a deliberately stomach-turning Jonsonian hyperbole, in scale with the huge scope of his satire, with the allegorical stature of Volpone himself. And yet I can recall a paragraph in a newspaper, at the time when Benito Mussolini was waging war in Abyssinia: it described the vast and curious wealth of a certain Abyssinian Prince, Ras Tafari, a cousin of the Emperor. Among his more fabulous possessions, he also kept a little human zoo; it contained a monk, a eunuch and a hermaphrodite. It would seem that Ben Jonson's fantasies are not entirely out of this world.

Half-wittedness, deformity and abnormality, seem to have been (historically speaking) the usual qualifications for the Fools or 'naturals' that, from time to time, were kept for a whim, or for the amusement of great households—a use for the village idiot.

At what time cunning, intelligence and talent took over from cretinism in the making of the Court Fool, it is hard to say. The Fool by Nature and the Fool by Art have always existed, and which is the more in vogue will depend on the taste of the age. In a civilized Court,

---

[1] Samuel Palmer, *Epitaphs and Epigrams* (London 1869).

like that of Richard II, we find that entertainment came from poets like Chaucer and Gower, and from tregetours such as those we read of in the *Franklin's Tale*. In a semi-barbarous Court, like that of Henry VIII, we find Will Sommers. It is hard to understand how educated people could relish the company of a freak of nature, and keep him, so to speak, as a pet. Shakespeare lifted the whole company of such Fools out of the slough of imbecility; his jesters have wit, pithiness; they can dance and sing and extemporize, their presence has point. It seems to say 'as, in the midst of life, we are in death, so, in the midst of sanity, we are in folly'.

But no actual Tudor Fool I ever heard of had such gift or quality. A good loud laugh or an agreeable gibe was as much as could be hoped for from Sommers, or even perhaps from Tarlton, except when he took to his tabor and pipe. If Will Sommers had no better jokes than those that Armin records of him, what are we to think of the taste and intelligence of Henry VIII?

We read in Armin's *Nest of Ninnies*, that the king, when sad, would cheer himself up by rhyming and riddling with this melancholy moron. The stooping, hollow-eyed figure would squinny at his monarch: ' "Now tell me," says Will, "if you can, what it is that, being borne without life, head, lippe or eye, yet doth runne roaring through the world until it dye?" "That is a wonder," quoth the King, "and no question; I know it not." "Why," quoth Will, "it is a fart." At this the King laught hartely and was exceeding merry.'

Richard Tarlton's verbal gifts seem to have been very little better, such, at least, as have come down to us in *Tarlton's Jests* and *News Out of Purgatory*; yet Fuller tells us that, 'when Queen Elisabeth was serious, dare not say sullen, and out of humour, he could undumpish her at his pleasure'. But he brought a frown to her face when he said of Sir Walter Raleigh, 'See, the Knave commands the Queen.' He was famous for his powers of extemporal rhyme, like Touchstone: but alas his published vein is no better than what one would expect to find in a ballad sold at a fair by Autolycus. Here is a sample:

> By rushing rivers late,
>   In Bedford town, no nay,
> Ful many a woeful state
>   May yeeld to fast and pray.
>
> At twelve oclock at night
>   It flowed with such a hed,

Yea, many a woful wight
Did swim in naked bed

Among the rest there was
A woful widow sure,
Whome God did bring to passe
The death she did procure.

Widow Spencer by name
A sleep she being fast,
The flood so rashly came
That she aloft was cast.

Which seeing started up,
Regarding small her pelf
She left beside her bed,
And so she drowned herself.[1]

And so on for thirty-six verses. Contrast them with Touchstone's lilting extemporizations:

If the cat will after kind,
So, be sure, will Rosalind. . . .

But before I go on to Shakespeare's imagination of Jesters, let me show you a few more authentic Tudor ones, for it is hardly possible to realize how much Shakespeare transfigured the whole tribe, if one does not know how raw his raw material was.

There was Jack Oates, Fool to a countrified knight.[2] Oates was a 'natural' given to almost senseless rages and jealousies whenever attention was paid to any entertainer other than himself. He broke a fiddle on a fiddler and beat up a bagpiper and burnt his bagpipes, not out of musical feeling, but out of envy. But his vendetta with the cook was crazier and more malicious. Sir William was particularly addicted to quince pies, and so, acting on an imperfectly thought-out plan to get the cook into trouble, Oates stole a quince pie. But it was too hot to hold, so the Fool jumped into the moat to cool it. Sir William's first reaction was to roar with laughter and sack the cook (presumably for having allowed the theft of the pie; he seems to have been almost as big a fool as Oates himself), but on learning that there was malice be-

---

[1] Tarlton's *Jests and News out of Purgatory*, ed. J. O. Halliwell, Shakespeare Society, 1844.
[2] See *Fools and Jesters*: with a reprint of Robert Armin's *Nest of Ninnies*, with an Introduction by J. P. Collier, Shakespeare Society, 1842

hind the incident, he 'bid the Cook enjoy his place againe'. Oates's best recorded joke is that he ran in to his master and some assembled guests, to announce that a country-wench in the servants' hall had eaten garlic, and seventeen men had been poisoned kissing her.

Then there was Jemy Camber, a fat Scotch dwarf, said to have been a yard and a nail high, and two yards round, with a small head, long hair, one ear bigger than the other, flaming eyes, a flat nose, a wide mouth, few teeth, short legs, pretty little feet and enormous hands. He seems to have been more butt than wit: ' "No," says Jemy, "the sun blowes very colde." "No," says the King, "the wind shines very hot." So simple hee was that he knew not whether it was the sunne or the winde made him sweat.'

Perhaps Edward Atienza had read this account of Jemy Camber in Armin's *Nest of Ninnies* when he contrived to perform Lavache in *All's Well That Ends Well* as a tubby dwarf—a miracle of costume, make-up and acting—at Stratford in 1955. There is, of course, no suggestion in Shakespeare that Lavache was a dwarf, but he is described as suffering from another inconvenience which he certainly shared with Jemy, namely a pressing sexual appetite.

'My poor body, Madam, requires it,' says Lavache when asking permission of the Countess to marry, 'if I may have your ladyship's good will to go to the world, Isbel the woman and I will do as we may.' Jemy Camber was sub-intelligent and could never so have expressed himself; nevertheless he got quite a long way towards seducing the laundress. She, however, was too much for him. She stuffed a heap of nettles under her bed; then, having lured him in beside her, she knocked the wall with her hand, as if someone were at the door. Jemy, terrified at being caught in the act, dived naked under the bed and found himself among the nettles.

One might think I had chosen my illustrations from specially oafish jests and jesters, but they are a disappointing lot; even Henry Pattensen, household Jester to Thomas More, was a crude-witted fellow; jokes about the size of a nose were about his level. Only More's charity can explain Pattensen's membership of the household.

What a world away from all such dolts and deformities are the Fools in Shakespeare! What a civilization breathes from Arden and Illyria, compared with what issues from Hampton Court! Armin's book shows us something of the actuality of Jesterdom, Shakespeare shows us jesters in the ideal, not what they were, but all they could never be.

Yet it was Armin who made this possible. Not his book, but himself, as an actor; *for* him, *through* him, Shakespeare created the witty Fool, the singing Fool, the fey, the tragic Fool. Armin joined Shakespeare's Company just before the turn of the century, in 1599; and from that moment began Shakespeare's vision of the Fool and his high art.

For the moment, however, let me return to the Wags and the Clowns. As I have already said, the three sub-categories of comic actor merge into one another in some of their tricks; what distinguishes the Wag is to strut along behind or beside his master. Some are blockish like the Dromios; some, like Launce and Speed, are fond of their own wit and ever ready to risk their bottoms for their tongues. The secret of their comedy is simple: word-play and horse-play. A good friendly knockabout or thrashing of the 'knock-me-on-the-door' style, for instance, is after all what everyone enjoys.

It may have been John Lyly who taught Shakespeare the dramatic charm of this master-to-boy relationship, from which it is so easy to create dialogue, catechism-wise when all else fails. Lyly's boys seem all to be in the top form of some Prep. School to Parnassus; they have been taught to utter in imagery. Here, for example, is young Half-penny, in *Mother Bombie*:

> HALFPENNY: Nay then, let me come in with a dream, short but sweet, that my mouth waters ever since I waked. Methought there sate upon a shelf three damask prunes in velvet caps and pressed satin gowns, like judges; and that there were a whole handful of currants to be arraigned of a riot, because they clung together in such clusters: twelve raisins of the sun were impannelled in a jury, and, as a leaf of whole mace, which was bailiff, was carrying the quest to consult, methought there came an angry cook, and gelded the jury of their stones, and swept both judges, jurors, rebels and bailiff into a porridge-pot; whereat I being melancholy, fetched a deep sigh that waked myself and my bedfellow.

This is excellent fooling. Youngest and smallest of Shakespeare's Wags, in a vein even more delicate and poetical, is Moth, servant to Don Adriano de Armado. Their happy sparring-partnership, so full of affectation, and, which is more, of affection, is a large part of the verbal magic of the play:

> ARMADO: Warble, child; make passionate my sense of hearing.
> MOTH (*singing*): Concolinel. . . .

ARMADO: Sweet air! Go, tenderness of years; take this key, give enlargement to the swain, bring him festinately hither; I must employ him in a letter to my love.

MOTH: Master, will you win your love with a French brawl?

ARMADO: How meanest thou? brawling in French?

MOTH: No, my complete master; but to jig off a tune at the tongue's end, canary to it with your feet, humour it with turning up your eyelids, sigh a note and sing a note, sometimes through the throat, as if you swallowed love by singing love, sometime through the nose, as if you snuffed up love by smelling love . . . with your arms crossed on your thin belly-doublet like a rabbit on a spit. . . . These are complements, these are humours, these betray nice wenches. . . .

ARMADO: How hast thou purchased this experience?

MOTH: By my penny of observation.

Lovely nonsense of this kind is a subliming of Lyly's dialogue, and indeed of the 'conceit' itself; the speakers feed each other with question and answer, and their relationship, of master and boy, is as if mellowed out of that between Sir Tophas and Epiton in Lyly's *Endymion*. An impudent variation of it is seen in Falstaff and his page:

FALSTAFF: Sirrah, you giant, what says the doctor to my water?

PAGE: He said, sir, the water itself was a good healthy water; but, for the party that owed it, he might have more diseases than he knew for.

This is a *visual* as well as a *verbal* use of the relationship—the enormous Falstaff, the infinitesimal page; verbally, it is amusing to see the first comic (might I say Dickensian?) use of the word *party* that I know of.

The main of Shakespeare's serving-boys are yokels in the egg, peasants like the Dromios, not gentry-pages like Moth; they are meant to be funny, not poetical; but they shade upwards socially, via Launce and Speed, to Biondello and to Tranio, who is well-enough bred to pass for his master Lucentio. But it would seem that there was a limit, even for Shakespeare, to what could be done with comic serving lads by way of stage effect; perhaps he found he was repeating himself; the soliloquies and name of Launce have much in common with those of Launcelot. The species seems to disappear from Shakespeare's work towards the turn of the sixteenth century; chronological order in this matter is not certain, but perhaps the last of the comic pages were the two imps who appear out of nowhere in the forest of Arden, sing, 'It was a lover and his lass . . .', and vanish as suddenly as they came.

B

But the Clown class goes right through Shakespearian comedy: and not only through the comedies, but through the histories and the tragedies. One of his first and most memorable is a tragic clown. He comes in at the height of the agony in *Titus Andronicus*, when the storm of passion is frothed with hysteria. Titus is as mad as the sea, but the tide is beginning to turn; hitherto he has only suffered, now he is beginning to act. As if to mark this moment, Shakespeare brings in a clown carrying a basket of pigeons, and the tension seems to be released a little; at last there will be something to laugh, or at least to smile, at. Titus mistakes the clown, in his crazy way, for a messenger from Jupiter: 'Shall I have justice? What says Jupiter?' 'Jupiter' however is a new word to the simpleton; he mixes it up, in baleful ignorance with 'Gibbet-maker': 'O! the gibbet-maker? He says he hath taken them down again for the man must not be hanged till the next week.' It is grim word-play, the beginning of Shakespearian malapropism, but grimmer is to come.

> TITUS: Why, didst thou not come from heaven?
> CLOWN: From heaven! alas! sir, I never came there. *God forbid I should be so bold to press to heaven in my young days.*

Could there have been, when this was first produced, experienced Shakespearian playgoers, they would have scented irony in airs such as these. Titus sends the fellow with a letter, demanding justice, to his enemy, the Emperor Saturninus: 'And when you come to him, at the first approach you must kneel; then kiss his foot; then deliver up your pigeons; and then look for your reward.' The simpleton moons off on his errand, the scene changes to the Emperor's court.

> TAMORA: How now, good fellow! wouldst thou speak with us?
> CLOWN: Yea, forsooth, an your mistership be emperial.
> TAMORA: Empress I am, but yonder sits the Emperor.
> CLOWN: 'Tis he. God and Saint Stephen give you good den.
> I have brought you a letter and a couple of pigeons here.
> (*Saturninus reads the letter.*)
> SATURNINUS: Go, take him away, and hang him presently.
> CLOWN: How much money must I have?
> TAMORA: Come, sirrah, you must be hanged.
> CLOWN: Hanged! By'r lady, then I have brought up a neck to a fair end.
> (*Exit, guarded.*)

Here is Shakespeare's first juxtaposition of madman, fool and death; his first use of comedy to heighten horror with surprise. The mention of Saint Stephen may put the fancy into one's mind that this clown is a first martyr to irony. But he has the last word: '*I have brought up my neck to a fair end.*' These effects are above what can be achieved with Wags. It is the *simplicity*, not the waggishness, of the clown that touches the scene with tragic feeling in its unique blend of lunacy and evil and rustic innocence.

Shakespeare's last tragic clown, if the clown that brings the asp to Cleopatra be he, is also a death-clown, also a simpleton; and in this case, that shimmers with ironies even more intense, his simpletonism is underlined by his attempts at waggery: 'You must not think I am so simple but I know the devil himself will not eat a woman.' He, too, has the last word in the interchange: 'I wish you joy of the worm.'

Apart from their vacuous innocence, these two tragic clowns have no 'character'. They do not need it. But most of the great clowns in Shakespeare are highly individual; they are among the most humanly perceived of all the members of their little worlds. One has only to think of Bottom and his companions.

It may be that we have to thank Will Kempe for this; we know, from the 1599 quarto of *Romeo and Juliet*, that he played Peter: from the Folio we know he played Dogberry too. If we unbridle our imagination a little, we may see him as a chief stimulus to Shakespeare's comic invention until Robert Armin took over from him, about 1599. Whatever quirks of individuality Shakespeare invented to give scope to the antics of Kempe, all the clowns have the great foundation-stone we have already noted, of simpletonism. Bottom is a simpleton who is also a genius. Suppose him, for a moment, anything but the pure innocent he is; suppose him a knowing wag; how intolerable would his relation with Titania become! But, as with the clown with the asp, such waggery as he has is the index of his innocence: 'And yet, to say the truth, reason and love keep little company together now-a-days. The more the pity, that some honest neighbours will not make them friends.' Bottom and the clowns of his class have, in their making, a hint of the aphorism of St Augustine that Langland quotes in *Piers Plowman*: '*Ecce ipsi idioti rapiunt celum, ubi nos·sapientes in inferno mergimur.*' See! very fools take Heaven by assault, where we, the wise, are sunk into the pit.

On this foundation of innocence, Bottom's genius as an artist is superimposed. I believe it was Mr J. B. Priestley who first noted that Bottom was essentially an artist, among companions whose only thought was for sixpence a day from the Duke. But Bottom cares

about *style*; he knows how to distinguish—'in the *true* performing'—
between the 'condoling' style of the lover and the cat-tearing manner
needed for the part of Ercles. His first thought is his make-up: 'Well,
I will undertake it. *What beard were I best to play it in?*' and he rattles off
half a dozen plausible alternatives from a glowing imagination. When,
later, problems in production arise, he overflows with exciting suggestions, and he rejects the proposal of Quince that the Prologue shall be
written in the trite metre of 'eight and six', preferring the full dignity
of octosyllabics: 'Let it be written in eight and eight.' Certainly style
is a great preoccupation with him, and inventiveness his special talent.
One would like to see a tapestry woven by Bottom the Weaver.

Dull and Elbow, the constables in *Love's Labour's Lost* and *Measure
for Measure*, are simpletons, both of them, too; but they have no
genius. They have character, however, far beyond what is needed for
their minimal plot-function. Dull is a model of obstinacy well-based in
ignorance. 'I said the deer was not a *haud credo*; 'twas a pricket,' he
asserts to Holofernes, and he can hold his own in a debate:

HOLOFERNES: . . . The allusion holds in the exchange.
     DULL: 'Tis true indeed; the collusion holds in the exchange.
HOLOFERNES: God comfort thy capacity! I say the allusion holds in the
          exchange.
     DULL: And I say the pollution holds in the exchange. . . .

Elbow, whose plot-function is the arrest of Pompey and Mistress
Overdone, is a product of the same constabulary, an adept in word-
mismanagement; but his endearing incompetence as an officer is used
not only to make us smile, but to show the patient tact of Escalus, who,
after a tiring morning with him and Pompey Bum, sees that Elbow
will have to be replaced and manages to make arrangements for this
without hurting his feelings. The patient justice and good feeling of
Escalus are, in turn, juxtaposed to the contemptuous attitude of
Angelo, who cannot be bothered with such matters and has left them,
with a sneer, to Escalus to handle. Thus the insufficiency of a comic
Constable is used by his creator to show the insufficiency of a protagonist.

The idea 'that out of the mouths of babes and sucklings hast thou
ordained strength', however, is more directly presented to us through
Dogberry, Verges and the Messina Watch in *Much Ado About Nothing*.
Once again we have a feast of malapropism and a good deal of ordinary
clowning ('We will rather sleep than talk; we know what belongs to a

Watch'); on top of that there is a sudden overflow of character in Dog-berry's last speech which instantly places him as a person—that is, as more than a Constable, in the social context of Messina: 'I am a wise fellow; and, which is more, an officer; and, which is more, a house-holder; and, which is more, as pretty a piece of flesh as any in Messina; and one that knows the law, go to; and a rich fellow enough, go to; and a fellow that hath had losses; and one that hath two gowns, and everything handsome about him.'

Pompey Bum, and his fellow-pander, Boult, in *Pericles*, are spirits of another sort, and yet the same actor may play them; they are in the Kempe tradition. To them are also allowed supererogatory moments of intimacy, brief glimpses of disarming candour, touches of grace. Pompey is brought to admit that his profession 'does stink in some sort': Boult, about to make the old and obvious joke about roses and prickles, suddenly stops short and says, 'O! sir, I can be modest.' Lysimachus retorts, 'That dignifies the renown of a bawd.'

Clowns make a class but Jesters are only a guild; that Shake-speare would ever have thought of that guild as a rich mine of drama without the advent of Robert Armin, seems unlikely. Yet his first Jester had been created some years before Armin replaced Kempe, and he sprang out of the Wag tradition, the tradition of the imp-servant in mischievous mood. It was Puck, court-fool to fairyland: 'I jest to Oberon, and make him smile. . . .'

The boy who played Moth could no doubt have played Puck too, but Touchstone is imagined for a matured actor: breathlessness and brio will carry Puck through his part, but Touchstone calls for timing. His lines are a study, an *étude*, for a professional, full of antitheses, alternatives, conditionals and qualifications: 'By my knavery, if I had it, then I were; but if you swear by that that is not, you are not fore-sworn; no more was this knight, swearing by his honour, for he never had any; or if he had, he had sworn it away, before he ever saw those pancakes or that mustard.' This and so many of his speeches depend for their effectiveness on infinitesimal changes of tone and tempo. Shake-speare seems to have discovered Armin's range gradually; it looks as if he did not at first know that he could sing, for the songs in *As You Like It* go to Amiens and the pages; but what he seized upon was the power of pulling off a set-piece in prose: and that means timing, and cadencing—the precise degree of emphasis required for the two demonstratives, for instance, *those* pancakes and *that* mustard. Touch-stone is a shallower, or at least a less complex character than Feste; he is the jester of prepared witticisms, the raconteur with a repertory. The story of Jane Smile, and the recital of the Seven Degrees of the Lie have evidently been made perfect by many previous repetitions. One feels he may even have tried out his dialogue with Corin on some previous occasion too, with some other shepherd, the reasons he gives fall so pat; court versus country was a stock debate, and Touchstone was prepared for it; indeed he initiates it. He is playing on home ground.

TOUCHSTONE: Wast ever in court, shepherd?
    CORIN: No, truly.
TOUCHSTONE: Then thou art damned.
    CORIN: Nay, I hope——
TOUCHSTONE: Truly, thou art damned like an ill-roasted egg, all on one side.
    CORIN: For not being at court? Your reason.
TOUCHSTONE: Why, if thou never wast at court, thou never sawest good
          manners; if thou never sawest good manners, then thy
          manners must be wicked; and wickedness is sin, and sin is
          damnation. Thou art in a parlous state, shepherd.

There is no bitterness in Touchstone: bitterness (mild though it be) in *As You Like It* is given to Jaques. Touchstone is there to be a blithe wit, and he knows it; he takes pleasure in it; he is a great exhibitionist. His name, no doubt, is chosen to tell his function—a debunker of romantic nonsense, whose triumphant common sense leads him to espouse Audrey. Jaques never made a worse guess than when he hazards that their loving voyage 'is but for two months victual'd'. An audience may well imagine it will outlast that of Rosalind and Orlando, even in that romantic world. Professor Hotson has reminded us that Armin had been apprenticed to a jeweller, and that may have given Shakespeare a hint for the Fool's name: for a touchstone is 'a piece of black quartz or jasper, used for testing the quality of gold and silver alloys, by the colour of the streak produced by rubbing them upon it'.

Feste does not seem to rely on set-pieces, but on extemporal wit; he has a repertory not of jokes, but of songs. He is a great reader of character; the first service he does for the audience in this regard is to make them realize that the Countess's 'mourning' for her brother is simply a mask she has assumed, in order to keep the Duke Orsino at arm's length. No one but Feste perceives this; he not only perceives it, but thinks the best way back into her favour is to tease her about the very man for whom she is so ostentatiously in grief:

FESTE: I think his soul is in hell, madonna.

COUNTESS: I know his soul is in heaven, fool.

FESTE: The more fool, madonna, to mourn for your brother's soul
being in heaven. Take away the fool, gentlemen.

COUNTESS: What think you of this fool, Malvolio? doth he not mend?

But a melancholy, not unlike the melancholy given to Jaques in *As You
Like It*, is in *Twelfth Night* allowed to tinge the wit of Feste; undaunted
co-operative jollity, such as we see in Touchstone, is exchanged for
touches of controlled, critical derision: 'Vent my folly! he has heard
that word of some great man, and now applies it to a fool; vent my
folly!' He is also coldly, wittily *mercenary*; no one ever hears Touchstone ask for money, but Feste is an adept:

CLOWN: Would not a pair of these have bred, sir?

VIOLA: Yes, being kept together and put to use.

CLOWN: I would play Lord Pandarus of Phrygia, sir, to bring a Cressida to
this Troilus.

VIOLA: I understand you, sir: 'tis well begg'd.

Above all he is malicious, a grudge-bearer, who has it in him to gird
at Malvolio, tormented and defeated as he has been; but the whirligig
of time brings its revenges even to Feste, for, at the end, he is left out of
things. When all the rest have moved off to the joyful *solemnitas* of
their journey's end, Feste, who has no Audrey to serve his turn, who
does not even seem to have a turn to serve, is left alone to sing his
melancholy song of the wind and the rain, the song he has in common
with the Fool in *Lear*. Feste seems to me the most complex of all the
Armin-Fools, the subtlest and bawdiest and coldest, the most attractive,
the most musical, the most talented; he has it in him to glitter in the
golden world, and yet to throw across it the long and deepening
shadow.

Having drifted into the romantic way of thinking about Touchstone
and Feste—as if they were real people, not characters in a play—let us
note that this is what the old magician so unfailingly contrives, and his
spell is a simple one; he gives his characters more character than they
actually need for the purposes of their play. This is the bamboozling
touch, that makes one think it is life, not a play; for in life the characters of men and women have similar surprises for us. Let us therefore,
for a moment, submit to the illusion, go the whole hog; the truth is
that Touchstone could easily become rather a bore, but Feste never.
You would be lucky if Feste even liked you. But then, of course, you

could always buy his liking—or a perfect imitation—and if you went on buying it, it would stay bought.

One has to try to keep one's head over Shakespeare's greatest Fool, the Fool in *Lear*; for, as Granville-Barker has warned us, it is possible to etherialize him to such a point that any actor would be a disappointment in the part. There are three things about him that differentiate him from all the other Jesters in the canon. First, he is a half-wit; that is, he is in the tradition of the 'natural' which, as we have seen, is the historic Tudor household-fool tradition, the village idiot taken into the family. Lear's Fool is an idiot of genius, just as Bottom is a simpleton of genius. Secondly he is a fierce critic of his master—no other 'allowed Fool' is allowed so much, because no other is a half-wit—and thirdly he is in total dependency on Lear; and this is also the effect of his native imbecility. He must be protected.

Lear's Fool thus does two things for an audience, both of which stem from his helpless, feeble-minded nature. It enables him to satisfy one of the strongest of an audience's wishes during Acts I and II, which is to hear someone give the insensate King a piece of their minds, for his treatment of Cordelia and trust of Goneril and Regan. It is true that Kent's gruff, bluff rebukes offer some expression to the indignation of an audience; but Kent cannot hit the King where it hurts most, because Kent's attack is *from outside*. Kent's attack can be repelled, and is so. Kent is banished. But the Fool is *inside*, under Lear's guard.

Because he is a helpless dependent, the Fool's attack cannot be repelled; he is inside Lear's armour, grafted to his compassion. He can, of course, be threatened with the whip, but what good is that? Lear would only be whipping himself for having heard and rebelled against the truth, as excellent a whipping as he advises later to the rascal beadle. The Fool's crazy versicles, riddles and proverbs sting Lear inwardly, and therefore give an 'I could have told you so' satisfaction to an audience; these are the satisfactions for which the Fool is so much beloved:

FOOL: The reason why the seven stars are no more than seven is a pretty reason.
LEAR: Because they are not eight?
FOOL: Yes, indeed: thou wouldst make a good fool.

The second great thing he does for us is to make visible the charity of Lear. This again is a consequence of the Fool's helplessness, of the *nuncledom* of their relationship.

Come on, my boy. How dost, my boy? art cold?
I am cold myself. Where is this straw, my fellow? . . .
Poor fool and knave, I have one part in my heart
That's sorry yet for thee. . . .

The action that must go with these lines makes one perceive the sincerity of Lear's prayer for the misery of others, the naked wretches, wherever they may be, that bide the pelting of the pitiless storm. His new-found charity and humbleness of heart are made manifest, are actable, are *seen*, in his tenderness towards the Fool. Seeing is believing.

That yet a fourth Fool, wholly different from all the others, and almost as dominating a figure, should have followed is one more example of a dramatic invention that seems never to repeat itself; the singing rogue-fool Autolycus, who has in his time been a gentleman and worn velvet, and is now reduced to the theft of lesser linen from farmers' wives, has to be considered. He is there to contribute an explosion of energy and rejuvenation at the very moment when *The Winter's Tale* needs the vigorous impulse of a new start. So he comes in singing, '*When daffodils begin to peer*'.

He has, of course, an infinitesimal part in the plot by which Camillo helps the escape of Florizel and Perdita; Florizel borrows his clothes. This could easily have been contrived in some other way, and it seems probable that Shakespeare made that rather mechanical use of Autolycus, to give countenance to his presence in the play, for a further, more significant purpose. Autolycus, it seems to me, is there not only for his energy but also for the stiffening of *roguery* he gives to what, without him, might have been indicted of pastoral sentimentality. Shepherd and shepherdess idealism and the pure airs of the country are all very well, but Shakespeare had always taken care to moderate such raptures. Silvius and Phoebe are brought to their senses even in Arden; Touchstone shows William off, and gets Audrey. One is kept down to earth. This earthiness is what Autolycus exists to provide, and with his earthiness he brings his country music; it has all the air of an Armin part.

Trinculo is the last and most deboshed of the race of Jesters. He is as different from those that preceded him as they are from each other; he seems only there to be bullied, to sink in the esteem of Caliban, to be jester to a drunken butler. He can just manage to sing a catch, but he seems to have no other talent; if he were not listed as 'a Jester' in the cast-list at the end of the play in the Folio, one might almost take him for a Clown, and a cowardly one. Unlike most of his fellow-fools in other plays, he has sunk into the sub-plot; he is even less than Lavache, the Fool in *All's Well*.

Trinculo, like the others, however, fits into his own play. Touchstone would have made rings round Caliban; Feste would have deserted Lear. Only Lavache, Jester to the old Countess of Roussillon, has moments which seem to qualify him for something better than his part and play. His actual function is to be a time-sandwich, that is, to keep a scene going which has no other purpose than to indicate a lapse of time between the scene before and the scene to follow, or to deliver a letter from one part of France to another. He has two or three creative touches lavished and lost upon him, for in spite of them he never comes into full view as a character. He builds no sympathy for Helena, as Lear's Fool does for Cordelia. He does little for the old Countess and nothing for Bertram. He is unimportantly rude to Parolles on two occasions, but whenever the play gets going, he is forgotten, or laid aside as not-for-the-moment necessary.

And yet this character which barely exists is given a lovely snatch to sing, one that deepens the enigma of what Shakespeare thought about the tale of Troy, which haunted him so long:

> Was this fair face the cause, quoth she,
>   Why the Grecians sacked Troy?
> Fond done, done fond,
>   Was this King Priam's joy?
> With that she sighed as she stood,
> With that she sighed as she stood,
>   And gave this sentence then;
> Among nine bad if one be good,
> Among nine bad if one be good,
>   There's yet one good in ten.

and he has one speech that rings strangely in the mouth of a jester: 'I am for the house with the narrow gate, which I take to be too little for pomp to enter; some that humble themselves may; but the many will be too chill and tender, and they'll be for the flowery way that leads to the broad gate and the great fire.'

'A shrewd knave and an unhappy' is Lafeu's wise comment on Lavache. He is an extreme example of what one finds in so many of Shakespeare's creations—there is more to them than they actually need for the plays in which they appear—they spill over into life.

2

'AS YOU LIKE IT'

by HELEN GARDNER

As its title declares, this is a play to please all tastes. It is the last play in the world to be solemn over, and there is more than a touch of absurdity in delivering a lecture, particularly on a lovely summer morning, on this radiant blend of fantasy, romance, wit and humour. The play itself provides its own ironic comment on anyone who attempts to speak about it: 'You have said; but whether wisely or no, let the forest judge.'

For the simple, it provides the stock ingredients of romance: a handsome, well-mannered young hero, the youngest of three brothers, two disguised princesses to be wooed and wed, and a banished, virtuous Duke to be restored to his rightful throne. For the more sophisticated, it propounds, in the manner of the old courtly literary form of the *débat*, a question which is left to us to answer: Is it better to live in the court or the country? 'How like you this shepherd's life, Master Touchstone?', asks Corin, and receives a fool's answer: 'Truly, shepherd, in respect of itself, it is a good life; but in respect that it is a shepherd's life, it is naught. In respect that it is solitary, I like it very well; but in respect that it is private, it is a very vile life.' Whose society would you prefer, Le Beau's or Audrey's? Would you rather be gossiped at in the court or gawped at in the country? The play has also the age-old appeal of the pastoral, and in different forms. The pastoral romance of princesses playing at being a shepherd boy and his sister is combined with the pastoral love-eclogue in the wooing of Phoebe, with the burlesque of this in the wooing of Audrey, and with the tradition of the moral eclogue, in which the shepherd is the wise man, in Corin. For the learned and literary this is one of Shakespeare's most allusive plays, uniting old traditions and playing with them lightly. Then there are the songs—the forest is full of music—and there is spectacle: a wrestling match to delight lovers of sport, the procession

17

with the deer, which goes back to old country rituals and folk plays, and finally the masque of Hymen, to end the whole with courtly grace and dignity. This is an image of civility and true society, for Hymen is a god of cities, as Milton knew:

> There let *Hymen* oft appear
> In Saffron robe, with Taper clear,
> And pomp, and feast, and revelry,
> With mask, and antique Pageantry.

The only thing the play may be said to lack, when compared with Shakespeare's other comedies, is broad humour, the humour of gross clowns. William makes only a brief appearance. The absence of clowning may be due to an historic reason, the loss of Kempe, the company's funny man. But if this was the original reason for the absence of pure clowning, Shakespeare has turned necessity to glorious gain and made a play in which cruder humours would be out of place. *As You Like It* is the most refined and exquisite of the comedies, the one which is most consistently played over by a delighted intelligence. It is Shakespeare's most Mozartian comedy.

The basic story is a folk-tale. The ultimate sources for the plots of Shakespeare's greatest tragedy and his most unflawed comedy are stories of the same kind. The tale of the old king who had three daughters, of whom the elder two were wicked and the youngest was good, belongs to the same primitive world of the imagination as the tale of the knight who had three sons, the eldest of whom was wicked and robbed the youngest, who was gallant and good, of his inheritance. The youngest son triumphed, like Jack the Giant Killer, over a strong man, a wrestler, joined a band of outlaws in the forest, became their king, and with the aid of an old servant of his father, the wily Adam Spencer, in the end had his revenge on his brother and got his rights. Lodge retained some traces of the boisterous elements of this old story; but Shakespeare omitted them. His Orlando is no bully, threatening and blustering and breaking down the doors to feast with his boon companions in his brother's house. He is brave enough and quick-tempered; but he is above all gentle. On this simple story Lodge grafted a pastoral romance in his *Rosalynde*. He made the leader of the outlaws a banished Duke, and gave both exiled Duke and tyrant usurper only daughters, as fast friends as their fathers are sworn enemies. The wrestling match takes place at the tyrant's court and is followed by the banishment of Rosalynde and the flight of the two

girls to the forest, disguised as shepherd and shepherdess. There the
shepherd boy is wooed by the gallant hero, and arouses a passion of
love-sickness in a shepherdess who scorns her faithful lover. The repentance of the wicked brother and his flight to the forest provide the
necessary partner for the tyrant's good daughter, and all ends happily
with marriages and the restoration of the good Duke. Shakespeare
added virtually nothing to the plot of Lodge's novel. There is no
comedy in which, in one sense, he invents so little. He made the two
Dukes into brothers. Just as in *King Lear* he put together two stories of
good and unkind children, so here he gives us two examples of a
brother's unkindness. This adds to the fairy-tale flavour of the plot,
because it turns the usurping Duke into a wicked uncle. But if he invents no incidents, he leaves out a good deal. Besides omitting the
blusterings of Rosader (Orlando), he leaves out a final battle and the
death in battle of the usurping Duke, preferring to have him converted
off-stage by a chance meeting with a convenient and persuasive hermit.
In the same way he handles very cursorily the repentance of the wicked
brother and his good fortune in love. In Lodge's story, the villain is
cast into prison by the tyrant who covets his estates. In prison he
repents, and it as a penitent that he arrives in the forest. Shakespeare
also omits the incident of the attack on Ganymede and Aliena by
robbers, in which Rosader is overpowered and wounded and Saladyne
(Oliver) comes to the rescue and drives off the assailants. As has often
been pointed out, this is both a proof of the genuineness of his repentance and a reason, which many critics of the play have felt the want of,
for Celia's falling in love. Maidens naturally fall in love with brave
young men who rescue them. But Shakespeare needs to find no
'reasons for loving' in this play in which a dead shepherd's saw is
quoted as a word of truth: 'Whoever lov'd that lov'd not at first sight.'
He has far too much other business in hand at the centre and heart of
his play to find time for mere exciting incidents. He stripped Lodge's
plot down to the bare bones, using it as a kind of frame, and created no
sub-plot of his own. But he added four characters. Jaques, the philosopher, bears the same name as the middle son of Sir Rowland de Boys
—the one whom Oliver kept at his books—who does not appear in the
play until he turns up casually at the end as a messenger. It seems possible that the melancholy Jaques began as this middle son and that his
melancholy was in origin a scholar's melancholy. If so, the character
changed as it developed, and by the time that Shakespeare had fully
conceived his cynical spectator he must have realized that he could not

be kin to Oliver and Orlando. The born solitary must have no family: Jaques seems the quintessential only child. To balance Jaques, as another kind of commentator, we are given Touchstone, critic and parodist of love and lovers and of court and courtiers. And, to make up the full consort of pairs to be mated, Shakespeare invented two rustic lovers, William and Audrey, dumb yokel and sluttish goat-girl. These additional characters add nothing at all to the story. If you were to tell it you would leave them out. They show us that story was not Shakespeare's concern in this play; its soul is not to be looked for there. If you were to go to *As You Like It* for the story you would, in Johnson's phrase, 'hang yourself'.

In an essay called 'The Basis of Shakespearian Comedy'[1] Professor Nevill Coghill attempted to 'establish certain things concerning the nature of comic form, as it was understood at Shakespeare's time'. He pointed out that there were two conceptions of comedy current in the sixteenth century, both going back to grammarians of the fourth century, but radically opposed to each other. By the one definition a comedy was a story beginning in sadness and ending in happiness. By the other it was, in Sidney's words, 'an imitation of the common errors of our life' represented 'in the most ridiculous and scornefull sort that may be; so that it is impossible that any beholder can be content to be such a one'. Shakespeare, he declared, accepted the first; Jonson, the second. But although *As You Like It*, like *A Midsummer Night's Dream*, certainly begins in sadness and ends with happiness, I do not feel, when we have said this, that we have gone very far towards defining the play's nature, and I do not think that the plot in either of these two lovely plays, or in the enchanting early comedy *Love's Labour's Lost*, which indeed has hardly any plot at all, can be regarded as the 'soul' or animating force of Shakespeare's most original and characteristic comedies. Professor Coghill's formula fits plays which we feel rather uneasy about, *The Merchant of Venice* and *Measure for Measure*. It is precisely the stress on the plot which makes us think of these as being more properly described as tragi-comedies than comedies. Neither of them is a play which we would choose as a norm of Shakespeare's genius in comedy. In *As You Like It* the plot is handled in the most perfunctory way. Shakespeare crams his first act with incident in order to get everyone to the forest as soon as he possibly can and, when he is ready, he ends it all as quickly as possible. A few lines dispose of Duke Frederick, and leave the road back to his throne

[1] *Essays and Studies* (English Association: John Murray, 1950).

empty for Duke Senior. As for the other victim of a wicked brother, it is far more important that Orlando should marry Rosalind than that he should be restored to his rights.

Mrs Suzanne Langer, in her brilliant and suggestive book *Feeling and Form*,[1] has called comedy an image of life triumphing over chance. She declares that the essence of comedy is that it embodies in symbolic form our sense of happiness in feeling that we can meet and master the changes and chances of life as it confronts us. This seems to me to provide a good description of what we mean by 'pure comedy', as distinct from the corrective or satirical comedy of Jonson. The great symbol of pure comedy is marriage by which the world is renewed, and its endings are always instinct with a sense of fresh beginnings. Its rhythm is the rhythm of the life of mankind, which goes on and renews itself as the life of nature does. The rhythm of tragedy, on the other hand, is the rhythm of the individual life which comes to a close, and its great symbol is death. The one inescapable fact about every human being is that he must die. No skill in living, no sense of life, no inborn grace or acquired wisdom can avert this individual doom. A tragedy, which is played out under the shadow of an inevitable end, is an image of the life pattern of every one of us. A comedy, which contrives an end which is not implicit in its beginning, and which is, in itself, a fresh beginning, is an image of the flow of human life. The young wed, so that they may become in turn the older generation, whose children will wed, and so on, as long as the world lasts. Comedy pictures what Rosalind calls 'the full stream of the world'. At the close of a tragedy we look back over a course which has been run: 'the rest is silence'. The end of a comedy declares that life goes on: 'Here we are all over again.' Tragic plots must have a logic which leads to an inescapable conclusion. Comic plots are made up of changes, chances and surprises. Coincidences can destroy tragic feeling: they heighten comic feeling. It is absurd to complain in poetic comedy of improbable encounters and characters arriving pat on their cue, of sudden changes of mind and mood by which an enemy becomes a friend. Puck, who creates and presides over the central comedy of *A Midsummer Night's Dream*, speaks for all comic writers and lovers of true comedy when he says:

> And those things do best please me
> That befall preposterously.

This aspect of life, as continually changing and presenting fresh

[1] Routledge, 1953.

opportunities for happiness and laughter, poetic comedy idealizes and presents to us by means of fantasy. Fantasy is the natural instrument of comedy, in which plot, which is the 'soul' of tragedy, is of secondary importance, an excuse for something else. After viewing a tragedy we have an 'acquist of true experience' from a 'great event'. There are no 'events' in comedy; there are only 'happenings'. Events are irreversible and comedy is not concerned with the irreversible, which is why it must always shun the presentation of death. In adapting Lodge's story Shakespeare did not allow Charles the wrestler to kill the Franklin's sons. Although they are expected to die, we may hope they will recover from their broken ribs. And he rejected also Lodge's ending in which the wicked Duke was killed in battle, preferring his improbable conversion by a hermit. But why should we complain of its improbability? It is only in tragedy that second chances are not given. Comedy is full of purposes mistook, not 'falling on the inventor's head' but luckily misfiring altogether. In comedy, as often happens in life, people are mercifully saved from being as wicked as they meant to be.

Generalization about the essential distinctions between tragedy and comedy is called in question, when we turn to Shakespeare, by the inclusiveness of his vision of life. In the great majority of his plays the elements are mixed. But just as he wrote one masterpiece which is purely tragic, dominated by the conception of Fate, in *Macbeth*, so he wrote some plays which embody a purely comic vision. Within the general formula that 'a comedy is a play with a happy ending', which can, of course, include tragi-comedies, he wrote some plays in which the story is a mere frame and the essence of the play lies in the presentation of an image of human life, not as an arena for heroic endeavour but as a place of encounters.

Tragedy is presided over by time, which urges the hero onwards to fulfil his destiny. In Shakespeare's comedies time goes by fits and starts. It is not so much a movement onwards as a space in which to work things out: a midsummer night, a space too short for us to feel time's movement, or the unmeasured time of *As You Like It* or *Twelfth Night*. The comedies are dominated by a sense of place rather than of time. In Shakespeare's earliest comedy it is not a very romantic place: the city of Ephesus. Still, it is a place where two pairs of twins are accidentally reunited, and their old father, in danger of death at the beginning, is united to his long-lost wife at the close. The substance of the play is the comic plot of mistakings, played out in a single place on a single day. The tragi-comic story of original loss and final restoration provides a frame. In what is probably his second comedy, *The Two Gentlemen of Verona*, Shakespeare tried a quite different method. The play is a dramatization of a *novella*, and it contains no comic place of encounters where time seems to stand still. The story begins in Verona, passes to Milan, and ends in a forest between the two cities. None of these places exerts any hold upon our imaginations. The story simply moves forward through them. In *Love's Labour's Lost*, by contrast, Shakespeare went as far as possible in the other direction. The whole play is a kind of ballet of lovers and fantastics, danced out in the King of Navarre's park. Nearby is a village where Holofernes is the schoolmaster, Nathaniel the curate, and Dull the constable. In this play we are given, as a foil to the lords and ladies, not comic servants, parasitic on their masters, but a little comic world, society in miniature, going about its daily business while the lovers are engaged in the discovery of theirs. Shakespeare dispensed with the tragi-comic frame altogether here. There is no sorrow at the beginning, only youthful male fatuity; and the 'putting right' at the close lies in the chastening of the lords by the ladies. The picture of the course of life as it appears to the comic vision, with young men falling in love and young women testing their suitors, and other men 'labouring in their vocations' to keep the world turning and to impress their fellows, is the whole matter of the play. Much more magical than the sunlit park of the King of Navarre is the wood near Athens where Puck plays the part of chance. Shakespeare reverted here to the structural pattern of his earliest comedy, beginning with the cruel fury of Egeus against his daughter, the rivalry of Lysander and Demetrius and the unhappiness of the scorned Helena, and ending with Theseus's over-riding of the father's will and the proper pairing of the four lovers. But here he not only set his comic plot of mistakings within a frame of sorrow turning to joy, he also set his comic place of encounters apart from the real world, the palace where the play begins and ends. All the centre of the play takes place in the moonlit wood where lovers immortal and mortal quarrel, change partners, are blinded, and have their eyes purged.

Having created a masterpiece, Shakespeare, who never repeated a success, went back in his next play to tragi-comedy, allowing the threat of terrible disaster to grow through the play up to a great dramatic fourth act. *The Merchant of Venice* has what *The Two Gentlemen of Verona* lacks, an enchanted place. Belmont, where Bassanio goes

C

to find his bride, and where Lorenzo flees with Jessica, and from which Portia descends like a goddess to solve the troubles of Venice, is a place apart, 'above the smoke and stir'. But it is not, like the wood near Athens, a place where the changes and chances of our mortal life are seen mirrored. It stands too sharply over against Venice, a place of refuge rather than a place of discovery. *Much Ado About Nothing* reverts to the single place of *The Comedy of Errors* and *Love's Labour's Lost*; and its tragi-comic plot, which also comes to a climax in a dramatic scene in the fourth act, is lightened not by a shift of scene but by its interweaving with a brilliant comic plot, and by all kinds of indications that all will soon be well again. The trouble comes in the middle of this play: at the beginning, as at the end, all is revelry and happiness. A sense of holiday, of time off from the world's business, reigns in Messina. The wars are over, peace has broken out, and Don Pedro and the gentlemen have returned to where the ladies are waiting for them to take up again the game of love and wit. In the atmosphere created by the first act Don John's malice is a cloud no bigger than a man's hand. And although it grows as the play proceeds, the crisis of the fourth act is like a heavy summer thunder-shower which darkens the sky for a time but will, we know, soon pass. The brilliant lively city of Messina is a true place of mistakings and discoveries, like the park of the King of Navarre; but, also like the park of the King of Navarre, it lacks enchantment. It is too near the ordinary world to seem more than a partial image of human life. In *As You Like It* Shakespeare returned to the pattern of *A Midsummer Night's Dream*, beginning his play in sorrow and ending it with joy, and making his place of comic encounters a place set apart from the ordinary world.

The Forest of Arden ranks with the wood near Athens and Prospero's island as a place set apart, even though, unlike them, it is not ruled by magic. It is set over against the envious court ruled by a tyrant, and a home which is no home because it harbours hatred, not love. Seen from the court it appears untouched by the discontents of life, a place where 'they fleet the time carelessly, as they did in the golden age', the gay greenwood of Robin Hood. But, of course, it is no such Elysium. It contains some unamiable characters. Corin's master is churlish and Sir Oliver Martext is hardly sweet-natured; William is a dolt and Audrey graceless. Its weather, too, is by no means always sunny. It has a bitter winter. To Orlando, famished with hunger and supporting the fainting Adam, it is 'an uncouth forest' and a desert where the air is bleak. He is astonished to find civility among men who

in this desert inaccessible,
Under the shade of melancholy boughs,
Lose and neglect the creeping hours of time.

In fact Arden does not seem very attractive at first sight to the weary
escapers from the tyranny of the world. Rosalind's 'Well, this is the
forest of Arden' does not suggest any very great enthusiasm; and to
Touchstone's 'Ay, now I am in Arden; the more fool I: when I was
at home, I was in a better place: but travellers must be content,' she can
only reply 'Ay, be so, good Touchstone.' It is as if they all have to
wake up after a good night's rest to find what a pleasant place they have
come to. Arden is not a place for the young only. Silvius, for ever
young and for ever loving, is balanced by Corin, the old shepherd, who
reminds us of that other 'penalty of Adam' beside 'the seasons' difference': that man must labour to get himself food and clothing. Still, the
labour is pleasant and a source of pride: 'I am a true labourer: I earn
that I eat, get that I wear, owe no man hate, envy no man's happiness,
glad of other men's good, content with my harm; and the greatest of
my pride is to see my ewes graze and my lambs suck.' Arden is not a
place where the laws of nature are abrogated and roses are without
their thorns. If, in the world, Duke Frederick has usurped on Duke
Senior, Duke Senior is aware that he has in his turn usurped upon the
deer, the native burghers of the forest. If man does not slay and kill
man, he kills the poor beasts. Life preys on life. Jaques, who can suck
melancholy out of anything, points to the callousness that runs through
nature itself as a mirror of the callousness of men. The herd abandons
the wounded deer, as prosperous citizens pass with disdain the poor
bankrupt, the failure. The race is to the swift. But this is Jaques's view.
Orlando, demanding help for Adam, finds another image from nature:

- Then but forbear your food a little while,
Whiles, like a doe, I go to find my fawn
And give it food. There is a poor old man,
Who after me hath many a weary step
Limp'd in pure love: till he be first suffic'd,
Oppress'd with two weak evils, age and hunger,
I will not touch a bit.

The fact that they are both derived ultimately from folk-tale is not
the only thing that relates *As You Like It* to *King Lear*. Adam's sombre
line, 'And unregarded age in corners thrown', which Quiller-Couch

said might have come out of one of the greater sonnets, sums up the
fate of Lear:

> Dear daughter, I confess that I am old;
> Age is unnecessary: on my knees I beg
> That you'll vouchsafe me raiment, bed, and food.

At times Arden seems a place where the same bitter lessons can be
learnt as Lear has to learn in his place of exile, the blasted heath. Corin's
natural philosophy, which includes the knowledge that 'the property
of rain is to wet', is something which Lear has painfully to acquire:

> When the rain came to wet me once and the wind to make me chatter, when
> the thunder would not peace at my bidding, there I found 'em, there I
> smelt 'em out. Go to, they are not men o' their words: they told me I was
> everything; 'tis a lie, I am not ague-proof.   .

He is echoing Duke Senior, who smiles at the 'icy fang and churlish
chiding of the winter's wind', saying:

> This is no flattery: these are counsellors
> That feelingly persuade me what I am.

Amiens's lovely melancholy song:

> Blow, blow, thou winter wind,
> Thou art not so unkind
> As man's ingratitude. . . .

> Freeze, freeze, thou bitter sky,
> That dost not bite so nigh
> As benefits forgot. . . ,

is terribly echoed in Lear's outburst:

> Blow, winds, and crack your cheeks! rage! blow!
> .   .   .   .
> Rumble thy bellyful! Spit, fire! spout, rain!
> Nor rain, wind, thunder, fire, are my daughters:
> I tax not you, you elements, with unkindness;
> I never gave you kingdom, call'd you children. . . .

And Jaques's reflection that 'All the world's a stage' becomes in Lear's
mouth a cry of anguish:

> When we are born, we cry that we are come
> To this great stage of fools.

It is in Arden that Jaques presents his joyless picture of human life, passing from futility to futility and culminating in the nothingness of senility—'sans everything'; and in Arden also a bitter judgment on human relations is lightly passed in the twice repeated 'Most friendship is feigning, most loving mere folly.' But then one must add that hard on the heels of Jaques's melancholy conclusion Orlando enters with Adam in his arms, who, although he may be 'sans teeth' and at the end of his usefulness as a servant, has, beside his store of virtue and his peace of conscience, the love of his master. And the play is full of signal instances of persons who do not forget benefits: Adam, Celia, Touchstone—not to mention the lords who chose to leave the court and follow their banished master to the forest. In a recent number of the *Shakespeare Survey* Professor Harold Jenkins has pointed out how points of view put forward by one character find contradiction or correction by another, so that the whole play is a balance of sweet against sour, of the cynical against the idealistic, and life is shown as a mingling of hard fortune and good hap. The lords who have 'turned ass', 'leaving their wealth and ease a stubborn will to please', are happy in their gross folly, as Orlando is in a love-sickness which he does not wish to be cured of. What Jaques has left out of his picture of man's strange eventful pilgrimage is love and companionship, sweet society, the banquet under the boughs to which Duke Senior welcomes Orlando and Adam. Although life in Arden is not wholly idyllic, and this place set apart from the world is yet touched by the world's sorrows and can be mocked at by the worldly wise, the image of life which the forest presents is irradiated by the conviction that the gay and the gentle can endure the rubs of fortune and that this earth is a place where men can find happiness in themselves and in others.

The Forest of Arden is, as has often been pointed out, a place which all the exiles from the court, except one, are only too ready to leave at the close. As, when the short midsummer night is over, the lovers emerge from the wood, in their right minds and correctly paired, and return to the palace of Theseus; and, when Prospero's magic has worked the cure, the enchanted island is left to Caliban and Ariel, and its human visitors return to Naples and Milan; so the time of holiday comes to an end in Arden. The stately masque of Hymen marks the end of this interlude in the greenwood, and announces the return to a court purged of envy and baseness. Like other comic places, Arden is a place of discovery where the truth becomes clear and where each man finds himself and his true way. This discovery of truth in comedy is made through errors and mistakings. The trial and error by which we come to knowledge of ourselves and of our world is symbolized by the disguisings which are a recurrent element in all comedy, but are particularly common in Shakespeare's. Things have, as it were, to become worse before they become better, more confused and farther from the proper pattern. By misunderstandings men come to understand, and by lies and feignings they discover truth. If Rosalind, the princess, had attempted to 'cure' her lover Orlando, she might have succeeded. As Ganymede, playing Rosalind, she can try him to the limit in perfect safety, and discover that she cannot mock or flout him out of his 'mad humour of love to a living humour of madness', and drive him 'to forswear the full stream of the world, and to live in a nook merely monastic'. By playing with him in the disguise of a boy, she discovers when she can play no more. By love of a shadow, the mere image of a charming youth, Phoebe discovers that it is better to love than to be loved and scorn one's lover. This discovery of truth by feigning, and of what is wisdom and what folly by debate, is the centre of *As You Like It*. It is a play of meetings and encounters, of conversations and sets of wit: Orlando versus Jaques, Touchstone versus Corin, Rosalind versus Jaques, Rosalind versus Phoebe, and above all Rosalind versus Orlando. The truth discovered is, at one level, a very 'earthy truth': Benedick's discovery that 'the world must be peopled'. The honest toil of Corin, the wise man of the forest, is mocked at by Touchstone as 'simple sin'. He brings 'the ewes and the rams together' and gets his living 'by the copulation of cattle'. The goddess Fortune seems similarly occupied in this play: 'As the ox hath his bow, the horse his curb, and the falcon her bells, so man hath his desires; and as pigeons bill, so wedlock would be nibbling.' Fortune acts the role of a kindly bawd. Touchstone's marriage to Audrey is a mere coupling. Rosalind's advice to Phoebe is brutally frank: 'Sell when you can, you are not for all markets.' The words she uses to describe Oliver and Celia 'in the very wrath of love' are hardly delicate, and after her first meeting with Orlando she confesses to her cousin that her sighs are for her 'child's father'. Against the natural background of the life of the forest there can be no pretence that the love of men and women can 'forget the He and She'. But Rosalind's behaviour is at variance with her bold words. Orlando has to prove that he truly is, as he seems at first sight, the right husband for her, and show himself gentle, courteous, generous and brave, and a match for her in wit, though a poor poet. In this, the great coupling of the play, there is a marriage of true minds. The other couplings run the gamut downwards from it, until we reach Touchstone's image of 'a she-lamb of a twelvemonth' and 'a crooked-pated, old, cuckoldy ram', right at the bottom of the scale. As for the debate as to where happiness is to be found, the conclusion come to is again, like all wisdom, not very startling or original: that 'minds innocent and quiet' can find happiness in court or country:

> Happy is your Grace,
> That can translate the stubbornness of fortune
> Into so quiet and so sweet a style.

And, on the contrary, those who wish to can 'suck melancholy' out of anything, 'as a weasel sucks eggs'.

In the pairing one figure is left out. 'I am for other than for dancing measures,' says Jaques. Leaving the hateful sight of revelling and pastime, he betakes himself to the Duke's abandoned cave, on his way to the house of penitents where Duke Frederick has gone. The two commentators of the play are nicely contrasted. Touchstone is the parodist, Jaques the cynic. The parodist must love what he parodies. We know this from literary parody. All the best parodies are written by those who understand, because they love, the thing they mock. Only poets who love and revere the epic can write mock-heroic and the finest parody of classical tragedy comes from Housman, a great scholar. In everything that Touchstone says and does gusto, high spirits and a zest for life ring out. Essentially comic, he can adapt himself to any situation in which he may find himself. Never at a loss, he is life's master. The essence of clowning is adaptability and improvisa-tion. The clown is never baffled and is marked by his ability to place himself at once *en rapport* with his audience, to be all things to all men, to perform the part which is required at the moment. Touchstone sustains many different roles. After hearing Silvius's lament and Rosa-lind's echo of it, he becomes the maudlin lover of Jane Smile; with the simple shepherd Corin he becomes the cynical and wordly-wise man of the court; with Jaques he is a melancholy moralist, musing on the power of time and the decay of all things; with the pages he acts the lordly amateur of the arts, patronising his musicians. It is right that he should parody the rest of the cast, and join the procession into Noah's ark with his Audrey. Jaques is his opposite. He is the cynic, the person who prefers the pleasures of superiority, cold-eyed and cold-hearted. The tyrannical Duke Frederick and the cruel Oliver can be converted; but not Jaques. He likes himself as he is. He does not wish to plunge into the stream, but prefers to stand on the bank and 'fish for fancies as they pass'. Sir Thomas Elyot said that dancing was an image of matrimony: 'In every daunse, of a most auncient custome, there daunseth together a man and a woman, holding eche other by the hande or the arme, which betokeneth concorde.' There are some who will not dance, however much they are piped to, any more than they will weep when there is mourning. 'In this theatre of man's life', wrote Bacon, 'it is reserved only for God and angels to be lookers on.' Jaques arrogates to himself the divine role. He has opted out from the human condition.

It is characteristic of Shakespeare's comedies to include an element that is irreconcilable, which strikes a lightly discordant note, casts a slight shadow, and by its presence questions the completeness of the comic vision of life. In *Love's Labour's Lost* he dared to allow the news of a death to cloud the scene of revels at the close, and, through Rosaline's rebuke to Berowne, called up the image of a whole world of pain and weary suffering where 'Mirth cannot move a soul in agony.' In the two comedies whose main action is motivated by hatred and with malice thwarted but not removed, *The Merchant of Venice* and *Much Ado About Nothing*, Shakespeare asks us to accept the fact that the human race includes not only a good many fools and rogues but also some persons who are positively wicked, a fact which comedy usually ignores. They are prevented from doing the harm they wish to do. They are not cured of wishing to do harm. Shylock's baffled exit and Don John's flight to Messina leave the stage clear for lovers and well-wishers. The villains have to be left out of the party at the close. At the end of *Twelfth Night* the person who is left out is present. The impotent misery and fury of the humiliated Malvolio's last words, 'I'll be reveng'd on the whole pack of you', call in question the whole comic scheme by which, through misunderstandings and mistakes, people come to terms with themselves and their fellows. There are some who cannot be 'taught a lesson'. In Malvolio pride is not purged; it is fatally wounded and embittered. It is characteristic of the delicacy of temper of *As You Like It* that its solitary figure, its outsider, Jaques, does nothing whatever to harm anyone, and is perfectly satisfied with himself and happy in his melancholy. Even more, his melancholy is a source of pleasure and amusement to others. The Duke treats him as virtually a court entertainer, and he is a natural butt for Orlando and Rosalind. Anyone in the play can put him down and feel the better for doing so. All the same his presence casts a faint shadow. His criticism of the world has its sting drawn very early by the Duke's rebuke to him as a former libertine, discharging his filth upon the world, and he is to some extent discredited before he opens his mouth by the unpleasant implication of his name. But he cannot be wholly dismissed. A certain sour distaste for life is voided through him, something most of us feel at some time or other. If he were not there to give expression to it, we might be tempted to find the picture of life in the forest too sweet. His only action is to interfere in the marriage of Touchstone and Audrey; and this he merely postpones. His effect, whenever he appears, is to deflate: the effect does not last and cheerfulness soon breaks in again. Yet as there is a scale of love, so there is a scale of sadness in the play. It runs down from the Duke's compassionate words:

> Thou seest we are not all alone unhappy:
> This wide and universal theatre
> Presents more woeful pageants than the scene
> Wherein we play in,

through Rosalind's complaint 'O, how full of briers is this working-day world', to Jaques's studied refusal to find anything worthy of admiration or love.

One further element in the play I would not wish to stress, because though it is pervasive it is unobtrusive: the constant, natural and easy reference to the Christian ideal of loving-kindness, gentleness, pity and humility and to the sanctions which that ideal finds in the commands and promises of religion. In this fantasy world, in which the world of our experience is imaged, this element in experience finds a place with others, and the world is shown not only as a place where we may find happiness, but as a place where both happiness and sorrow may be hallowed. The number of religious references in *As You Like It* has often been commented on, and it is striking when we consider the play's main theme. Many are of little significance and it would be humourless to enlarge upon the significance of the 'old religious man' who converted Duke Frederick, or of Ganymede's 'old religious uncle'. But some are explicit and have a serious, unforced beauty: Orlando's appeal to outlawed men,

> If ever you have look'd on better days,
> If ever been where bells have knoll'd to church. . . ;

Adam's prayer,

> He that doth the ravens feed,
> Yea, providently caters for the sparrow,
> Be comfort to my age!

and Corin's recognition, from St Paul, that we have to find the way to heaven by doing deeds of hospitality. These are all in character. But the God of Marriage, Hymen, speaks more solemnly than we expect and his opening words with their New Testament echo are more than conventional:

> Then is there mirth in heaven,
> When earthly things made even
> Atone together.

The appearance of the god to present daughter to father and to bless the brides and grooms turns the close into a solemnity, an image of the concord which reigns in Heaven and which Heaven blesses on earth. But this, like much else in the play, may be taken as you like it. There is no need to see any more in the god's appearance with the brides than a piece of pageantry which concludes the action with a graceful spectacle and sends the audience home contented with a very pretty play.

3

A CLASSICAL SCHOLAR LOOKS AT SHAKESPEARE

by H. D. F. KITTO

IF A classical scholar is asked to look at Shakespeare, and does it, let no state of rage and disappointment be declared if he sees no more than what is seen, perhaps more clearly, by everyone else. I am not come professing to bring any new ideas, and as I am no Shakespeare scholar there must be many excellent old ideas of which I am ignorant.

Both for my convenience and for yours, I am not going to look at the whole of Shakespeare. I shall say nothing about Greek comedy and Shakespearian comedy; and among the Shakespearian tragedies I am going to limit my view to *Hamlet* and the series of historical tragedies that begins with *King John* and ends with *King Richard the Third*. If I ventured into *Lear*, *Othello* and the rest, I think that the generalities I shall offer would be much the same, and I know that my task in organizing one single paper out of the more abundant material would have become much more difficult.

On turning from the Greeks to Shakespeare, one is at first impressed, naturally, by the differences between them—differences of style, structure, presentation; Shakespeare so varied, so rich, the Greeks so austere. Within the art of tragic drama, they seem to be the polar opposites. It might be extremely interesting to discuss these differences: Shakespeare with his freedom; the Greeks with their maximum of three actors, their omnipresent Chorus, and the famous Three Unities of which the neo-classics were so much more conscious than the classical dramatists themselves. But all this I shall pass over, except in so far as these differences may become relevant incidentally; I wish to discuss what is to me at least the much more interesting topic of their resemblances. The formal differences are relatively superficial.

Since what one sees whether in Shakespeare or in anything else depends very much on the point from which one looks, it is only fair that I should at once try to give you some rough idea of the point from which this particular classical scholar is looking, for not all Greek scholars look at Greek tragedy in the same way. Our lives would be duller if we did.

There is one major question, I think, that the interpretative critic of tragic drama must settle with himself before he ventures to hang out his sign: what balance was struck, in his judgment, by the dramatist between his preoccupation with individuals and particulars, and his preoccupation with universals? In Greek drama, this question involves our taking one of several possible views about the gods, who in one way or another play so large a part in it. We can say, at one extreme, that it is a grim drama of implacable Fate, one in which the human actors are little more than puppets, going through motions that omnipotent gods decree. A recent editor of the *Agamemnon*, taking this view, maintains that Paris, Agamemnon and the rest had no choice; all was decreed for them. To me, this is nonsense—and I claim credit for Hellenic restraint that to my word 'nonsense' I prefix no objurgatory epithets. I will not argue this; I am not defending, but only trying to indicate my own point of view. The opposite extreme is to give one's best attention to the individual characters—and they do indeed deserve and reward it; to admire the splendour of Clytemnestra or Antigone, to speculate about hidden motives and conflicts, to call Euripides' *Medea* 'a profound psychological study'—which in my opinion it isn't; and, doing all this, to treat the gods as an obligatory religious appanage to what was, *ex officio*, a religious art.

A short survey of the *Antigone* will illustrate this; it will also give us material that will come in handy later on.

Classical scholars, from time to time, criticize adversely the structure of this play: to some extent, we are told, it lacks unity, since for most of the play our attention is concentrated, naturally, on the heroine, but in the concluding scenes—the last 150 verses or thereabouts—she is not mentioned; what is more surprising, when Sophocles brings back Creon from the cavern he brings with him the body of Haemon, Creon's son, but not the body of Antigone. A recent critic has said that his interest in the play is very much attenuated when Antigone disappears from it; Sophocles leaves us with Creon and his troubles, and Creon, as a dramatic character, is small beer after the splendid Antigone.

It is no doubt possible that Sophocles, though an experienced and not incapable dramatist, made an elementary blunder of this kind; it is also possible that a modern critic has taken hold of the wrong end of the stick. It is clear to me that the critics, in this case, commit a simple

fallacy—a typically modern one: they strike the wrong balance between preoccupation with the particular and preoccupation with the
universal. I will restate the criticism in this form: 'I find Antigone one
of the most sublime characters in dramatic literature. I find her resis-
tance to Creon one of the most moving of all tragic conflicts. When
her tragedy is consummated and I am left with the second-rate Creon,
I lose interest.'

The fallacy lies not in the estimate of the two characters, but in the
assumption that the play is, first and foremost, a play about Antigone.
The interpretation which I have summarized leaves out the gods as
actors in the piece. It allows for the fact, of course, that Antigone is doing what the gods approve; it takes no account of the part in the
action which Sophocles allots to them, and therefore throws the play
off its balance. It gravely attenuates the amplitude of the action; it
makes the play too small. Let us look, with all brevity, at these gods. I
mention them in the order of their coming on.

The first ode is a triumphant hymn of thanksgiving for the deliverance of the city: the traitor's foreign army has been repelled. One
part of the ode runs like this:

> For the arrogant boasts of an impious man
> Zeus hateth exceedingly. So, when he saw
> This army advancing in war-like flood
> In the pride of their golden equipment,
> He struck them down from the rampart's edge
>   With a fiery bolt
> In the midst of their cry of 'Triumph!'

The last words of the play—in that part of the play which is not so very
interesting—refer to Creon, now a broken man, confessing that he has
brought his disasters on his own head by his own obstinate folly. The
chorus observes:

> Proud words of the arrogant man, in the end,
> Bring punishment, great as his pride was great,
> Till at last he is schooled in wisdom.

The parallel may be significant; at all events, let us bear it in mind for
the present.

I move on to the point where the Watchman comes in with his news
that the body has been buried; he is terrified what Creon may do to
him, and he stands first on one leg then on the other before he can
bring himself to tell his story. When he has told it—that someone has

cast dust on the body, and that no animals have touched it—the chorus-leader says:

> My lord, I have been pondering on this:
> Do we not see in it the hand of God?

Creon flies into a rage at the idea: 'What, you old fool? You think the gods have any concern for the body of a traitor who came to destroy their city and temples?' No, he says; it is some political enemy who has done it. Presently, he will learn better.

Antigone is caught and condemned to death. They say to Creon: she is betrothed to your son; are you really going to kill her? His reply is coarse and brutal: 'There are plenty of women about; he can go to bed with another.' I invite your attention to the way in which Sophocles uses the love-theme here. Haemon, the lover, arrives, hoping to reason with his father, doing his best to control himself. Once more, Creon is coarse and brutal; the result is that his son rushes out in despair and rage. Then Sophocles does an interesting thing: he writes a short ode for the Chorus about the power of Aphrodite; she sits enthroned beside the other great gods and has sway over gods, men, animals. No one can defy her. 'A comment,' we say, 'on the preceding scene, in which, because of his love, a son has threatened his father.' —No doubt; but let us remember it, for it is a comment also on what is going to happen to Creon later.

Antigone at last is led off to her death. Then, unexpectedly, a prophet arrives—and I may remined you that Shakespeare too uses prophecy quite a lot. The prophet and what he says deserve attention. Very elaborately, he describes certain unnatural happenings: birds have been tearing each other to pieces, with unnatural cries; the fat of sacrifice, dripping into the flames, will not catch fire. To the prophet, the cause of this perturbation in nature is plain enough: 'You are to blame,' he says to the King; 'you have angered the gods—the gods of the upper world because you have buried one who is alive, the gods of the nether world because you will not bury one who is dead. For the life that you are wantonly destroying, you will soon have to pay with the life of one of your own; the Erinyes, the Avengers of the gods, are lying in wait for you.'

So it happens—though there is no divine intervention, no onset of black-robed Erinyes. Indeed, Sophocles makes it plain that the ruin of Creon comes in the most natural way imaginable: Creon has decided that he must release Antigone; arriving at the cavern, he finds that he has been forestalled by his son; Haemon himself, however, had been forestalled by Antigone, for she, passionate creature that she was, had hanged herself rather than wait for death by starvation. When Haemon sees his father, in his mad rage he tries to murder him; failing in this, he kills himself. The Queen, hearing of the disaster, also kills herself; she has lost one son already; she cannot endure the loss of the other; and she dies, cursing Creon.

> Proud words of the arrogant man, in the end,
> Bring punishment, great as his pride was great.

But it is a complete misconception to say that the gods have not intervened and have done nothing, that events have simply taken their natural course. Indeed, it would be nearer the truth to say that the gods have done everything, since the gods, collectively, *are* the natural course of things. This is the point at which we may recall the ode on the power of Aphrodite, and the folly of trying to oppose it. Creon told his son that one girl is as good as another; he was wrong. When the maddened Haemon turned on his father, sword in hand, we see the power of Aphrodite in action. In several ways Creon has presumed to defy certain of the deep sanctities of life: the instinctive respect that we pay to a dead body, the loyalty of a sister towards a brother and towards her whole family, the love that joins a man and a woman. All these things are, in the Greek sense, divine. Creon defied them, and inevitably they recoil on him and crush him. It is dangerous to anger the gods.

Now perhaps we see how superficial is the complaint that the play is deficient in unity, and that the dramatist leaves us in the last scenes with a character, Creon, much inferior in interest to Antigone. It is a criticism that misses the true dimensions of the play, which is so much more than simply a play about the tragic heroine Antigone. Creon may be a second-rate man, but the spectacle of such a man defying the gods in his ignorance, and being overwhelmed by them, is not a second-rate dramatic spectacle. The fallacy is the belief that tragedy has to do with exciting and tragic individuals. It has indeed, but in so wide a setting; with the gods, so to speak, keeping the ring. They do not control the actions of the individuals; rather do they work in and through the actions of individuals. Their power, their laws, are the unalterable framework of the universe within which we have to live our lives. The decisions are ours; the results, in the long run, will work out in accordance with certain laws. In the action of a Greek play, the activity of gods is always interwoven; that is to say, the Greek dramatist consciously sets his tragic action within a universal framework.

I have said so much about one Greek play in order to indicate the point of view from which this particular Greek scholar looks at Shakespeare. I am reluctant to go on talking about Greek plays, but perhaps I ought to say a word about the *Oedipus*, because this play is usually cited to prove the puppet-theory: Oedipus was doomed before ever he was born to kill his father and to marry his mother. Well, *what* about Oedipus? Sophocles expressly makes the play a defence of religion, and that puzzles us. As Sophocles handles it, it is a story in which the parents of Oedipus are told, 'If you have a son, this and that will happen.' But they say, in effect, 'Oh, we will look after *that*.' Then we have Oedipus before us: intelligent, resolute, Man at his most splendid and self-confident. He too is told, 'You are going to murder your father and marry your mother.' But Oedipus will look after *that*. He knows where his father and mother are: they are in Corinth—though in fact he has had a straight hint that the king and queen of Corinth are *not* his parents. He will not go back to Corinth; he makes his way to Thebes—and he does, for all his wisdom and resolution, precisely what was predicted. Now, Sophocles was writing in an age in some ways like our own: an age of triumphant intellectualism, new techniques, intoxicating self-confidence. It perturbed Sophocles; for him, there were more things in Heaven and Earth than were dreamed of by this new and cocksure philosophy. He was for more humility, more piety, less confidence that human confidence can take control. Therefore he wrote the *Oedipus*.

Let me jump straight into Shakespeare from the *Oedipus*, into *Hamlet*; there is, I think, an impressive resemblance in one not unimportant detail. The main argument of this paper will be that when one turns from Greek tragedy to Shakespearian tragedy, one is impressed more and more with the feeling that they have one thing in common—and it is the great thing: the spaciousness or amplitude that I tried to bring out by discussing the *Antigone*; a sense that the action is being played out with reference not simply to exciting and tragic individuals, but to the whole framework of our universe. The resemblance may be put negatively also: that as the *Antigone* is both attenuated and slightly distorted in structure so long as we approach it in a quasi-romantic way, with our eyes glued upon the heroine, so too are certain tragedies of Shakespeare distorted or attenuated, by some critics and producers, though not of course by all. Thus *Hamlet* has

often been reduced to the study of the fascinating character of Hamlet
—and this has been read in very diverse ways. The real dimensions of
the play have sometimes, in consequence, not been suspected. You will
remember the very respectable film of the play, and its sub-title: 'The
tragedy of a man who could not make up his mind.' But if *this* is what
Shakespeare thought he was writing, there is an indecent disproportion
between the size of his theme and the structure which he designed to
hold it; for the action of the play concerns two houses, that of King
Hamlet and that of Polonius, and by the end of the play both of them
are wiped out, and the Crown of Denmark passes to a comparative
outsider. Rather a large penalty for the crime of not being able to make
up one's mind! As in that criticism of the *Antigone*, the real amplitude
of the play has not been perceived.

But I was speaking of the *Oedipus*. At the beginning of the play,
Thebes is being ravaged by a plague, and Sophocles makes much of it.
Apollo declares the source of it: the city is polluted by the two unnatural, though innocent, offences against natural sanctities—and the
nature of the plague is nicely proportioned to its cause, for it is sterility;
crops, animals, the human kind, are afflicted with barrenness. The
dramatic imagery is the same as that which we have met already in the
Antigone, where Creon's offences against the laws of Nature and the
gods issue in the unnatural behaviour of the birds and of the fat which
will not burn. It is the same as that with which *Hamlet* opens: murder
most foul, foul and unnatural, causes that to happen which is quite
outside the ordinary course of Nature:

> The sepulchre,
> Wherein we saw thee quietly inurn'd,
> Hath op'd his ponderous and marble jaws,
> To cast thee up again—

making night hideous, so different from that holy night, 'Wherein our
Saviour's birth is celebrated'. Evil is abroad, Nature herself is in revolt
against it. We do not even begin to see the dimensions of *Hamlet* until
we see that it begins with foul sin, which, gathering head, spreads
corruption everywhere.

This is one familiar thing which one Hellenist sees, or thinks he sees,
when he turns to Shakespeare. Let us look a little further in *Hamlet*. Did
Sophocles or Aeschylus ever contrive more terrible tragic irony than
the scene in which Claudius is at his prayers? Both in effect and intention it is, I think, very like some of the most awful strokes of irony in

D

the *Oedipus*; and again, it is easily made nothing in particular, as it is by those who turn Hamlet into an irresolute procrastinator; as it was by the last actor I saw in the part, who did melodramatic stuff with a sword and so distracted one's attention from the irony. The speech of Claudius: 'O! my offence is rank. . . . May one be pardon'd, and retain the offence?' offers a terrifying spectacle, and one which has nothing to do with the tragedy of a man who could not make up his mind: it is the spectacle of a man who knows that he is bound for everlasting damnation, and cannot do the only thing that may save him. (His speech, incidentally, ends with the same delusive words, 'All may be well,' which are used in the *Agamemnon*, twice by the doomed King, and once by the doomed Queen.) On top of this, '*Enter* Hamlet'. The poet has so designed the play that it is the only chance Hamlet is to have of killing Claudius in security; moreover, the chance comes when he has just found all the proof that he could possibly desire of Claudius's guilt; also, when his passions are attuned to it: 'Now could I drink hot blood.' Why does he *not* do it? A Laertes would have cut his throat i' the church; Horatio, one suspects, would have gone straight to his point; but Hamlet has a finer mind than these, as Oedipus has a finer mind than the sober Creon of that play—but it is Creon who survives. Hamlet will not be satisfied with the mere death of Claudius; he will have him damned as well; he will therefore not 'take him in the purging of his soul'. He is arrogating to himself—a man—the judgment which must be left to God; and, like Oedipus time after time, he is using 'god-like reason' in disastrous ignorance of a material fact:

> My words fly up, my thoughts remain below:
> Words without thoughts never to Heaven go.

One reason for looking forward to Heaven is the possibility of hearing Sophocles and Shakespeare discussing tragic irony.

We speak of the 'inevitability' of Greek tragedy. It rests on the belief, which experience does not wholly contradict, that as in the physical universe certain laws manifestly prevail, so that a basic Order is maintained—an Order, or a general Balance between things—so do certain comparable laws in that other Universe of human action and suffering; as, for example, the law that underlies the *Agamemnon*, that violence will provoke counter-violence, until the inevitable end comes: chaos. The student of Greek drama finds this same inevitability in *Hamlet* also; he is, after all, on familiar ground. In Shakespeare's imagery here, the poison which Claudius poured into King Hamlet's ear spreads everywhere, corrupting everything, especially friendship, loyalty, and love, until at the end it emerges again from a metaphorical to a literal poison, and destroys Claudius and Gertrude, Laertes and Hamlet. Here one thinks of Aeschylus, who also uses imagery like this: Paris the sinner is described as one who 'treads underfoot the beauty of holy things', and then, later, we see Agamemnon entering his palace, trampling underfoot the crimson tapestry which he knows should be offered to gods. Again, the chorus, singing of Agamemnon's destruction of Troy, tells us that Zeus cast such a net around the city that none could escape—and later we see Agamemnon lying dead in the net that was cast over him by Clytemnestra, a 'net woven by the Erinyes'.

The whole of the second part of *Hamlet* is strongly marked by this tragic inevitability. To say nothing about the way in which Claudius is driven from one crime into another, there is the opening of Act IV, Scene 2—surely one of the greatest of tragic openings: 'I will not speak with her.' It is certainly one of the important themes of the play that so many in it wish to keep the evil hidden; Shakespeare wrote one of his most extraordinary scenes, of the Ghost in the cellarage, to emphasize this very point. But it is impossible; in the end it is proclaimed to all:

> Foul deeds will rise,
> Though all the earth o'erwhelm them, to men's eyes.

Just as the foul deeds of Oedipus could not remain hidden, so here. Gertrude tries to hide the evil from herself: 'I will not speak with her,' —but she must:

> 'Twere good she were spoken with, for she may strew
> Dangerous conjectures in ill-breeding minds.

At one point this feeling of inevitability is concentrated in a stroke of dramatic irony which has its exact parallels in Sophocles. One of the things corrupted by Claudius's poison, as we have seen, is Friendship. Rosencrantz and Guildenstern are at least old associates of Hamlet's, on friendly enough terms with him, at the beginning. There is already irony when, on his arrival, Guildenstern says to the King and Queen:

> We both obey,
> And here give up ourselves, in the full bent,
> To lay our service freely at your feet,
> To be commanded.

Giving oneself up to the service of such as these is some danger, as they discover. But it is a later irony which is so Sophoclean. In the *Antigone*, Sophocles regularly puts into the mouth of his wise chorus observations about Antigone which are true, but only when we refer them to Creon; for example, 'To the one whom God will ruin, evil seems good.' So is it with that speech made by Rosancrantz to Claudius:

> The cease of majesty
> Dies not alone, but, like a gulf doth draw
> What's near it with it; it is a massy wheel,
> . . . which, when it falls,
> Each small annexment, petty consequence,
> Attends the boisterous ruin:

This is said to King Claudius; but how much more pertinent when we refer it to the death of King Hamlet; and realize that Rosencrantz himself is a small annexment whom sin will engulf.

It is high time we escaped from this inexhaustible play, lest we never escape; but there remains one point so interesting to a Hellenist that it may not be passed over: the pirate-ship. About this, Bernard Shaw somewhere makes the illuminating comment that it is a threadbare device that would be scorned by a second-rate melodrama, but the magnificent Shakespeare didn't mind. What the comment illuminates is not Shakespeare but Shaw, among whose gifts imagination is not notable. Again the student of Greek drama knows at once where he is —or thinks he does; for the Greek too did this: namely, uses an incident that looks like pure chance in order to make us feel that the gods—that is, some universal order—is visible in the events. Twice—for example, in his *Electra* and in the *Oedipus*—Sophocles uses this sequence: the Queen makes a solemn sacrifice and petition to Apollo; when the prayer is ended, a messenger arrives with news—good news, for the Queen. He comes apparently by chance; yet the dramatic timing of his arrival is such that we, the audience, cannot but feel that it is the god's answer to the prayer; in Clytemnestra's case, at least, a blasphemous one; in each case, the message leads directly to the Queen's death. Heaven is ordinant. But the plot does not *need* the gods at all; the gods move along with the human actors, but they do nothing to help them, still less to command them. One could cut them out, here and from many another Greek play, and the play would still be intelligible and stage-worthy. But it would be much smaller; it would become only an exciting play of character and intrigue; a particular, and not a universal.

The half-hidden presence of the gods forces us to see that the ven-
geance is the recoil upon Agamemnon's murderers of their own crime; a
grim universal law is at work. The pirate-ship is a Shakespearian equi-
valent—and he has others, such as prophecy. His plays, too, are universals: Heaven is ordinant; certain unchanging laws can be discerned in
the succession of events. The course of evil begun by Claudius will
destroy the two chief houses in Denmark, but it will not be given to
Claudius to destroy Hamlet and himself to escape.

But there are other plays than *Hamlet*, and it is time to look at them.
A few years ago—if I may for a moment be autobiographical—I took
advantage of a brief and blessed illness to do what I had never done
before: to read right through the Histories of Shakespeare in order.
Naturally, I had read and seen some of them, and certain things lived
in the memory: the villainy (rather overdone, as it had seemed) of
Richard III, the tragically misguided Richard II, the splendid rhetoric
in *Henry V*; but I had no firm grip on the whole series, only the general
impression that is conveyed by the common phrase 'a grand pageant of
English history'. I read them all straight through, and the effect was
overwhelming; a 'pageant' if you will, but one which has that same
tragic amplitude of which we have been speaking. The margins of my
Shakespeare are now full of scribbles like, 'Cf. Aeschylus, *Agam.*', or
'See *Trachiniae*', or '*Trojan Women*, chorus'; on one passage, the word
'*Iliad!*'

What sent me back to the *Iliad* was the scene in the Temple Garden
in *King Henry VI*, Part I. You will recall how Richard Plantagenet has
quarrelled violently with young Somerset. These two are in the Garden
with Suffolk, Warwick, Vernon, and—a most interesting addition—a
Lawyer to whom Shakespeare does not bother to give a name; he is
just 'A Lawyer'. What the quarrel is about we are not told, but
Somerset plucks a red rose, asks that those who think with him shall do
the same, and agrees to abide by the decision of the majority. Only
Suffolk plucks the red; Warwick and Vernon pluck a white rose with
Plantagenet, and the Lawyer says to Somerset:

> Unless my study and my books be false,
> The argument you held was wrong in you,
> In sign whereof I pluck a white rose too.

Not very Homeric—not yet; but Plantagenet says, 'Now, Somerset,
where is your argument?' and the reply is, 'Here, in my scabbard.'—
So much for Law.

At the end of the scene, Warwick says:

> And here I prophesy: this brawl today,
> Grown to this faction in the Temple garden,
> Shall send between the red rose and the white
> A thousand souls to death and deadly night.

The *Iliad* begins like this:

> Sing, goddess, of the anger of Achilles the son of Peleus, that baleful anger which brought endless misery to the Achaeans, and sent the souls of many brave heroes to Hades, and left their bodies to be devoured by dogs and birds; and the plan of Zeus was fulfilled. Begin where Agamemnon the King and great Achilles came to strife and enmity.

The *Iliad* is a tragic poem, and it has a strong unity, because, in spite of its length and the richness of its episodes it does keep to its central theme, announced in these opening words: an outburst of hot wrath between two violent men not only sends 'a thousand men to death and deadly night', but also brings shame to Achilles, and such bitter grief too, over the death of his dear Patroclus, that when at length Agamemnon is ready to make extravagant amends Achilles finds them hardly worth the taking, for Patroclus is dead. And the 'plan of Zeus' does not mean that Zeus, for inscrutable reasons of his own, stirred up this quarrel, but that such violence is bound to have such results. Warwick's prophesying means the same.

The Histories are full of prophecy, and so are Greek plays, and in neither case is prophecy a mere dramatic ornament or convenience. Its real purpose is to relate the particular instance to a general law; to give it amplitude. We have seen how Teiresias prophesied to Creon what the gods, in their anger, were going to do with him; the purpose of the prophecy is not merely to break Creon's obstinacy; it is, much more, to make us feel that what happens to him is not merely bad luck, but is a typical recoil on a man of his own inhumanity and folly. Prophecy is possible only because there are general laws which operate in these things. Take, for example, King Richard's prophecy, as recollected by Henry IV:[1]

> But which of you was by,—
> You, cousin Nevil, as I may remember,—
> When Richard, with his eye brimful of tears,
> Then check'd and rated by Northumberland,

[1] *King Henry IV*, Part 2, III. i. 65 ff.

> Did speak these words, now prov'd a prophecy?
> 'Northumberland, thou ladder, by the which
> My cousin Bolingbroke ascends my throne;'
> Though then, God knows, I had no such intent,
> But that necessity so bow'd the State
> That I and greatness were compelled to kiss:
> 'The time shall come', thus did he follow it,
> 'The time will come, that foul sin, gathering head,
> Shall break into corruption:'—so went on,
> Foretelling this same time's condition
> And the division of our amity.

It is one difference between Comedy and Tragedy that comedy depends on surprise while Tragedy, on the whole, avoids it; that is to say, there may be surprise at the magnitude of the disaster, but not at the disaster itself. The tragic poet will discount surprise by prophecy; and his prophecies are not arbitrary, but have their roots in universal human experience.

Let us pursue this matter of prophecy a little further; Shakespeare gives us examples in plenty. In *King John*, Constance, whose cause has been taken up by King Philip and Austria, is thrown over by them when they strike their bargain with John—the bargain by which the Dauphin is to marry Blanche. Constance is beside herself with fury and despair, and presently cries:[1]

> Arm, arm, you heavens, against these perjur'd kings!
> A widow cries; be husband to me, heavens!
> Let not the hours of this ungodly day
> Wear out the day in peace; but, ere sunset,
> Set armed discord 'twixt these perjur'd kings!
> Hear me! O, hear me!

Immediately, in comes Pandulph the Papal Legate; he, by excommunicating John, causes Philip to renounce the bargain. A battle ensues, and by sunset Austria is dead. So is the prayer answered; Heaven has passed its own judgment on the perjured Kings. It is an exact parallel, in technique, effect and purpose, with what Sophocles does in the *Electra* when he brings in his Messenger pat upon Clytemnestra's prayer to Apollo. Another Greek example, though one which works in reverse, can be found in the denouement of Euripides' *Medea*—a scene which the logic of Aristotle failed to understand. When Medea has murdered her children, the Chorus, in horror, sings a stanza in

[1] *King John*, III. i. 107 ff.

which it calls upon the Sun-god, as the source of purity, to avenge the crime. But what the Sun-god does is to send an airborne chariot to rescue the murderess and take her safe to Athens. This is one reason why the play makes no sense if we try to turn it, in our modern way, into something of a psychological study of Medea; from this sequence we must infer either that Euripides could not make a decent plot, or that he could, and wanted to suggest that Medea's wild cruelty is something elemental which is not alien from the nature of Man and of the universe.

There is one form of prophecy, namely the ironic, the apparently mocking prophecy, at which we may look a little more closely. It is fairly common in folk-lore; a classical instance is the tale about Croesus the King of Lydia: that he, contemplating an attack on Persia, consulted Delphi and was told that if he crossed the River Halys he would destroy a mighty empire; so he did cross the river, and did destroy a mighty empire. Unfortunately, it was his own. What this type of story signified to the minds of those who invented them must remain a matter of speculation; but Sophocles and Shakespeare also used the type, and here we can do more than speculate.

I have mentioned the *Trachiniae*, the play which deals with the death of Heracles. In this play, he is a hero whose whole life is encompassed with oracles. The one that will concern us is that the Labour on which he is at present engaged is to be his last; it will end either in his death or in unbroken peace. He returns from it in safety; therefore all will now be well. Before he reaches his home, having fallen violently in love with a young Princess, and having failed to persuade her father to let him have her as his mistress, he storms and sacks her city, destroys all its men, takes the girl, and sends her home where his faithful wife is awaiting him. She, to win back his love, sends to him the robe which she has anointed with a love-charm. She does not know that the love-charm, given to her years back by an enemy of Heracles, is deadly poison. It destroys him; and so is the oracle fulfilled: this recent Labour does end in lasting peace, but it is the peace of death.

The classical scholar now present is forcibly reminded of this in reading *King Henry IV*, with its prophecy about Jerusalem; but before discussing that, we might glance at one or two others which are at least similar, even if not the same. In *King Richard III*, Buckingham is executed on All-Souls' Day—that same day, as he says, on which he had falsely sworn loyalty to Edward, 'his children, and his wife's allies':

> That high All-Seer which I dallied with
> Hath turn'd my feigned prayer on my head,
> And given in earnest what I begg'd in jest.[1]

We speak sometimes of the mocking irony of the gods; in this case at least the gods were doing more than simply amuse themselves at Buckingham's expense. It is a typical instance of the meaningful way in which the tragic poet will use coincidence. In *King John* the ironic fulfilment of prophecy is used in reverse. Peter of Pomfret, a rude and turbulent fellow, prophesies that on Ascensiontide ere noon John will have delivered up the crown; which John duly does, though it is in submission to the Papal Legate, from whom he immediately receives it again. *King John* I find a difficult play to understand, but as it ends in peace, with Pandulph—in spite of his not very edifying conduct earlier in the play—appearing as an anticipation of Prospero:

> It was my breath that blew this tempest up
> Upon your stubborn usage of the Pope;
> But since you are a gentle convertite,
> My tongue shall hush again this storm of war—[2]

I assume that the function of the prophecy is to underline the re-establishment of order in the kingdom by the acceptance of the Pope's authority, a kingdom in which form has been formless, order orderless.

Henry IV is very close to Sophocles. At the opening of Part I we find Henry looking forward to the end of civil tumult, and planning a Holy War, 'As far as to the sepulchre of Christ'. But Northumberland's rebellion intervenes, with all its treachery and bloodshed—treachery on both sides—and it is not until near the end of Part 2 that the dream recurs:

> We will our youth lead on to higher fields
> And draw no swords but what are sanctified.[3]

To this theme, the full-close is the illness, and then the death, of Henry in the Jerusalem-chamber:

> It hath been prophesied to me many years
> I should not die but in Jerusalem,
> Which vainly I suppos'd the Holy Land.

---

[1] *King Richard III*, v. i.   [2] *King John*, v. i.
[3] *King Henry IV*, Part 2, IV. iv.

> But bear me to that chamber; there I'll lie:
> In that Jerusalem shall Harry die.[1]

The resemblance to the oracles given to Heracles is unmistakable; how deep does it go? Deep enough, I think. As for Heracles, it is made quite plain that he falls because of his habitual and violent disregard of the rights of others—in this instance, of a loyal and understanding wife, whom, without a thought, he is going to supersede with the beautiful young girl Iole. We may reflect—and I think Sophocles intended us to reflect—that it was open to Heracles to return from this final Labour and live henceforth in peace; but his ungovernable passion, not for the first time, got the better of him, so that his wife was induced to use the love-charm. It was his own action which determined that the promised peace should be the peace of death. It might have been otherwise; the gods were not simply mocking him. The fulfilment of the Jerusalem-prophecy is no less tragic; but this fact is not to be seen except in its full context, and this embraces *King Richard II* as well as the two parts of *King Henry IV*.

It is, no doubt, possible to think of *King Richard II* as being the tragedy of a young king led into evil courses and then to disaster by bad advisers. It is possible to think of the *Antigone* as the tragedy of the heroic young Antigone. Both Sophocles and Shakespeare were pretty good at portraying character. But if we think of either play on this level only, we gravely diminish its importance. From such a point of view we might object to *King Richard II* what has been objected to the *Antigone*, that it lacks unity, inasmuch as the last scenes concern Bolingbroke quite as much as Richard; to which, I suppose, one answer might be that this is one of the Chronicle-plays, and one must not expect them to be very good in construction. (This answer, I may say, is not mine.)

Richard, at the beginning of the play, is under grave suspicion of having caused Gloster's death. Gaunt speaks about this, though with more restraint, as Constance speaks about her wrongs in *King John*:[2]

> When law can do no right,
> Let it be lawful that law bar no wrong ...
> For he that holds his kingdom holds the law:
> Therefore, since law itself is perfect wrong,
> How can the law forbid my tongue to curse?

[1] *King Henry IV*, Part 2, IV. v. 235 ff.   [2] III. i. 185 ff.

Gaunt does not conclude, with Constance, that when law can do no right, no law can bar wrong; Gaunt, indeed, is the only important character in this tragic series of plays who does *not* agree with Constance. He has every incentive to stir against Gloster's butchers, but he will not take Heaven's justice into his own hands; it will be the tragedy of his son Henry that he does. You will recall Gaunt's reply to the Duchess:[1]

> Since correction lieth in those hands
> Which made the fault that we cannot correct,
> Put we our quarrel to the will of heaven;
> Who, when they see the hours ripe on earth,
> Will rain hot vengeance on offenders' heads.

Gaunt, in fact, agrees with Socrates, that it is better to suffer than to do wrong.

In the matter of the accusations which pass, on this score, between Hereford and Mowbray, I am on unfamiliar ground, but I assume that the formal ordeal by battle is the symbol of Heaven's judgment; and not only does Richard prevent this, but also he metes out his own justice to Hereford and Mowbray in a singularly capricious manner. Perhaps it is not over-subtle to see some tragic irony in the reason which Richard gives for preventing the duel; it is:

> For that our kingdom's earth should not be soil'd
> With that dear blood which it hath fostered.[2]

At the end of the play it is Richard's own blood that soils his kingdom's earth.

Having given a partial judgment on this quarrel, Richard goes on to plunder Gaunt's estate—that is to say, Hereford's—to farm his kingdom, to reduce England to chaos; to give Hereford every apparent justification, barring its lawlessness, to reclaim his dukedom and estates by force, with the support of others, like Northumberland, who can tolerate Richard no longer; with the result that, almost by force of circumstances, Bolingbroke is led to assume the crown. Henry is speaking truly when he says, in a passage that I quoted earlier:

> Though then, God knows, I had no such intent,
> But that necessity so bow'd the State
> That I and greatness were compelled to kiss.

---

[1] *King Henry IV*, Part 2, I. ii. 4 ff.   [2] *King Richard II*, I. iii. 125 f.

This 'necessity' is very like one in the *Agamemnon* which has puzzled some commentators: the 'yoke of necessity' to which Agamemnon submitted at Aulis when, to prosecute his war, he sacrificed his daughter to Artemis. Why did the gods present him with so bitter a choice? What primitive theological ideas was Aeschylus entertaining? Primitive ideas very like those of Shakespeare: that to avenge wrong through blood and violence can leave behind it only a legacy of more blood and violence. Both poets live in the same world. In the *Agamemnon*, Aeschylus calls the first crime of the long chain of crime in the house of Atreus the πρώταρχος ἄτη, the blind sin that began it all; a like succession has been started by the lawlessness of Richard; it leads directly to his deposition, and you know very well how that deposition re-echoes in the plays that are to follow. Richard, in his extremity, is willing to adopt Bolingbroke as his heir and to yield the high sceptre freely, but it is too late for the voice of reason and peace to be heard. As the uncomfortable Bishop of Carlisle observes: 'What subject can give sentence on his King?' Richard himself says:[1]

> I find myself a traitor with the rest;
> For I have given here my soul's consent
> To undeck the pompous body of a king.

Now, nothing can stop it. Bolingbroke may do his best to be moderate towards Richard: 'Urge it no more, my lord Northumberland.'[2] But Richard's crimes and follies have produced the crime of crimes, deposition; the consequences must follow. Even before the coronation the Abbot of Westminster is speaking to Aumerle and Carlisle about laying a plot against Henry; Henry can be magnanimous enough to pardon Aumerle, but he says, 'Have I no friend will rid me of this living fear?' —and the officious Exton murders Richard. For his service he receives from Henry the curse of Cain, and Henry says:[3]

> I'll make a voyage to the Holy Land,
> To wash this blood from off my guilty hand.

But the blood is not so easily to be washed off, either from Henry or from his kingdom. Blood spilt on the ground, as Aeschylus also knew, invokes fresh blood.

It is the first announcement of the Jerusalem theme; the new king is already beginning to take on the lineaments of a tragic figure.

One point I have passed over, and I think it is a not unimportant one;

---

[1] *King Richard II*, IV. i. 248 ff.   [2] IV. i. 271.   [3] V. vi. 49 f.

it relates to Shakespeare's handling of Richard in the second part of the play. That he becomes a tragic figure goes without saying, but Shakespeare also writes some rather good poetry for him, and perhaps we may be in some danger of thinking that he was merely characterizing Richard as a poetic soul. Perhaps he was; but there is something more. I am thinking in particular of the scene of Richard's return from Ireland.[1] He says:

> I weep for joy
> To stand upon my kingdom once again.
> Dear earth, I do salute thee with my hand. . . .

Carlisle reassures him:[2]

> Fear not, my lord: that Power that made you king
> Hath power to keep you king in spite of all.

This, no doubt, is true; what bishops say must be believed.
    Richard's reply, as you will remember, contains the passage:[3]

> Not all the water in the rough rude sea
> Can wash the balm from an anointed king;
> The breath of worldly men cannot depose
> The deputy elected by the Lord.
> For every man that Bolingbroke hath press'd
> To lift shrewd steel against our golden crown,
> God for his Richard hath in heavenly pay
> A glorious angel: then, if angels fight,
> Weak men must fall, for Heaven still guards the right.

True; but Richard is pitifully deceiving himself. The Power that made him king does not choose to keep him king; the Angels do not turn up. The breath of worldly men *can* depose the deputy anointed by the Lord—though they must pay the inevitable price for doing it. Richard did not enjoy the advantage of having read Aeschylus. He might have learned from the *Agamemnon* that the gods are stern and inflexible; from the *Suppliants* of Aeschylus that the gods do not automatically protect the wronged if they themselves are in the wrong; from the *Electra* of Sophocles that the prayers of one who is a criminal may be answered in devastating fashion. To all Richard's fine poetry Heaven is remarkably insensitive: Heaven is concerned, in these sombre plays, to visit upon men the inevitable consequences of what they have done—upon them, and (as in the *Agamemnon* too) upon the innocent as

---

[1] *King Richard II*, III. ii. 4 ff.   [2] Ib. 27 f.   [3] Ib. 54 ff.

well, as is so terribly portrayed in *King Henry VI*, Part 3, in those antistrophic scenes, reminiscent of some of the choruses in the *Trojan Women*, of the Son who has killed his Father, and the Father who has killed his Son.

Such is the context in which we should consider Henry's dream of a holy war against the infidel, and the ironic fulfilment of the prophecy that he should die in Jerusalem. It could not be, not in a world in which foul sin, gathering head, has broken into corruption; a world in which there is always argument why an oath should not be kept, an offer of friendship and forgiveness not trusted; 'Form formless, order orderless.'

The tragic thought of Sophocles is based on the conception of a universe which is grounded on Dikê, principles of Order, which, when violated, will reassert themselves, maybe just as violently. The Shakespearian basis appears to be not very different. It is said by Faulconbridge, in his speech on Commodity: 'the world ... is peized well, made to run even upon even ground'. When it does not run even, the fault is in those who have made it uneven.

As for the unevenness, it is notable how many times in these plays a character is given only the choice between two evils, placed in a dilemma. There is Blanche, in *King John:* her marriage-feast must be stained with blood; she can, she says, wish success neither to husband nor uncle, nor to father nor grandmother. There is the good York, in *King Richard II*:[1]

> Both are my kinsmen:
> The one is my sovereign, whom both my oath
> And duty bids defend; the other again
> Is my near kinsman, whom the King hath wrong'd,
> Whom conscience and my kindred bids to right.

There is Henry VI, who time after time vainly tries to end the strife by composition, to whom Clifford harshly says:

> My gracious liege, this too much lenity
> And harmful pity must be laid aside;[2]

for Henry can avoid war only by disinheriting his own son. The same sort of thing happens in the Greek plays, and for the same reason: not that the President of the Immortals is malignant, but that human conduct has made the ground uneven. There is Agamemnon, faced with

[1] II. ii. III ff. · [2] *King Henry VI*, Part 3, II. ii. 9 f.

his choice at Aulis—because he is obeying a violent conception of justice. There is King Pelasgus in the *Suppliants* of Aeschylus: because, away in Egypt, violence is offered to certain women who are of Greek descent, they fly for refuge to Greece and invoke the rights of suppliants; the King therefore has to choose: will he, on behalf of unknown women, lead his subjects into war with the Egyptians, or will he reject the suppliants and thereby brave the wrath of the offended gods?

The classical scholar looking at Shakespeare finds at least one other point of interest which I should like to discuss, however briefly. There is extant only one Greek play, *The Persians*, which in the strict sense is a historical tragedy. It deals with events which were only eight years old, events in which most of his audience must have been involved actively. Yet in some important ways his plot diverges from history— to the occasional embarrassment of ancient historians, who think that the poet should have done better. But it can be shown, I think, that the divergences are purposeful, and, when we see what the play is really about, very effective: Aeschylus was not writing a patriotic chronicle-play, but a tragedy about a king who defied the gods. Now, my domestic *Shakespeare* is a pleasant Victorian edition, and in it I find, at *King Henry VI*, Part III, iii, 2, the following note: 'This seems a needless departure from fact. Sir John Grey fell in the second battle of St Albans, fighting on King Henry's side; and his lands were not seized by the Queen [Queen Margaret], who conquered in that battle, but by King Edward after the battle of Towton. Shakespeare has the matter correctly in *King Richard III*, i, 3.' Shall we look for a moment at this scene, in which Shakespeare contradicts not only history, but also himself?

It is the scene in which Lady Elizabeth Grey appears before Edward IV to ask for the restoration of her late husband's lands. By pretending that Grey had suffered in defence of the House of York, Shakespeare lays Edward (as he admits) under a debt of honour to Lady Elizabeth. Nevertheless, Edward will not at first repay this debt of honour unless she will accept a proposal of dishonour, upon her rejecting of which he persuades her to become his Queen, although in fact he has already sent Warwick to Paris to ask for the hand of the Lady Bona. Clearly, Shakespeare wished to suggest that Elizabeth became Queen in circumstances of folly and dishonour. This is the reason why he gets his history wrong here.

In the tragic poets, I think, close parallels are not accidental. I therefore go back to *King Henry VI*, Part I, v, 5; to the remarkable scene in

which de la Pole takes prisoner at Angiers a beauteous maiden, decides
that he can hardly make her mistress, being married, and so decides to
make her young Henry's Queen. This he does, although Gloster the
Lord Protecter is against it—for an interesting reason:

> So should I give consent to flatter sin.
> You know, my lord, your Highness is betroth'd
> Unto another lady of esteem;
> How shall we then dispense with that contract,
> And not deface your honour with reproach?

The parallel with Edward IV is fairly close; Shakespeare makes it
closer. Queen Margaret he represents as turning out an implacable and
vindictive stirrer-up of civil war; and as for Edward's Queen Elizabeth,
he makes the advancement of her relatives—Rivers and the rest—a
potent cause of dissension and bloodshed. Folly, dishonour and con-
cupiscence bear their natural fruit. Finally, we have those appalling
scenes in *King Richard III* in which these two discarded and bereaved
Queens, like a band of Furies, join in cursing both each other and
everyone else; and in order to engineer these scenes, Shakespeare again
departs from history: he pretends that Queen Maragaret was not either
in the Tower or in France, but at large in London. Both *The Persians*
and these plays of Shakespeare are good illustrations of Aristotle's
dictum that Poetry is more serious and philosophical than History.

Therefore, to sum up: the classical scholar, when he journeys from
Athens to Stratford-on-Avon—or rather to the Globe Theatre—
though indeed he has to accustom himself to a different style of
dramatic architecture, to different clothes and different manners, very
soon finds himself at home; for these are great tragic poets. They speak
the same language, though in different dialects: those in Greek, this one
in English. They speak about the same things; whether they tell us of
an Agamemnon or a Creon, or of a King Richard or a Hamlet, they
are speaking in the same grave and spacious way of nothing less than
the terms on which the gods will let us live; and though each of them
speaks in his own voice and with his own accent, about this one thing
they do not speak differently.

4

THE QUESTION OF CHARACTER IN SHAKESPEARE

by L. C. KNIGHTS

ET me begin with an unashamed bit of autobiography. In 1932 I was asked to give a paper to the Shakespeare Association in London. I was a comparatively young man, dissatisfied with the prevailing academic approach to Shakespeare, excited by the glimpses I had obtained of new and, it seemed, more rewarding approaches, and I welcomed the opportunity of proclaiming the new principles in the very home of Shakespearian orthodoxy, whilst at the same time having some fun with familiar irrelevancies of the kind parodied in my title, *How Many Children had Lady Macbeth?* I gave my paper and waited expectantly for the lively discussion that would fol-low this rousing challenge to the pundits. So far as I remember, nothing happened, except that after a period of silence an elderly man got up at the back of the room and said that he was very glad to hear Mr. Knights give this paper because it was what he had always thought. The revolution was over, and I went home. It was hardly a historic occasion, and the only reason for mentioning it is that when my paper was published as one of Gordon Fraser's Minority Pamphlets it ob-tained a certain mild notoriety that has never since entirely deserted it: only a few years ago a writer in *The Listener* called it 'the Communist Manifesto of the new critical movement'. Well of course it was no-thing of the kind. *How Many Children had Lady Macbeth?* has earned its footnote in the history of modern criticism partly, I like to believe, because it says a few sensible things about *Macbeth*, partly because of its sprightly title (which was suggested to me by F. R. Leavis), and partly because it reflected the conviction of an increasing number of readers that the prevailing language of Shakespeare criticism didn't quite fit what seemed to them of deepest importance in the experience of Shakespeare's plays. In the last twenty-five or thirty years there has certainly been a movement away from the older type of 'character' criticism which had for so long held the field and which culminated in

A. C. Bradley's *Shakespearean Tragedy*.[1] But so far as any one book can be said to herald the new movement it was G. Wilson Knight's *The Wheel of Fire* (1930), shortly to be followed by *The Imperial Theme* (1931).[2]

Now what I am here to do today is to try to get one aspect of that movement into perspective; more specifically I want to ask, after some twenty-five years of Shakespeare criticism that has not on the whole been on Bradleyean lines, what we now understand by the term 'character' when we use it in giving an account of Shakespeare's plays, to what extent—and within what limitations—'character' can be a useful critical term when we set out to define the meaning—the living and life-nourishing significance—of a Shakespeare play.

I don't want to burden you with a history of Shakespeare criticism, ancient or modern, but a few historical reminders are necessary. Since Shakespeare criticism began, people have praised Shakespeare for the lifelikeness of his characters. But it was not until the end of the eighteenth century that Shakespeare's remarkable power to make his men and women convincing led to a more and more exclusive concentration on those features of the *dramatis personae* that could be defined in terms appropriate to characters in real life. The *locus classicus* is of course Maurice Morgann's *Essay on the Dramatic Character of Sir John Falstaff* (1777). Twelve years before, in 1765, Dr. Johnson, in his great Preface, had given the more traditional view:

> Nothing can please many, and please long, but just representations of general nature. . . . Shakespeare is above all writers, at least above all modern writers, the poet of nature. . . . His persons act and speak by the influence of those general passions and principles by which all minds are agitated, and the whole system of life is continued in motion. In the writings of other poets a character is too often an individual; in those of Shakespeare it is commonly a species.
>
> It is from this wide extension of design that so much instruction is derived. . . .[3]

[1] Macmillan, 1904.
[2] Methuen.
[3] We may compare Johnson's characteristic comment on *Macbeth*: 'The play is deservedly celebrated for the propriety of its fictions, and solemnity, grandeur, and variety of its action; but it has no nice discriminations of character, the events are too great to admit the influence of particular dispositions, and the course of the action necessarily determines the conduct of the agents. The danger of ambition is well described. . . .' Johnson, it is true, also says of Shakespeare, 'Perhaps no poet ever kept his personages more distinct from each other.'

Morgann, on the contrary, is interested in what is uniquely individual
in the character he describes, and these individual traits, he affirms, can
be elicited from the stage characters in much the same way as one
builds up the character of an acquaintance in real life: 'those characters
in Shakespeare, which are seen only in part, are yet capable of being
unfolded and understood in the whole'.

> If the characters of Shakespeare [he goes on] are thus *whole*, as it were
> original, while those of almost all other writers are mere imitation, it may be
> fit to consider them rather as Historic than Dramatic beings; and, when
> occasion requires, to account for their conduct from the *whole* of character,
> from general principles, from latent motives, and from policies not avowed.

It is this principle that allows him to distinguish between 'the *real*
character of Falstaff' and 'his *apparent* one'. What R. W. Babcock, in
his useful book, *The Genesis of Shakespeare Idolatry, 1766–99*,[1] calls 'the
psychologizing of Shakespeare' was well established even before Coleridge gave his lectures; and Coleridge's influence, though of course
more subtly, worked in the same direction. It seems true to say that in
the nineteenth century Shakespeare's characters became 'real people',
and—with varying degrees of relevance—the plays were discussed in
terms of the interaction of real people for whom sympathy or
antipathy was enlisted. Bradley's tremendously influential *Shakespearean Tragedy* was published in 1904, and, for Bradley, 'the centre of
the tragedy . . . may be said with equal truth to lie in action issuing
from character, or in character issuing in action': 'action is the centre of
the story', but 'this action is essentially the expression of character'.

Now Bradley had the great virtue of being thoroughly immersed in
what he was talking about, and I am sure that his book has helped very
many people to make Shakespeare a present fact in their lives. Also
there is no need to make Bradley responsible for all the vagaries of the
how-many-children-had-Lady-Macbeth? kind, which mostly lie on
the fringes of criticism. But Bradley's book did endorse a particular
kind of preoccupation with 'character', and once 'character'-criticism
became the dominant mode of approach to Shakespeare, certain important matters were necessarily obscured, and people's experience of
Shakespeare became in some ways less rich and satisfying than it might
have been. For one thing genuine perceptions became entangled with
irrelevant speculations—'How is it that Othello comes to be the companion of the one man in the world, who is at once able enough, brave

[1] University of North Carolina Press, 1931.

enough, and vile enough to ensnare him?'; Macbeth's tendency to ambition 'must have been greatly strengthened by his marriage'. And if the critic who accepts too naïvely the character-in-action formula is liable to disappear down by-paths outside the play, he is almost equally likely to slight or ignore what is actually there if it does not minister to his particular preoccupation—witness the ease with which the old Arden edition of *Macbeth* dismissed as spurious scenes that do not con‑ tribute to the development of character or of a narrowly conceived dramatic action. Even at its best the focus is a narrow one. Shake- spearian tragedy, says Bradley, 'is pre-eminently the story of one person, the "hero", or at most of two, the "hero" and "heroine" '; and the mark of the tragic hero, besides his greatness, is that there is a 'conflict of forces' in his soul. I suppose, if you look at matters in this way it doesn't necessarily mean that you idealize the hero as Bradley does Othello, missing the critical 'placing' determined by the play as a whole. But it does mean that you are likely to ignore some important matters, such as the structure of ideas in *Macbeth*. After all, in his greater plays, Shakespeare was doing more than merely holding a mirror up to nature, more even than representing conflict in the souls of mighty characters: he was exploring the world and defining the values by which men live. In short, Shakespearian tragedy, any Shake- spearian tragedy, is saying so much more than can be expressed in Bradleyean terms. It was some such perceptions as these—combined with an increasing knowledge of Elizabethan dramatic usage and con- vention—that prompted exploration of Shakespeare, not necessarily in opposition to Bradley, but to a large extent outside the Bradleyean frame of reference.

Simplifying for the sake of clarity, I would say that as a result of critical work done in the last quarter of a century, the approach to Shakespeare of an intelligent and informed reader to-day is likely to differ in three important respects from that of the intelligent and in- formed reader of a generation ago. To start with, he is likely to take it for granted that any one of Shakespeare's greater plays is very much more than a dramatized story; that it is, rather, a vision of life—more or less complex and inclusive—whose meaning is nothing less than *the play as a whole*. This is what Wilson Knight meant when he sometimes referred to his work in terms of 'spatial analysis', as distinguished from the analysis of a series of steps in time. Ideally, we try to apprehend each play as though all its parts were simultaneously present: there is an obvious analogy with music, and criticism of this kind tends to describe

Shakespeare's meanings in terms of 'themes' rather than in terms of motive, character-development, and so on. Wilson Knight speaks of cutting below 'the surface crust of plot and character', and remarks that in *Macbeth*, for example, 'the logic of imaginative correspondence is more significant and more exact than the logic of plot'. He also, of course, told us that 'we should not look for perfect verisimilitude to life, but rather see each play as an expanded metaphor, by means of which the original vision has been projected into forms roughly corre- spondent with actuality', and the fact that this remark has been quoted in innumerable examination papers shouldn't obscure its crucial im- portance in determining the kind of approach to Shakespeare that I am trying to define.[1] In the second place, our contemporary reader is likely to take for granted that the essential structure of the plays is to be sought in the poetry rather than in the more easily extractable elements of 'plot' and 'character'. I think our age is more aware of the complex structure, of the depth of life, of Shakespeare's verse, than any of its predecessors. Critics have written at length about his imagery, his ambiguities and overlaying meanings, his word-play, and so on; and there is no doubt that such studies have sharpened our sense not only of the tremendous activity of Shakespeare's verse—its generative power—but of the strong and subtle interconnections of meaning within the imaginative structure of the plays. It is significant that 'in- terpretation' relies heavily on extensive quotation and detailed analysis.[2] Finally—abandoning my hypothetical intelligent reader—I should say that our whole conception of Shakespeare's relation to his work, of what he was trying to do as an artist whilst at the same time satisfying the demands of the Elizabethan theatre, has undergone a very great change indeed. The 'new' Shakespeare, I should say, is much less impersonal than the old. Whereas in the older view Shakespeare was the god-like creator of a peopled world, projecting—it is true—his own spirit into the inhabitants, but remaining essentially the analyst of 'their' passions, he is now felt as much more immediately engaged in the action he puts before us. I don't of course mean that we have re-

---

[1] 'And Shakespeare's was a mind that thought in images, so that metaphor packs into metaphor, producing the most surprising collocations of apparently diverse phenomena: he thought of time, and death, and eternity, in terms of a candle, a shadow, and an actor. Is it not likely that the large and composite image of the story as a whole would serve him as a metaphor or symbol for his attitudes to certain aspects of experience?'—S. L. Bethell, *Shakespeare and the Popular Dramatic Tradition* (Staples, 1948), p. 115.

[2] A method that has its dangers, for we sometimes seem to run the risk of having the play read for us.

turned to Frank Harris's Shakespeare, engaged in drawing a succession
of full-length portraits of himself, but that we feel the plays (in Mr.
Eliot's words) 'to be united by one significant, consistent, and developing personality': we feel that the plays, even if 'in no obvious form',
'are somehow dramatizing . . . an action or struggle for harmony in
the soul of the poet'.[1] We take it for granted that Shakespeare thought
about the problems of life, and was at least as much interested in working towards an imaginative solution as he was in making a series of
detached studies of different characters, their motives and their passions.
Here again, specialist studies are indicative: we think it reasonable that
a scholar should inquire what evidence there is that Shakespeare had
read Hooker, and if so what effect it had on his plays; we inquire into
Shakespeare's political ideas and their background; we are prepared to
examine *Shakespeare's Philosophical Patterns*[2] (which is the title of a book
by the American scholar, W. C. Curry). In short, we take seriously
Coleridge's remark that Shakespeare was 'a philosopher'; the vision of
life that his plays express is, in a certain sense, a philosophic vision. But
at the same time we remember—at least, I should like to be able to say
we remember—that the plays are not dramatizations of abstract ideas,
but imaginative constructions mediated through the poetry. If Shakespeare's verse has moved well into the centre of the picture, one reason
is that linguistic vitality is now felt as the chief clue to the urgent
personal themes that not only shape the poetic-dramatic structure of
each play but form the figure in the carpet of the canon as a whole.[3]

This short and imperfect account may serve as an indication or re-
minder of the main lines of Shakespeare criticism since 1930, or thereabouts. Happily my job is not to award marks of merit to different
critics, and I don't intend to offer a list of obligatory reading. We all
have our own ideas about the recent critics who have helped us most
in our understanding of Shakespeare, and I don't suppose that we
should all agree about all of them. But I think we should agree that
there have been some books offering genuinely new insights, and that
where criticism has been most illuminating it has usually been on quite
non-Bradleyean lines. At the same time let us recall certain facts. If
'plot' and 'character'—mere 'precipitates from the memory'—sometimes seem to be described in abstraction from the full living im-

[1] See T. S. Eliot's essay on John Ford.
[2] Louisiana State University Press, 1937.
[3] A few sentences in this paragraph are borrowed from my essay on the
Tragedies in the Pelican Guide to English Literature (ed. Boris Ford), 2, *The Age
of Shakespeare*.

mediacy of our direct experience of the plays, and therefore to lead away from it, so too 'themes' and 'symbols' can be pursued mechanically and, as it were, abstractly. Whereas it is equally obvious that criticism in terms of 'character' can be genuinely revealing; John Palmer's *The Political Characters of Shakespeare*[1] is an example. And of course you can't get away from the term. Not only does the ordinary theatregoer or reader need it to explain his enjoyment, but even critics least in sympathy with Bradley at times naturally and necessarily define their sense of significance in terms appropriate to living people. Clearly the critical field has not been given over to those whom J. I. M. Stewart calls 'the new Bowdlers, whom man delights not, no nor woman neither, and who would give us not merely *Hamlet* without the Prince but the Complete Works without their several *dramatis personae*'. The notion of 'character', in some sense, has not disappeared, and is not going to disappear, from Shakespeare criticism. What we need to do is simply to clear up our minds about it, to make our handling of the term both more flexible and more precise.

Before I go on to give my own simple summing up of things as I see them I should like to mention two books that have a direct bearing on the matters we are pursuing. The first is J. I. M. Stewart's witty, entertaining and instructive *Character and Motive in Shakespeare*.[2] Stewart not only has some shrewd knocks at those who over-play the element of Elizabethan dramatic convention in Shakespeare and those who would tailor the plays too closely to the pattern of their own proprieties, he has some illuminating comments on particular plays. But his main interest, in the present connexion, lies in the way he develops the conception of character-presentation beyond the bounds of naturalism. To the extent that Shakespeare is concerned with character and motive— and he does 'present "man" and reveal psychological truths'—he works not through realistic portrayal but through poetry—that is, through symbolism and suggestion as well as by more direct means; and in this way he makes us aware not—or not only—of what we normally understand by character but of its hidden recesses.

The characters, then (but I mean chiefly those major characters with whom the imagination of the dramatist is deeply engaged), have often the superior reality of individuals exposing the deepest springs of their action. But this superior reality is manifested through the medium of situations which are sometimes essentially symbolical; and these may be extravagant or merely fantastic when not interpreted by the quickened imagination, for it is only

[1] Macmillan, 1945.   [2] Longmans, 1949.

during the prevalence of a special mode of consciousness, the poetic, that the underlying significance of these situations is perceived. (pp. 9–10)

Of just what Shakespeare brings from beyond this portal [of the depths of the mind], and how, we often can achieve little conceptual grasp; and often therefore the logical and unkindled mind finds difficulties which it labels as faults and attributes to the depravity of Shakespeare's audience or what it wills. But what the intellect finds arbitrary the imagination may accept and respond to, for when we read imaginatively or poetically we share the dramatist's penetration for a while and deep is calling to deep. (p. 30)[1]

   The other book I want to refer to is *Character and Society in Shakespeare*[2] by Professor Arthur Sewell. It is a small book but, I think, an important one. Briefly, Mr Sewell's contention is that the characters of a play only exist within the total vision that the play presents: 'in Shakespeare's plays the essential process of character-creation is a prismatic breaking-up of the comprehensive vision of the play' (p. 19). There is, therefore, an absolute distinction between a dramatic character and a person in real life whose conduct can be accounted for 'from general principles, from latent motives, and from policies not avowed'. 'We can only understand Shakespeare's characters so long as we agree that we cannot know all about them and are not supposed to know all

---

[1] This insistence on the imaginative—on the non-rational but not therefore irrational—portrayal of character, and on the need to respond to it imaginatively, is important, and, as I have said, Mr. Stewart can be illuminating. But it also seems to me that his method, as he pursues it, can sometimes lead outside the play, as in his use of psycho-analytic concepts to define Leontes' jealousy. The main criticism of any psycho-analytic account of Shakespeare's characters is not simply that it is irrelevant—though it may be—but that it reduces the material it works on to a category that can be known and docketed. To accept it is to feel that you know about a character something of importance that has been simply handed over, and that can be received alike by every reader, whatever the degree of his concern, the extent of his actual engagement, with the plays. It obscures not only the uniqueness but the *activity* of the work of art; whereas any play only exists for you to the extent that *you* have grappled with its meanings. Thus Mr. Stewart's account of Leontes' repressed homosexuality (reactivated by the presence of Polixenes, and then 'projected' on to Hermione) is relevant inasmuch as it points to the presence in what Leontes stands for of unconscious motivations, of motives beyond conscious control. But within the context of the play as a whole their exact nature is irrelevant: they are simply an X within the equation which is the play. What the play gives us is the awakening of new life that can enlist the same impulses which, in the first part, have been shown as the material of an unruly aberration. All we need to know of the aberration is that it is a representative manifestation: to pin it down exactly as Mr. Stewart does, is to make Leontes' jealousy something that we *know about* instead of something we *respond to* as part of the total generative pattern of the play.
[2] Clarendon Press, 1951.

about them' (p. 12). What is relevant for us is not an assumed hinterland of motives but simply the particular 'address to the world' that is embodied, with different degrees of explicitness, in the different characters. In the comedies the characters tend to be static and, so to speak, socially conditioned: they represent attitudes and modes of judgment that serve for the presentation and critical inspection of our everyday world. In the great tragedies the characters speak from out of a deeper level of experience—'metaphysical' rather than social, though the distinction is not absolute; the vision they embody is transformed in the full working out of the attitudes to which they are committed; and their reality is established by our own active commitment to the drama's dialectical play. Of both comedy and tragedy it can be said that 'unless Shakespeare had set our minds busy—and not only our minds—on various kinds of evaluation, his characters could never have engaged us and would have lacked all vitality' (p. 18). And again, there is the suggestion 'that character and moral vision must be apprehended together, and that when character is understood separately from moral vision it is not in fact understood at all' (p. 59).

Where, then, at the end of all this, do we come out? Perhaps only among what many people will regard as a handful of commonplaces. Let me start with the most thumping platitude of all: in Shakespeare's plays *some* impression of character is constantly being made upon us. It is likely to begin as soon as a major character is introduced.

> Why, I, in this weak piping time of peace,
> Have no delight to pass away the time,
> Unless to see my shadow in the sun
> And descant on mine own deformity.

> Though yet of Hamlet our dear brother's death
> The memory be green, and that it us befitted
> To bear our hearts in grief and our whole kingdom
> To be contracted in one brow of woe,
> Yet so far hath discretion fought with nature. . . .

I pray you, daughter, sing; or express yourself in a more comfortable sort.

Here, and in innumerable other instances, we have what Mr. Sewell calls the 'distillation of personality into style'. We know these people by the way they speak; as Mr. Stewart puts it, 'In drama the voice *is* the character'—though we also have to add that often Shakespeare

speaks *through* the person with a meaning different from, or even
contrary to, that apparently intended by the character.

At the same time we have to admit that our sense of character—of a
complex, unified tissue of thought and feeling from which a particular
voice issues—varies enormously not only as between different plays,
but as between the different figures within a single play. *All's Well
That Ends Well* is nearer to a morality play, and is less concerned with
characterization, in any sense, than is *Othello*. In *Measure for Measure*
'analysis of character' may take us a long way with Angelo; it is
utterly irrelevant as applied to the Duke.

Let me give another example—which will serve to illustrate Mr.
Sewell's remark about the characters embodying 'an address to the
world', in case anyone should have been left uneasy with that phrase.
Here is Don John introducing himself in conversation with Conrade
in Act I of *Much Ado About Nothing*.

> I wonder that thou, being—as thou say'st thou art—born under Saturn, goest
> about to apply a moral medicine to a mortifying mischief. I cannot hide
> what I am: I must be sad when I have cause, and smile at no man's jests; eat
> when I have stomach, and wait for no man's leisure; sleep when I am
> drowsy, and tend on no man's business; laugh when I am merry, and claw no
> man in his humour.

Conrade advises that he should apply himself to winning the good
opinion of his brother the Duke, with whom he is lately reconciled,
and Don John goes on:

> I had rather be a canker in a hedge than a rose in his grace; and it better fits
> my blood to be disdained of all than to fashion a carriage to rob love from
> any: in this, though I cannot be said to be a flattering honest man, it must
> not be denied but I am a plain-dealing villain. I am trusted with a muzzle and
> enfranchised with a clog; therefore I have decreed not to sing in my cage. If
> I had my mouth, I would bite; if I had my liberty, I would do my liking:
> in the meantime, let me be that I am, and seek not to alter me.

A good many things are plain from this—Don John's exacerbated
sense of superiority ('I . . . I . . . I . . . .'), his particular kind of 'melancholy', and his affectation of a blunt, no-nonsense manner. Clearly he
is related to Richard of Gloucester and to Iago. Their common
characteristic is an egotism that clenches itself hard against the claims of
sympathy, and that is unwilling to change—'I cannot hide what I am;
I must be sad when I have cause . . . let me be that I am, and seek not
to alter me.' It is, in short, the opposite of a character 'open' to others

and to the real demands of the present. That is all we know about Don
John and all we are required to know: we are not asked to consider his
bastardy or his other grievances. He is simply a perversely 'melancholy'
man who serves as villain of the piece, the agent of an otherwise
unmotivated evil.

What is true of a minor figure like Don John is true of all the
characters of Shakespeare: we know about them only what the play
requires us to know. Even to put the matter in this way is—as we shall
see in a minute—over-simplified and misleading, but it serves to remind us that however we define for ourselves a character and his rôle,
there is a strict criterion of relevance: he belongs to his play, and his
play is an art-form, not a slice of life. The fact that this at least is now
a commonplace is a guarantee that we shall never again have to waste
our time on the complete irrelevance of some forms of character-
analysis as applied to Shakespeare's *dramatis personae*.

But we still haven't got to the heart of the matter. What is the 'play
as a whole', to which we say the characters are subordinate? To this
question there is no simple answer, but we can at least attempt an
answer that will help our reading.

Poetic drama offers a vision of life, more or less complex, more or
less wide-embracing, as the case may be. Shakespeare's poetic drama as
a whole is different from Jonson's or Racine's; and within Shakespeare's poetic drama as a whole there are many different kinds. Even
at its simplest there is some degree of complexity, of dialectical play,
as persons embodying different attitudes are set before us in action and
interaction. Of course when we are watching them we don't think of
them as the embodiment of attitudes—of different addresses to the
world: we say simply, Rosalind is in love with Orlando. Yet while we
know that two addresses to the world can't fall in love, we also know
—and this knowledge moves from the back of our minds and comes
into action when, having seen or read the play several times, we try to
bring it into sharper focus—that Shakespeare is doing something more
significant with Rosalind and Orlando than showing us how interesting
it is when boy meets girl. *As You Like It*, which is a fairly simple play,
will help us here. *As You Like It* is of course a romantic comedy, with
its own interest and entertainment as such. But the plot and the structure of the incidents point to an interest in the meaning of a life lived
'according to nature'. Duke Senior's idyllic picture ('Hath not old
custom made this life more sweet Than that of painted pomp?' etc.) is
an over-simplification, as the play makes plain; but it is a possible atti-

tude, put forward for inspection, and as the play goes on it is clear that we are meant to take an intelligent interest in the varying degrees of naturalness and sophistication—each playing off against the other— that are put before us. *As You Like It*, in short, rings the changes on the contrasting meanings of 'natural' (either 'human' or 'close down to the life of nature') and 'civilized' (either 'well nurtured' or 'artificial')— all especially pointed with reference to the passion of love. It is largely an entertainment; but at the same time it is a serious comedy of ideas— not abstract ideas to be debated, but ideas as embodied in attitude and action. So that by playing off against each other different attitudes to life, the play as a whole offers a criticism of various forms of exaggeration and affectation—either 'romantic' or professedly realistic—with Rosalind as arbiter, although of course she is not above the action but involved in it herself.[1]

What is true of *As You Like It* is also true of greater plays, such as *Measure for Measure*, *King Lear*, or *Antony and Cleopatra*, though here of course the play of varied sympathies and antipathies, of imaginative evaluation as different possibilities of living are put before us, is more complex, and the experience handled is more profound. But of all the greater plays it is true to say that *all* the characters are necessary to express the vision—the emergent 'idea' or controlling preoccupation— and they are necessary only in so far as they do express it. Gloucester's part in *King Lear* is not to give additional human interest, but to enact and express a further aspect of the Lear experience; for with Gloucester, as with Lear, confident acceptance of an inadequate code gives place to humble acceptance of the human condition, and there are glimpses of a new wisdom:

> I have no way, and therefore want no eyes;
> I stumbled when I saw.

The striking parallels between the two men are proof enough of deliberate artistic intention in this respect.

What *King Lear* also forces on us, even when we are prepared to see the different characters as contributing to a pattern, is the inadequacy of terms relating to 'character'. What character has Edgar in his successive transformations? In the storm scenes, where Lear's vision of horror is built to a climax, we are acted on directly by the poetry, by

---

[1] See James Smith's excellent essay on *As You Like It* in *Scrutiny*, IX. i. June, 1940, reprinted in *The Importance of Scrutiny*, ed. Eric Bentley (Grove Press, New York, 1957).

what is said, in some respects independently of our sense of a particular person saying it. So too in the play as a whole, and in the other greater plays, our sense of the characters—of what the characters stand for in their 'address to the world', their 'moral encounter with the universe'—is inseparable from the more direct ways in which, by poetry and symbolism, our imaginations are called into play. To take one simple example. When Macbeth, on his first appearance, says, 'So foul and fair a day I have not seen,' he does far more than announce himself as a character—tired, collected, brooding; echoing the Witches' 'Fair is foul, and foul is fair', he takes his place in the pattern of moral evaluations which make the play so much more than the story of a tragic hero, which make it into a great vision of the unreality, the negative horror, that evil is. In reading Shakespeare our sense of 'character', defined and limited as I have tried to define and limit it, is important; but so is our responsiveness to symbolism (the storm in *Othello* and Othello's trance, Lear's bare heath and Gloucester's Dover Cliff, Hermione's moving statue), and so is our responsiveness to imagery (the imagery of darkness conveying spiritual blindness in *Macbeth*), to verse rhythm, and to all the inter-acting elements of the poetry: it is from these that there emerges a controlling direction of exploratory and committed interests—of interests involving the personality as a whole—that we indicate by some such word as 'themes'.

Mr. John Holloway has recently objected to the use of 'theme' in Shakespeare criticism:[1] it is a sign that the work in question is to be reduced to a generalized moral reflection, whereas literature does not provide us with general truths, only with particular instances. 'What *Macbeth* does . . . is to depict for us, in great and remarkable detail, one imagined case and one only.' 'Narrative', he suggests, is 'the fundamental quality of the full-length work', the essential principle of imaginative order. Now both these conceptions of the work of art as 'one imagined case and one only', and of 'narrative' as the controlling principle, seem to me to be, in their turn, open to objection. But I think we are dealing with something far greater than the particular question—Is Shakespeare most profitably discussed in terms of 'character' or 'theme' or 'narrative'? What has come into sight, what we must take account of, is nothing less than the depth of life of any great work of art, its capacity to enter into our lives as power. What do we mean when we say that a great work of art has a universal appeal?

[1] 'The New "Establishment" in Criticism', *The Listener*, September 20th and 27th, 1956.

Surely something more than that it tells a story likely to interest every-body. We mean that the special case (and I grant Mr. Holloway the artist's 'passion for the special case') brings to a focus a whole range of awareness, that it generates an activity of imaginative apprehension that illuminates not only the 'case' in question but life as we know it in our own experience: it can modify, or even transform, our whole way of seeing life and responding to it. It is this capacity to generate mean-ings that is the 'universal' quality in the particular work of art. And it is the presence of the universal in the particular that compels the use of such generalizing terms as 'themes' or 'motifs'. Of course, like other critical terms, they can be used mechanically or ineptly, can harden into counters pushed about in a critical game. But as simple pointers their function is to indicate the *direction* of interest that a play compels when we try to meet it with the whole of ourselves—to meet it, that is (using De Quincey's term), as literature of power.

To read Shakespeare, then (and in reading I include seeing his plays performed), we need to cultivate a complex skill. But there is no need to make heavy weather of this. That skill can be largely intuitive; we can reach it in many ways, and there is no need (especially if we are teachers) to be too insistent on any one approach. In 'Demosius and Mystes', a dialogue appended to *Church and State*, Coleridge refers to a mighty conflict between two cats, 'where one tail alone is said to have survived the battle'. There is always a danger of critical squabbles be-coming like that; and I for one would rather see among my pupils an honest and first-hand appreciation of what is offered by way of 'character' than a merely mechanical working out of recurrent imagery and symbolic situations. We should remember also that the life of the imagination runs deeper than our conscious formulations. T. S. Eliot (in his Introduction to S. L. Bethell's book on Shakespeare), says of the persons of the play of a modern verse dramatist,

> they must on your stage be able to perform the same actions, and lead the same lives, as in the real world. But they must somehow disclose (not neces-sarily be aware of) a deeper reality than that of the plane of most of our conscious living; and what they disclose must be, not the psychologist's intellectualization of this reality, but the reality itself.

'They must somehow disclose (not necessarily be aware of) a deeper reality': I think that what Eliot says of the persons in verse plays like his own, applies—*mutatis mutandis*—to the spectators of poetic drama. To the extent that a Shakespeare tragedy truly enlists the imagination (and this means enlisting it for what is in the play, not for a display of virtuosity) it is precisely this deeper level of apprehension—the hidden potentialities, wishes, and fears of the individual spectator—that is being worked on, even though the spectator himself may not be conscious of it, and thinks that he is simply watching someone else's 'character issuing in action'.

All the same, even when this is admitted, there is no reason why the common reader should not be encouraged to see rather more. For it is in our imaginative response to *the whole play*—not simply to what can be extracted as 'character', nor indeed to what can be simply extracted as 'theme' or 'symbol'—that the meaning lies; and Shakespeare calls on us to be as fully conscious as we can, even if consciousness includes relaxed enjoyment and absorption as well as, sometimes, more deliberate attention to this or that aspect of the whole experience.

5

SHAKESPEARE'S PASTORAL COMEDY

by MARY LASCELLES

CRITICISM bearing on the pastoral strain in Shakespearian comedy belongs to two widely separated groups: that of the distant past, broadly based, both as to what it asserts and what it takes for granted—which is why I mean to begin with it; and that, more pointed and particular, of the immediate present. It is this which poses a problem for me. When you have been teaching for more years than you care to reckon, a piece of fresh criticism will sometimes make its impact in successive waves. First: 'Why yes, but isn't this what I have been trying to say all this while?' Second (in the voice of conscience): 'Trying is the operative word—when have you succeeded in formulating this idea?' Nevertheless, the conclusion must always be: 'For me, it is never completely uttered until I have said it myself—or said what arises from this encounter of old and new ideas.' Thus, while it is the least I can do, to acknowledge indebtedness (bluntly, for brevity's sake) to a number of writers whose work has appeared of late—notably, in the eighth and eleventh volumes of the annual *Shakespeare Survey*[1]—it is also the most. For it still remains for me to find my own way forward, asking such questions as I can frame, and seeking answers for which I can find words.

Hazlitt prompts the first of these questions, by what he says about Shakespearian comedy. The immediate context is *Twelfth Night*, but I think that his comments on this play apply—and that he would have been willing that they should apply—more widely; at least to include all those of Shakespeare's comedies that are called romantic. 'This,' he says, '. . . is perhaps too good-natured for comedy. . . . It makes us laugh at the follies of mankind, not despise them, and still less bear any ill-will towards them.' And, after contrasting it with the artificial and

[1] Cambridge University Press. I must single out for special gratitude Professor Harold Jenkins (on *As You Like It*, in *Shakespeare Survey* 8).

satirical comedy of the Restoration, he proceeds to generalize: 'Shakespeare's comedy is of a pastoral and poetical cast. Folly is indigenous to the soil, and shoots out with native, happy, unchecked luxuriance. Absurdity has every encouragement afforded it; and nonsense has room to flourish in.'[1]

I propose to consider what these conjunctions mean: comedy *but* good-natured; inviting laughter that is free from contempt, and of a pastoral, poetical cast. Why, in the first place, did Hazlitt plant that (implied) *but* between comedy and all these agreeable things—the laughter of sheer enjoyment, poetry, the world of the pastoral?

Perhaps I may be allowed a personal illustration. I happened once to be lecturing on *Henry IV*—to an audience that was, or chose to appear, decidedly non-committal. Therefore I was the more surprised when one member of it—a particularly grave-looking graduate from overseas—joined me as I walked back and told me that he had never really thought Falstaff funny until he listened to me. I replied with proper modesty that it was George Robey he should have heard. No, that was not what he meant. All the literary, all the learned people he had met hitherto had been insistent that comedy was meant to do something beneficial to you—to make you better, not to make you laugh. Now, if this seems far-fetched, let me point out that, according to some eminent scholars and critics, Falstaff *cannot* have been meant to amuse the judicious, since he is merely the traditional figure of Riot misleading Youth—an interpretation which, as Miss Gardner points out, has had an enervating effect on some recent productions of the play, 'in which Falstaff has seemed so oppressed by awareness that he is temptation incarnate that he has hardly had the spirit to present any serious temptation.'[2]

Were we meant to enjoy the rogues and fools of Shakespearian comedy? And does that enjoyment touch hands with liking? (Enjoyment and liking must, surely, go along together in actual life; but I think that they need not in art; we can enjoy the representation of what we by no means like—and that, in most other kinds of comedy, is what we are invited to do.)

Coleridge's theory of comedy may help: he was hardly likely to devise one which would exclude Shakespeare. He calls it 'poetry in unlimited jest'. It entails, he says, 'the apparent abandonment of all definite aim or end, the removal of all bounds in the exercise of the

[1] *Characters of Shakespeare's Plays*: 'Twelfth Night'.
[2] Helen Gardner: *The Limits of Literary Criticism* (O.U.P. 1956).

F

mind'. It is (he continues) 'a display of intellectual wealth squandered in the wantonness of sport without an object'.[1]

Now I believe that such comedy as this description comprises asks certain conditions, a particular climate of the imagination. The world in which this pure comic spirit can operate must be at once like and unlike our own. Thus, there are in this world laws of cause and effect; but, against their very nature, they act intermittently. Here, as in our world, you may, if you touch fire, burn your fingers; for it is not a world in which fire never burns, but, rather, one in which it sometimes forgets to burn—or even burns the wrong man, the one who has kept well out of its way. Retribution is not, as in satire, inexorable; the dispenser of justice may be entreated—or may prove absent-minded. The proper consequence of an act is sometimes suspended—now in favour of the fox, now on behalf of the goose. (Suspended only; where would be the sport if all law were annulled?)

Here, a doubt occurs. This is all very well so long as we are concerned with pure comedy: a game in which there is no finality—if the players desist, it is only because they wait for the impulse to renew itself; a country dance tune, whose last phrase is an irresistible invitation to a new beginning. It is natural and reasonable to contrast this 'intellectual wealth squandered in the wantonness of sport' with satire, which closes with a clang—the villain punished, the fools frightened into prudent behaviour. But what are we to make of romantic comedy? It also has its close, much like a resolution of discord in music. Theseus turns back to Athens with the words:

> . . . in the temple, by and by, with us,
> These couples shall eternally be knit.[2]

Moreover, the knitting follows a pattern of poetic justice—or purports to do; we may have to exercise a little kindly forgetfulness in favour of Demetrius—and even of Helena. He was unfaithful before ever the magic juice touched his eyelids; she has made us wonder whether faithfulness is really a virtue. After all, it is Shakespeare's way to overlook shortcomings; and the total impression stands: romantic comedy closes on true love rewarded. But will not its rewards be as alien to 'the abandonment of all definite aim or end', to 'sport without an object', as are the punishments of satire? So there *is* a problem involved in the conjunction of qualities which Hazlitt remarked—a conjunction

---

[1] *Lectures and Notes on Shakespeare*, ed. T. Ashe (1884), p. 188.
[2] *A Midsummer Night's Dream*, IV. i. 186, 7.

peculiarly Shakespearian: comedy; good nature; pastoral—which, for
the Elizabethan dramatist, signified first and foremost pastoral romance,
a literary species brought from abroad, but naturalized with the good
gardener's intuitive skill and boldness. It was (I believe) by way of this
very Elizabethan approach to the pastoral way of writing—and thinking, and feeling—that Shakespeare attained what Milton calls 'heart-
easing Mirth', and Johnson 'the greatest end of comedy—making an
audience merry'. For the qualities which set Shakespearian comedy
apart from all other kinds are Elizabethan qualities, though raised to a
higher power. The men who were born not far from the middle of the
sixteenth century and grew up in the sixties, seventies and eighties, rediscovered the lost land of pastoral on their own frontiers, recognizing
that its language and customs were not strange. This discovery, like a
fine early morning, was too good to last; it had to give way to the
sultry brilliance of Jacobean romantic fashions; but Shakespeare never
wholly relinquished his vision—even his last plays, which have provoked such a variety of explanations, ranging from boredom to theo-
phany, are best understood in the light of this pastoral morning.

To support this proposition I should need the space of a sizeable book.
For example, why 'lost'? Why 'rediscovered'? I can only say that what
I assume to be the true significance of pastoral must have been overlaid
by the use as a school textbook of Mantuan's Eclogues—satiric dia-
tribes, attributed to shepherds, but resembling the original pastoral
eclogues no more than a lecturer on drama resembles a dramatist—and
seven worlds away from pastoral romance. What, then, was recovered,
and where, and in what form? To answer this I shall have to ask your
patience while I trace one tradition of pastoral writing a little way back
towards its source.

Pastoral romance (as the Elizabethans practised it) derives—at some
distance—from those long, leisurely, extravagant prose tales written in
the decline of the ancient world, among the Greek colonies in the
islands and on the farther shore of the Mediterranean. One alone can
truly be called pastoral—*Daphnis and Chloe*; yet all had something to
contribute to the tradition of pastoral romance. Revived in the
Renaissance, given currency in Latin and vernacular translations, they
gained an influence out of all proportion to their merits, and took new
life from better men than their original authors. (So it may happen that
some vigorous future writer will derive inspiration from this or that
group of minor novels which to our eyes shimmer only with the
phosphorescence of decay—and a still more distant critic will wonder

what he found in them.) Intricately patterned stories—the theme of love prevailing in Italy and France, of chivalry in Spain—captured the imagination of courtly audiences and were presently popularized. We, of course, expected to have it all ways: hence our mingling, on the stage and in print, of conventions proper to tales of both love and chivalry, to exotic and to homely narrative art. There was indeed some warrant for this boldness. I count it significant that three seminal pieces of Renaissance story-telling—Boiardo's *Orlando Innamorato*, Montemayor's *Diana*, and Sidney's *Arcadia*—were left each at the death of its author in a state to invite completion. For such romance, with its hint of improvisation to please a particular audience, seems to engage our imagination in such a way that, if the narrator cannot finish, it becomes an office of friendship to dream out his dream for him. (Imagine Walter Scott dying in his early thirties, with *The Lay of the Last Minstrel* incomplete—who but would wish to carry it further?) The *Arcadia*, which Sidney had relinquished in the midst of revision, owed its ending, as the Elizabethans knew it, partly to his sister. It has the air of an unfinished building which loving care and some regard for the original design have made habitable, and indeed elegant, but which still guards the secret of that full purpose which was growing in the builder's mind even as he worked. For this reason, and also because it has lately been studied in particular relation to Shakespeare, I prefer to use for my principal illustration that other romance which may have been Sidney's initial inspiration, and was surely one of Shakespeare's: the *Diana* of Montemayor. About a year after its first appearance in print, its author was killed, leaving his slight but intricate tale with some threads still to be tied up—and therefore (like Boiardo's) at the mercy of continuators. What they added tended to stick, and, by the time that an English translation appeared,[1] Montemayor's pretty little book had become a bulky folio.

How am I to describe in a few words the total impression left in my own mind by the *Diana*—let alone its intrinsic character? If I assert—where I should rather suggest, substantiate and so persuade—it is because I am forced to take the nearest way to a place which, when I reach it, will be no more than my point of departure. First, then: never believe those travel-weary historians of literature who tell you that this romance is unreadable—nor that its English dress is an ungainly make-shift. The translator, Bartholomew Young, has been hardly used. His original, like most of its kind, was a medley of prose and verse, and the

[1] In 1598—it had, however, been completed in 1583.

ill luck of inclusion in an Elizabethan miscellany has made some of his songs familiar; for them I will not enter the smallest plea. But his prose, which is often tart and fresh, and never insipid, has come to us only in those well-meaning, insidious, unavoidable extracts called Shakespearian sources—there must be few notable romances of his age which Shakespeare did not know and lay under contribution. But, here, as so often, virtue resides in the whole, not in the part he can be shown to have used.

The pattern of the stories which (folded one within another) compose this whole can be intimated thus: A loves B, but B loves C—who loves nobody until, mistaking D for E, and being mistaken by G for H, he endeavours to extricate himself by feigning love for A, supposing her to be—well, you see how it goes, and with no more reason than that, as Puck says, 'Cupid is a knavish lad.' All this is set in a world where we may reckon with some three or four *constants*. The pastoral region is a place of refuge, and the dominant symbol of relief from danger, weariness, want, every ill, is water. By stream or spring forlorn lovers may linger, recounting their former vicissitudes, until the completion of a prescribed cycle, the fulfilment of some oracular prediction, brings lost opportunity round again, and they—wiser than before —reach out and take it. Thus, time has a strange circular movement; it accords with the rhythm of the revolving seasons. True, the pastoral poet has often lamented that, while nature renews itself, man goes his way once for all. (This is, of course, mere human make-believe—the pretence that it is last year's rose or nightingale come back to us.) In pastoral romance, however, man may sometimes share in this self-renewal. It is as though, tilting the hour-glass (a much more vivid symbol than our clock), he could give himself, not the next hour, but the past hour over again. And so, surprisingly, the oracle, which in Greek myths of the prime had signified the inescapability of a man's destiny, and had usually been charged with tragic implications, has now, in the silver age and in tales deriving from it, assumed an almost contrary character and become a symbol of the second chance. In such a world, the shepherd boy may well pipe as though he should never be old, and the parents of a lost child make light of the years of waiting.

Here is another constant in such romance: loss and recovery—identity itself is very easily lost or mislaid, to be reassumed when the time is ripe. (The deserted girl who seeks redress in boy's disguise is much older than the need to provide fitting parts for boy actors.) Where none is known until he chooses to disclose himself, the odds are strongly in favour of an unknown champion proving a woman—or, if a man, one alienated from his rights, or his very name. And, where many do not know themselves for what they are, a shepherdess may well find herself a queen, or an outlaw the heir to a kingdom.

So far, you might truly say, the characteristics I have described could belong equally to romance or pastoral—and indeed these are not very easily distinguished in their Elizabethan forms. But there is this difference. Whereas, in romance, the final pattern is composed of rewards and punishments, ideally distributed, pastoral has a variant of its own. Here innocence is a protection, and contentment, set high among the virtues, is in a special sense its own reward, since the contented mind receives no injury from the blows of adverse fortune. An ideal world —yes; but not the world of enervating daydream.

I have now in my hands the main threads of my argument, and can gather illustrations (particularly from the *Diana*), and weave in Shakespearian analogies. Montemayor's story is, as you will have inferred, too cobweb-like to bear retelling, but one strand may be followed to its conclusion. Felismena, whose birth was attended by dark sayings, is deserted by her lover, follows him in boy's dress (as Julia follows Proteus) and serves him in his courtship of Celia (as Viola serves Orsino). Parted from him once more, she takes to arms and, championing the oppressed, finds herself in the midst of a shepherd community. After many exchanges of tale and song among these pastoral people gathered round a spring, all of them resolve on visiting the wise lady Felicia and the temple of Diana. For some lovers of small consequence, Felicia has magical remedies, not unlike Oberon's. To another, the man she mourns is restored; his death, which she believed herself to have witnessed, was an eye-cheating trick—one very common in the Greek romances. For Felismena, however, according to the oracular Felicia, further trials and greater happiness are reserved. Setting out on her quest again, she comes among other shepherds—gentle, dark-skinned, and speaking Portuguese, her native tongue, and Montemayor's likewise, though he wrote in Castilian. On an island in the river by whose banks they live, she rescues a hard-pressed knight. He is, of course, her lost love, and Felicia has only to give him the water of remembrance to bring about a perfect reconciliation. How much of all this (my general propositions and particular instances) may we, without ever labouring a point, relate to Shakespeare? I suggest that refuge among unworldly people and resort to a benevolent oracular power recur significantly in his pastoral comedy.

When Le Beau, in *As You Like It*, warns Orlando of the enmity of
the usurping Duke, he is to all appearance acting out of character.
Shakespeare can be very peremptory with one of his minor *dramatis
personae* if he wants something done and there is nobody else at hand
to do it. But the words in which this apparently shallow and time-
serving courtier takes leave of the man whose life he has saved at some
risk to his own are even more surprising than his action:

> Hereafter, in a better world than this,
> I shall desire more love and knowledge of you.[1]

And what else can this 'better world' be than Arden? And what is
Arden but a pastoral region where lost children are found, parted
lovers reunited, dispossessed men come to their own again, and repentance and reconciliation grow like the leaves on the trees? To support
this I must ask your patience while I reach back and draw in yet another
strand of argument.

I believe, first, that exotic myths will most readily take possession of
minds familiar from childhood with story-patterns that in some way
resemble them; and, secondly, that the English counterpart of that
pastoral world in which

> earthly things made even
> Atone together[2]

was a legendary forest: Sherwood Forest, ruled by the gentle outlaw.
It is evident that Shakespeare was familiar with the Robin Hood
ballads and pageants and popular plays—these may have been the
'Whitsun pastorals' Perdita recalled—and the recollections he cherished
of them seem to have been pleasant. The references to them are, it is
true, given to disreputable characters or spoken in jest; but so are those
to all figures of popular, native story in his plays, and this I take to be
no more than a concession to the clever young men in the audience. It
is certain at least that an undercurrent of allusion to the dispossessed
man and the gentle outlaw runs through no fewer than three plays:
The Two Gentlemen of Verona, *As You Like It* and *Cymbeline*.

The first is a mere sketch: bold, even careless. Valentine, 'in disgrace
with fortune and men's eyes',[3] is welcomed by the outlaws; he is the
very man they have been waiting for, and he undertakes to lead them
on condition that none shall offer violence to women or mere travellers.
(So Robin Hood in the ballad claims:

[1] I. ii. 301, 2.   [2] v. iv. 116, 7.   [3] Sonnet 29.

I never hurt woman in all my life,
Nor man in woman's company.)

He muses on life in the forest, as Duke Senior will teach his followers
to do in Arden. And, again as in Arden, when the end comes it will
compass the three conditions necessary to a happy ending in Shakespearian comedy: truth will be revealed; those on whom this revelation
casts an ugly light will repent; the oppressed and the oppressor will be
reconciled. Indeed, Valentine has but to find his enemy at his mercy to
forgive him freely. Even the outlaws turn out to be 'men endu'd with
worthy qualities'—or so Valentine tells the Duke.[1] Had he forgotten
their original confessions, or did he claim that his brief rule had
reformed them? Perhaps the forest had worked its magic.

Now in *As You Like It* we find such a strange mixture of the old
Robin Hood legends and the newly rediscovered pastoral romance
that I must remind you briefly of its origins. The oldest to survive is the
Tale of Gamelyn: a lay (longer and more circumstantial than a ballad;
more downright and homely than a romance) belonging to the second
quarter of the fourteenth century, but, from the fifteenth onwards,
attributed to Chaucer; shining, therefore, with a borrowed lustre.
Rough it certainly is, probably representing an early phase in the
development of that legend whose outcome is the cycle of Robin
Hood ballads. It is a tale of rights lost and recovered; taken by cunning,
regained by strength. The youngest of three brothers (hardy, bold,
but something of a simpleton) is cheated of his due by the eldest, and
calls into the balance against him other simple, wronged men. Their
fortunes swing to and fro; but right finally gets the upper hand in that
forest world where the outlaws have established a rule of their own.
They have been driven from their homes by oppression; and, even if
they are not quite so gentle as the foresters of later tradition, they
know how to maintain order: that is, they are ruled by a king, not by
force, fraud or fortune. Before him Gamelyn is summoned to give an
account of himself—together with Adam, his brother's steward, who
has helped him to escape, and shared his wanderings and hardships.

Than seide the maister kyng of outlawes,
'What seeke ye, younge men under woode-schawes?'
Gamelyn answerde the kyng with his croune,
'He moste needes walke in woode that may not walke in towne.'[2]

---

[1] v. iv. 153.   [2] Ed. Skeat (Oxford, 1926), ll, 669-72.

At the end, it is by summoning his friends the outlaws that he redresses the balance of justice—in an episode suggesting the outlines of a popular cartoon: the poacher on the bench, the squire and parson in the dock. And, with a flourish of legality, the King of England himself makes Gamelyn and Adam justices of the peace, and hangs all their enemies.

Presently, the Robin Hood ballads bear this story some way down towards the rich lowland pastures of romance. There, the knight who has fallen into the clutches of the Church (by bankruptcy, not heresy) wanders gently and disconsolately about the forest, until the outlaws (rather by show of strength than outright violence) regain his lands for him. (It is strange to consider that, when we reach the broad plains of Elizabethan romantic comedy, the Church—once the most powerful landowner in all England—will be reduced to a few friars and hermits who offer sensible advice, perform convenient but slightly irregular marriage ceremonies and convert usurping dukes in forest glades.) The ballads vary, of course, in tone; but their general tendency is towards a softening of the Gamelyn story, and this continues into Elizabethan drama, and probably the Robin Hood pageants also—which, with a touch of sentimental archaism, glorified the old English long-bow while it was falling out of use as a weapon of war. (Contrariwise, that mercenary soldier, Falstaff, carries a pistol—long before it was invented.)

Lodge's *Rosalynde*, the immediate precursor and substantial source of *As You Like It*, is a gay and graceful mixture of the old stories of Sherwood justice with the new, fashionable, pastoral romances. Lodge, an adventurous reader, was familiar with *Gamelyn*, Sidney's *Arcadia* (probably in manuscript) and, we may be sure, popular versions of the Robin Hood legend. And he had his share of the authentic Elizabethan magic, 'gilding pale streams with heavenly alchemy'. He has caught the happy timelessness of pastoral; any of his characters might say with Orlando: 'There's no clock in the forest.'[1] It has become the realm of 'love in idleness'. Replacing the 'wife good and fair' whom Gamelyn married in the last line but four—and a line is all she is allowed—princesses and shepherdesses (the princesses disguised as shepherdesses, the shepherdesses as courtly in their bearing as the princesses) await the approach of their suitors, sonnet in hand. And these are better love-poems than Orlando's. Was it Shakespeare's whim, or was it his wisdom, to give us the very poetry of love—and not allow so much as one

[1] III. ii. 321.

of his lovers to write a respectable piece of verse? Perhaps his motive
was akin to Chaucer's, when he took for himself the Tale of Sir Thopas.

These unreckoned riches of pastoral leisure belong rather to narrative
than to drama, and I think there are signs that Shakespeare recognized
this as a problem confronting him. Orlando, though he is driven from
his brother's house within the narrow compass of the play, is indeed
the lost child of traditional romance: he has been reared as though a
foundling; nevertheless 'he's gentle, never schooled and yet learned,
full of noble device'.[1] Then, time-inconsistencies have been apparent
to the critics, and by some set down to revision:[2] the rightful Duke's
banishment seems to be news when Charles tells it to Oliver—yet, by
Celia's account, it happened when she was too young to plead for her
cousin; and the Duke himself speaks of his forest life as though it had
endured the season's change. Presently, the usurping Duke gives Oliver
a year in which to find his brother, though our impression of the play's
duration is a few fleeting days. (The change from winter to summer, in
a recent production, was—to my thinking—an innovation enjoyable
while fresh, but not fit to establish a new theatrical tradition). Is it
fanciful to suggest that Shakespeare, when he began to write, had
hardly counted the cost of the alterations he must make and, if he later
noticed discrepancies, did not care to efface them, preferring a *past-
indefinite* tense? The passage of the seasons, especially as it is reflected in
the talk of the older men (Duke Senior and Adam), signifies an acceptance of the terms of mortal life:

> my age is as a lusty winter,
> Frosty, but kindly.[3]

The condition of this acceptance of change is the contented mind. In
Arden, love fosters its own peculiar impatience, but those who are
free 'fleet the time carelessly, as they did in the golden world'.[4] Their
contentment extends even to little things: Jaques' failure to disturb the
equanimity of any but the lovers—and *they* give as good as they get. I
suspect that a small illustration of this has been swept away in the process of tidying the text, and I would plead for its restoration. Who
should sing the third stanza of 'Under the greenwood tree'? Jaques
offers it to Amiens who, according to the First Folio, agrees to sing
and launches into it with the words, 'Thus it goes.' But the subsequent
Folios and modern editions and (so far as I can tell) stage tradition have

[1] I. i. 175.   [2] Notably by the New Cambridge editors.
[3] II. iii. 52.   [4] I. i. 127.

transferred those three words, together with the stanza, to Jaques—
only the New Cambridge editors offering a hesitant defence of the
Folio text in a note. Now, the actor who plays Jaques is rarely a singer,
and the stanza is usually declaimed to a little audience (Amiens and
anyone else who can be mustered) with such acrimony that Amiens'
subsequent question loses its point. But, let Jaques put a paper into
Amiens' hand, and let *him* sing innocently this parody of his own two
stanzas, asking with unruffled good humour, at the close, 'What is
Ducdame?'—and there is some reason for Jaques' exasperated retort:
' 'Tis a Greek invocation to call fools into a circle.'[1] The satirist is
baffled by the world of comedy.

Unexpectedness ranks high among the distinctive qualities of *As You
Like It*. The play tingles with questions. I deny altogether the claim that
it is a satire on pastoral convention. True, it returns an echo to the
pastoral idea; but the tone of this echo has not the heart-searching
melancholy of Raleigh's:

> If all the world and love were young,
> And truth in every Sheepheards tongue,
> These pretty pleasures might me move,
> To live with thee, and be thy love——

nor the scorching irony of Donne's:

> Come live with mee, and bee my love,
> And wee will some new pleasures prove. . . .

It is the tone rather of a brisk challenge—one to which the sequel may
yet be: 'Pass friend, and all's well;' and, if the pastoral idea is challenged, that is because it *is* an idea, a pattern for living laid up in the
mind, and such ideas are in full flight, and the people of the play in full
cry after them, all up and down the glades of Arden. Everything is set
off by contrasts; and the alternations are so swift that we might as
well try to tell the colour of a field of ripening barley combed by the
wind as capture any of the successive moods by definition. If the
idealism of the Duke is called in question by Jaques, why, so is the
cynicism of Jaques by the Duke. Rosalind, herself 'many fathom deep
in love' and pursued by Celia's keen raillery, undertakes to turn every
convention of love-making inside-out; and against her romantic
friendship with Celia is set her astringent treatment of Phoebe. None
of the disputants has the last word; but, with the possible exception of

[1] II. v. 48-58.

Jaques, none of them wants it. The pursuer lets the quarry escape, sure that he will not go far, for fear of ending the pursuit. This is indeed Coleridge's 'intellectual wealth squandered in the wantonness of sport without an object'. How is it to be reconciled with the need inherent in romance, to resolve all discords in a full close?

In the first place, it is necessary that all the characters should go back where they belong. Do not quarrel with this; it is required by the pattern of loss and recovery. Dekker confuses this issue when—turning the story of patient Griselda into a play—he makes her father's home, to which she returns bringing her children, a place of pastoral felicity, where the loveliest of all his songs is sung. Only her brother, a spoiled scholar and a character of Dekker's own invention, is ignorant of what Griselda knows:

> . . . adversity
> Dwells still with them that dwell with misery,
> But mild content hath eas'd me of that yoke;
> Patience hath borne the bruise, and I the stroke.[1]

Thus, when the story is pulled back into its course, we are haunted by remembrance of his pastoral world and would be glad to return to it. But the ring which is the proper symbol of pastoral romance is not rounded into completion until each of the characters has fulfilled the destiny to which he, or she, was born; and, to this end, the Duke must reassume his office—in a court where (as Professor Jenkins points out)[2] goodness has been restored and Jaques' occupation's gone, Rosalind must reign after him with Orlando, the dispossessed man come to his own again, and benignant powers must operate.

Now, I freely admit that Hymen is not a very impressive counterpart even of the *romantic* oracle. Nevertheless, I find it significant that Shakespeare should have employed, for the ending of *As You Like It*, these three agents: a symbolical figure, speaking such archaic verse as he gives to Jupiter and the ghosts in *Cymbeline*, Juno and Ceres in *The Tempest*; a mood of half-belief in Rosalind's tale of her uncle the magician ('most profound in his art and yet not damnable'); and a pattern of riddling stipulations, propounded by Rosalind in her character as *magician's boy*, to which the lovers must subscribe—and which, being fulfilled, resolve all discords.

The oracle in *Cymbeline* has proved a stumbling-block; and—not to

---

[1] *Patient Grissill* (attributed to Dekker, Chettle and Haughton), v. ii.
[2] *Shakespeare Survey* 8, p. 45.

pursue this question further than our purpose requires—it performs its function awkwardly: it bears no intelligible relation in time to those confessions by which the skein of the plot will presently be unravelled, nor any in place to that ideal country which Imogen has found and lost again, where outlaws offer refuge to the oppressed, and recognize an imposter, even in a true man's clothes. And yet I believe the use of this device to be in keeping with those pastoral intimations—with Imogen's wish, before ever she set out on the journey which led to the outlaw's cave, that she and Posthumus had been herdsmen's children; with the mountain-bred boy's victory over the court-bred ruffler and braggart. Suppose that Shakespeare was finding his way back to a source of imaginative fulfilment which had charmed him some years earlier, but was cumbered with too weighty and intricate a story, and had to rest content with something short of his full purpose.

Within a year or so, he recognized what he sought, hidden away in that old-fashioned and unprepossessing little tale, Greene's *Pandosto*. It had something he needed: an oracle which, as a source of infallible truth, could be credited with authority, even sanctity; which would inevitably punish the unbeliever and yet—so far had tragedy given ground to romance—let punishment teach repentance, and repentance cherish hope; and shepherds, the traditional guardians of that place of refuge in which hope might be realized.

To show why I believe that *The Winter's Tale* transcends the models on which it is framed by obtaining their ultimate purpose, I shall have to ask a question which must sound very simple and matter-of-fact: in those ancient tragic stories which turn upon oracular prediction, what would have happened if the people whom it threatens had taken no notice of it? If King Acrisius, warned that he would be killed by his grandson, had not imprisoned his daughter, nor, when her child was born, put them both to sea in an open boat, Perseus would not have caused the death of an unknown man, and found himself the slayer of his grandfather. For the point of these stories seems to be that it is a man's efforts to avert his fate which fasten it upon him. We are therefore (I take it) to understand that a man so visited can no more desist from struggling than could an animal caught in a trap. Does Shakespearian pastoral comedy shirk this knowledge, or see beyond it?

All I can now attempt is to point out some ways in which oracular truth—absolute truth regarding past, present, even future events—operates in *The Winter's Tale*. Notice, first, that Leontes no sooner acknowledges his suspicions than he sends to the oracle, supposing that he will obtain confirmation of them—a departure from *Pandosto*, in which the Queen asks that Apollo be consulted. Next, the crucial scene representing the messengers on their way back from 'the Isle of Delphos' is set as prelude to Hermione's trial: in some twenty lines it conveys an extraordinary impression of serenity and sanctity. Cleomenes and Dion are unshakeably convinced of the truth of the sealed statement they carry; convinced, also, that it will clear the Queen.[1] It is evidently established that, while we remain in Sicily—that is, until the end of Act III, Scene ii—things are what they seem, to us and to everyone in the play, *except* Leontes.

Now, if I may revert to my simple question: what would have happened if Leontes had accepted the truth thus delivered? The prediction that 'the king shall live without an heir' would have been inexplicable; indeed, at the time when it was entrusted to the messengers, Leontes would still have a wife and two children with him. But, possessed by the insane conviction that he and oracular truth are ranged together against false seeming, he does not wait for the revelation: he condemns the child he supposes Polixenes' to death. It is Shakespeare's way to accept character as the ultimate source of event. Therefore, when truth is revealed and he finds himself standing alone, Leontes is already committed to the utterance of his final, fatal blasphemy: 'There is no truth at all i' the oracle.'[2] Immediately and inexorably, the wheels begin to turn: word comes of Mamilius's death, and he interprets it as divine retribution:

> Apollo's angry; and the heavens themselves
> Do strike at my injustice.

Paulina's 'this news is mortal to the Queen' threatens complete fulfilment of the prediction, and Leontes' public confession and vow of amendment are answered by her passionate cry that repentance prolonged beyond the span of mortal life would not atone. Nothing further is said of reparation, nor is the oracle's stipulation, 'if that which is lost be not found', remembered again until the very eve of finding. It is mere critical officiousness to demand an oracular injunction against second marriage; Leontes has accepted the full implications of his misdeed.

Presently, a speaker only less august than the oracle intervenes. Time, in appropriately archaic verse, explains his own function as composed of contrarieties:

[1] III. i.   [2] III. ii. 141.

> ... it is in my power
> To o'erthrow law, and in one self-born hour
> To plant and o'erwhelm custom.[1]

He is alike founder, destroyer, renewer. He cannot (in the agonized words of Lucrece) 'return and make amends'; but, given time and kindly shelter, the seed will yield next year's harvest, and we have but now seen the lost child received into the pastoral refuge.

> I turn my glass ...
> ... but let Time's news
> Be known when 'tis brought forth.

From now on, growth proceeds underground: things will not be what they seem; honest characters (Paulina and Camillo) will be involved in a tissue of subterfuge; the truth, if it is told, will be uttered uncomprehendingly—as when Polixenes tests Perdita with gardeners' talk of crossing strains, and she maintains that like must mate with like. One certainty alone holds: in the pastoral world, the promise of the oracle will be fulfilled as surely as were its threats, and the lost will be found.

What, then, does this pastoral world signify? Not 'wish-fulfilment' —a new name for an old misuse of the imagination. *That* requires obliteration of the boundary which separates the imagined from the actual. But the world of true pastoral is always known for a country of the mind, to be attained only by force of the imagination. This, doubtless, holds good for all great imaginative story-telling (whether cast in narrative or in dramatic form). Pastoral fiction, however, has a distinction of its own to observe, and this may best be indicated in terms of time and space. Tragedy shakes us with its tremendous *here* and *now* (no matter how remote its subject). History (Shakespearian history, at least) makes a sharp impact of *there* and *then*—the sun rising on St. Crispin's day over the field of Agincourt. But pastoral romance is, and must always remain, *elsewhere* and *some other time*. Thus, though it is simply and immediately enjoyable, in a kind and degree beyond that of other story-telling, it no more invites us to identify ourselves with its happy people than the rainbow invites us to climb. In its realm, Shakespearian comedy is free to flourish. Its happy endings are not flattering fantasies, but tokens of a fulfilment to be imagined only, not hoped for. In this fulfilment, the partial and piecemeal returns and

[1] Prologue to Act IV.

renewals which life grants us are capable of completion; not only does the future stretch before us, with its assured rhythm of the seasons and the generations—the past itself is no longer irretrievably lost. Not Perdita alone comes back, but Hermione also.

6

THE HEIGHTS AND THE DEPTHS:
A SCENE FROM 'KING LEAR'

by HARRY LEVIN

SPEAKING of depths and heights, I hope that my title has not provoked a wider curiosity than can be sharply focused by my sub-
title. I shall not be talking about the periods of Shakespeare's
development, or looking for his autobiography in his dramaturgy, or
assuming—with Edward Dowden and others—that he wrote his
tragedies out of some private grief and later, when he felt mellower,
turned back to comedies. The moods and changes that continue to
interest us today are not those which we attribute to the artist in person, but those which we experience through his art. Its characteristic
transitions from splendour to torment, from *O altitudo* to *de profundis*,
seem to accord with a basic principle of tragic vicissitude. What I
propose to discuss, in some contextual detail, is one extremely specific
illustration of that principle, a text often cited but seldom re-ex-
amined, probably because our modes of stagecraft have strategically
changed.

'Gain Shakespeare's effects by Shakespeare's means when you can.'
Such was the sound advice of Granville-Barker for the modern interpretation of Shakespeare. However, there are times when the theatrical
interpreter cannot use Shakespearian means, even though the academic
interpreter may know how a certain Shakespearian effect was accom-
plished. We cannot cast a boy as Cleopatra, though Shakespeare did;
very few actresses are up to the part in our time, even after a long and
respectable career in the theatre. Shakespeare would never have been
able to spread his drama of *Antony and Cleopatra* through forty-two
scenes, crossing and recrossing the Mediterranean, had he been forced
to compress it within a proscenium, relying upon a succession of back-
drops or a revolving stage. Working within an adaptable but permanent structure—mainly a forestage flanked by adequate exits or

entrances, backed by some sort of curtained area and an upper balcony
—Shakespeare achieved unlimited effects by limited means.

These were primarily verbal. To one with his gift for turning words
into pictures, the absence of scenery was a stimulus to the pictorial
imagination. Hence Shakespeare did his own scene-painting, verbally.
'This castle hath a pleasant seat,' says Duncan, praising the air; and
Banquo goes on to enlarge our mental picture of Glamis Castle with
his lyrical speech about the temple-haunting martlet, the pendent bed,
and the heaven's breath. This delicate imagery has the quality of repose
in painting, or so Sir Joshua Reynolds has commented. Repose indeed!
for here the gentle Duncan will all too soon be taking his last repose;
before morning that heavenly courtyard will be all the drunken porter
fancies, when he envisages it as a gateway to hell; and we shall have
been transported, as it were, from the heights to the depths.

Shakespeare used no programmes, and does not seem to have put
much faith in locality-boards.

> Alack! the night comes on, and the bleak winds
> Do sorely ruffle,

says Gloucester, thereby setting the time and place at the end of the
Second Act of *King Lear*:

> for many miles about
> There's scarce a bush.

And with a clatter of doors being closed and shutters banged, the clang-
ing of gates and other sound effects which are actually verbal, the stage
is set—that vastest and barest of stages—for the storm scenes of Act III,
which alternate between the indoors and the open air, and gain the
effect of wind and rain by means of the old King's efforts to outscorn
them. Granville-Barker's preface to *King Lear* is a practical refutation
of A. C. Bradley's influential and paradoxical argument that, though it
may be Shakespeare's greatest achievement, it is too huge for the stage.
This, in turn, was a philosophical rationalization of Charles Lamb's
opinion that performance was unbearable. Now Lamb was more of a
theatre-goer than Bradley, but he could only have witnessed the play in
productions which were cruelly cut and badly adulterated. He therefore
concluded that the spectacle of an old man, tottering about in a storm
with a stick, could only be painful or disgusting.

Other critics have recoiled more strongly from that terrifying scene
where Gloucester's eyes are put out *coram populo*, not behind the scenes

as in *Oedipus Rex*, but in full view of the audience and in complete
violation of classical decorum. It is a deliberate and definitive breach, a
more flagrant gesture of indecorum than the Elizabethan intermixture
of hornpipes with funerals, or the abasement of kings to the level of
clowns in the companionship of Lear and his Fool. Yet even that hor-
rendous act has a certain propriety as a literal climax to a whole train of
metaphors involving eyesight and suggesting moral perception, the
lack of which is so fatal for Gloucester and Lear. None so blind as those
who have eyes and see not. Their eyes may be open, but—like those of
Lady Macbeth in her sleep-walking scene—their sense is shut. This
visual metaphor is generalized into *hybris*, the pride that goes before a
tragic fall, with the self-denunciation of Antony:

> But when we in our viciousness grow hard—
> O misery on't!—the wise gods seel our eyes;
> In our own filth drop our clear judgments; make us
> Adore our errors; laugh at's while we strut
> To our confusion.

When we become too intimately involved in the tragic experience,
we tend to feel pain and disgust as Lamb did, rather than pity and fear.
Catharsis, if it clears the mind through those classic emotions, does so
by placing the object at an aesthetic distance from the spectator. He
must, of course, apprehend it through sympathy, empathy, or some
sort of identification with it. But he also achieves a sense of perspective
through his detachment from it. Recent dramatic theory would stress
this latter stage, which Bertolt Brecht terms estrangement, as the most
important aspect of the emotional process. But long ago Lucretius
evoked the intellectual pleasure of looking out on troubled waters
when one was safe ashore, of looking down on the violent conflicts of
men from the heights of philosophy. Tragedy presents such knowledge,
not in philosophic abstraction but in concrete exemplification. Thus,
though it cries to us out of the depths, it offers us a way of temporarily
detaching ourselves from the human predicament, and rising above
those situations in which it has vicariously involved us.

The example for which I should like to claim your particular attention is neither the pitiful involvement of Lear in the storm nor the
terrible blinding of Gloucester. It is a subsequent and incidental episode,
the sixth scene of Act IV, a curiously didactic scene best known for its
purple passage describing Dover Cliff. How near we really come to
Dover Cliff is a moot question, as I shall try to show in my attempt to

recover an unique effect which could only have been attained through Shakespearian means. Elsewhere in drama it has certain precedents and analogies, but none of them comes very close to the matter at hand. In the *Plutus* of Aristophanes, the others threaten to throw the blind god over a precipice, and the threat is averted when he reveals his name. In the repertory of Japanese Kabuki, the dance-drama *Shakkyo* concerns an old lion who pushes a young one off a cliff as a kind of test: by climbing back, the cub proves his manhood—or, rather, his lionhood.

That would seem to be the normal relationship between the two generations, father and son. Shakespeare reverses it, when Edmund accuses Edgar of maintaining that 'the father should be as ward to the son'. The accusation will come true ironically, when the disguised Edgar leads the blinded Gloucester. 'In this play,' Dame Edith Sitwell has aptly observed, 'we see the upheaval of all Nature, the reversal of all histories.' Tragedy always seems to hinge upon a reversal, or peripety. Here a peripety is the starting-point, when the King reverses his traditional role by stepping down from the throne. As the tragedy broadens, moving out of the realm of history into the sphere of nature, it sets off a series of further reversals. The antagonism between crabbed age and flaming youth, always a latent tension in Shakespeare's plays, breaks into overt conflict in *King Lear*. It was implicit in classical comedy, to be sure, and terribly explicit in the dire prophecy of Matthew: 'And brother shall deliver up brother to death, and the father his child: and children shall rise up against parents, and cause them to be put to death.'

This abrogation of the most fundamental commitments, straining family ties beyond endurance and turning simple affections into complex hatreds, is still a major source of power in literature. Filial ingratitude is an obsessive theme with Proust, just as parricide is with Dostoevsky. Like the sons of old Karamazov, Edgar and Edmund incarnate the good and evil of their father's character. Science, natural philosophy, 'the wisdom of nature can reason it thus and thus, yet nature finds itself scourged by the sequent effects', the superstitious Gloucester laments at the outset, anxious to blame his fate upon the stars. The worst of the many symptoms of upheaval that he enumerates is 'the bond cracked between son and father'. In Gloucester's own case, it is 'son against father', though he suspects the wrong son as it turns out. In the King's case, it is 'father against child', and Gloucester underlines the parallel. Shakespeare never made bolder use of the double plot than when he matched the dynastic struggle of the main plot with its domestic counterpart, the Gloucester underplot. To take a *donnée* so exceptional, to hit upon so unheard-of a set of circumstances and double them, was to call the entire moral order into question, as A. W. Schlegel pointed out.

The story in outline harks back, far beyond the old play that Shakespeare adapted, through chronicle and legend, to the mounds of British prehistory and the fens of Druidical myth. But Shakespeare, shrewd folklorist that he was, found the same archetype at work in the most fashionable book of romantic fiction among his contemporaries, Sir Philip Sidney's *Arcadia*. Two heroes of that romance, in the course of their princely adventures, had encountered the blind King of Paphlagonia begging his dutiful son to lead him to headlong death from the top of a rock because, as he put it, 'I cannot fall worse than I am.' From the doleful speeches of father and son, it emerged that a bastard son and brother had betrayed them both through his 'unnatural dealings'—a protesting phrase which Gloucester echoes at the moment when the two plots first come together in the play. The interpolated narrative ends in a battle and a reinstatement, with the blind King dying joyfully and the rightful heir forgiving his perfidious half-brother.

Sidney devotes a single chapter to this minor encounter; yet he tells us it is 'worthy to be remembered for the unused examples therein, as well of true natural goodnes, as of wretched ungratefulnesse'. Edgar and Edmund, then, are exemplary figures, models of filial conduct, for better and worse. The worse of the two has an obvious dramatic advantage. It is always easier to portray an effectual villain than a young man of simple-minded goodwill. Some of Milton's critics have sympathized more with his Satan than with his Son of God. Yet the title-page of the First Quarto leaves no doubt as to who, after Lear himself, is the male protagonist: who is, so to speak, the *jeune premier*. It reads in part: '*With the unfortunate life of Edgar, sonne and heire to the Earle of Gloster, and his sullen and assumed humor of Tom of Bedlam.*' Instead of remaining just a nice young man, rather pallid and timid, Edgar is allowed to rival Shakespeare's dynamic villains by assuming a dangerous and colourful role.

Edmund has played his part from the beginning, though he already looks toward a *dénouement* of some sort when he summons Edgar from hiding: 'and pat he comes, like the catastrophe of the old comedy'. Even while Edmund is soliloquizing, he is rehearsing his initial interview with his half-brother, and the notes he sings—*mi contra fa*—significantly form the forbidden interval known as *diabolus in musica*. His

own 'cue', as it happens, will become Edgar's: 'a sigh like Tom o'
Bedlam'. But Edgar, at this point, is no less credulous than their father.
With Gloucester he falls into Edmund's trap, is suspected of parricidal
intentions, and proscribed as an outlaw. In his fugitive soliloquy, he
determines

> To take the basest and most poorest shape
> That ever penury, in contempt of man,
> Brought near to beast.

He will disguise himself, paradoxically, by taking off his clothes and
exposing himself to the elements. 'With presented nakedness', when
we next see him, he will be attempting to

> outface
> The winds and persecutions of the sky.

And Edgar seems to anticipate the storm, even as Lear seems to conjure
it up with his imprecations of blast and fog.

As Edgar goes on to describe the role of Poor Tom, we can understand why it made him so popular on the Elizabethan stage. But,
though it is quasi-comic, we can scarcely regard it as comic relief;
rather, with its vagrant grotesquerie, it intensifies the tragic pathos.
Those Bedlam beggars were harmless madmen released from their
lunatic asylum, the notorious Hospital of St. Mary's of Bethlehem in
London. Wandering aimlessly about the countryside, with their teeth
chattering from exposure and their bare flesh lacerated by self-torture,
they besought the stranger's alms with their prayers or curses. Edgar
not only dresses the part; he fills it in with apt charms and exorcisms
and brilliant bits of histrionic improvisation. He even seems to have
worked up the names of devils from a current theological pamphlet:
Turleygod, Flibbertigibbet, Frateretto, the last a likely name for a
diabolical brother. Not the least of many ironies is that this innocent
youth must pretend to be the victim of demonic possession, haunted
by the foul fiend in many shapes—albeit these demons, on naturalistic
inspection, are merely vermin.

Dramatic tradition gave Tom of Bedlam a forerunner in the person
of Diccon the Bedlam, the Vice or mischief-maker in the crude old
Cambridge comedy of *Gammer Gurton's Needle*. Edgar, too, will play
the Vice in his later manipulations, when he intervenes on behalf of
Gloucester. Meanwhile he acts as an object-lesson for Lear. The extent
of Lear's reversal may be grasped by contrasting the first scene of

Act I with the last in Act II. In the former the bidding goes up, as Goneril and Regan bid for the kingdom with their large speeches of love. In the latter the haggling goes down, as the daughters cut down the retinue of their father. An hundred, fifty, five-and-twenty knights. 'Ten, or five.' 'What need one?' By that time we are ready to move on with Lear from the court, the world of superfluity, to the heath, the world of necessity—from the heights toward the depths. His retort in farewell is the first of his speeches on need and its opposite, luxury, especially luxurious clothing and the difference it makes between the sophisticated courtier and the basest beggar, between man's life and beast's.

When Lear has exposed himself to the pinch of necessity, when he has felt the storm and first expressed a new insight into the houseless lives of naked wretches, it is then that the ragged Edgar appears as the personification of abject poverty and misery. 'Is man no more than this?' the King demands, striving to emulate Tom by removing his own regal garments. 'Unaccommodated man'—the naked wretch in the state of nature—'is no more but such a poor, bare, forked animal as thou art.' Commentators have told us how richly the prose of this passage is interlarded with primitivistic speculations from Montaigne, whom Shakespeare knew so well through Florio's translation, and who had inspired so much of Hamlet's self-questioning. Lear has his own version of Hamlet's exclamation, 'What a piece of work is a man!' Unaccommodate him, banish him from the commodities of the court, take away the trappings of civilization, complete his exposure to the elements. What is there left to differentiate him from all the other animals, by whose sharpened fangs we feel increasingly surrounded? Will he be naturally good, as Rousseau would argue? Or is he inherently evil, as Hobbes would have it, a wolf to his fellow man?

The Machiavellian bastard, Gloucester's natural son Edmund, dedicates himself to the goddess Nature, as he ruthlessly envisions her; while, through his cruel machinations, Edgar is placed in such a false position that their father calls his legitimate son an 'unnatural villain'. On the other hand, Edgar stands closer to nature; Lear hails him as a natural philosopher, who should be able to answer his questions concerning 'the cause of thunder' and the other mysteries of the cosmos. This affinity, based on the fact that Edgar is Lear's godson, is confirmed by their respective plights, as Edgar keenly realizes: 'He childed as I father'd!' As the pair enter the hovel together, Edgar's snatches of balladry and fairy-tale transform it into a legendary dark tower, where

a young squire is undergoing a ritual of knightly initiation while nameless giants objurgate: 'Fie, foh, and fum.' Edgar is more of a spectator
than a feature of the spectacle in the ensuing scene, summing it up in
the sententious understatement that 'grief hath mates' or misery loves
company.

This is the hallucinatory arraignment, where his own half-hearted
pretence meets Lear's actual madness, accompanied by the half-witted
folly of the natural fool with his one pathetic joke: the rain rains every
day for those who are excluded from the sunshine of royal favour. The
only person present who can speak sanely, Kent in his servant guise of
Caius, counsels patience. Edgar is so moved at times that his tears interfere with his impersonation, 'mar' his 'counterfeiting'. Gloucester,
whom Edgar has welcomed as a squinting fiend, re-enters to terminate
the scene by ordering that the King be conveyed on a litter to Dover.
Thereafter, in his master's absence, he becomes the scapegoat. What
follows is the scene of his sacrifice, upon which there is no temptation
to dwell, except for pointing out that this reversal—despite its extreme
brutality—is humanely mitigated by a recognition. Peripety, according
to Aristotle, is most effective when it coincides with such a recognition,
anagnorisis.

When Cornwall inquires 'Where is thy lustre now?', Gloucester responds, 'All dark and comfortless.' Then, when the malicious Regan
apprises him of Edmund's villainy, he suddenly recognizes that Edgar
is innocent. Thus, at the very moment of blinding, Gloucester sees how
blind he has been all along. 'I stumbled when I saw,' he will live to say.
Now, in the absence of eyesight, he will be guided by a kind of ethical
illumination. One of the servants, an old man, suggests that the
'roguish madness' of 'the Bedlam' would qualify him to be Gloucester's guide. Their conjunction is brought about in the first scene of
Act IV. Kent has previously consoled himself with the thought that he
could fall no lower than the stocks, and that any turn of Fortune's
wheel would mean a rise in the world for him. Similarly, Edgar *solus*
now views himself as 'The lowest and most dejected thing of fortune,'
whose condition any change would improve. But alas, he speaks too
soon. The sight of his bleeding father is worse than anything he has
met so far.

'The worst is not,' Edgar thereupon reflects, 'so long as we can say,
"This is the worst."' This may be regarded as Shakespeare's variation
on the tragic theme of Sophocles, 'Call no man happy until he is dead,'
or the cry from the depths when Job curses the light and gropes in the

dark. Gloucester, in spite of his infirmity, half-recognizes Edgar as that thing between a madman and a beggar which makes him 'think man a worm', but also made him think of his son. And it is at this significant juncture that Gloucester voices his pessimistic view of the human condition:

> As flies to wanton boys, are we to the gods;
> They kill us for their sport.

The world-view that opens up is as hopeless as Hardy's, governed by nothing more serene or secure than crass casualty and blind chance. It seems proper to Gloucester that a madman should lead a blind man, so long as he knows the way to Dover Cliff. 'From that place,' he declares with grim succinctness, 'I shall no leading need.' In his desperation, faced with what seems to be the pointless hostility of the universe, what can he do but dispatch his own 'nighted life'? That is the last resort of Stoicism; and Shakespeare, in his Roman plays, consistently treats suicide as an honourable mode of death. In his tragedies with a Christian background, his attitude is shaded with disapproval, and he cites God's canon against self-slaughter.

King Lear is supposed to take place in prehistoric Britain, and to be roughly contemporaneous with the ancient Kings of Judea. Shakespeare has taken pains to have his characters invoke 'the gods' in the plural and swear by conspicuously pagan divinities. But Edgar, that Good Samaritan with his faith, humility, and charity, seems to be *anima naturaliter christiana*. Curiously enough, in the original legend, where Lear regains his crown and Cordelia is dethroned again after his death, she ends by committing suicide in prison. It is her ghost which arises to retell the family history and point the moral in the standard Elizabethan collection of poetic case-histories, falls of princes or sad stories of the deaths of kings, the *Mirror for Magistrates*. There the usual reversal, the change of fortune from prosperity to adversity, from the heights to the depths, is presented as a warning to those who are highly placed, lest they be precipitated

> From greatest haps, that worldly wightes atchieue:
> To more distresse then any wretche aliue.

So Cordelia's monologue concludes. Comparably the first play performed before Queen Elizabeth, *Gorboduc*, one of whose collaborators was co-author of the *Mirror for Magistrates*, warned the queenly magistrate against the division of her realm and even foreshadowed *King*

Lear in introducing a dissension between rival Dukes of Cornwall and Albany.

Downfall was the formula for tragedy that Shakespeare inherited and elaborated, not only in plot and characterization but in language and staging as well. The dying fall is its traditional posture. Its vicissitudes, such as the ups and downs of Richard II's reign, lend their thematic pattern to his tragedy, wherein his fall is a come-down literally as well as figuratively. Aloft, on the upper stage, the imagined walls of Flint Castle, Richard compares himself to Phaeton; descending to the lower stage, he condescends to pun about the 'base court'. Descent is even more desperate in *King John*, where Prince Arthur is killed in escaping from the Castle of Angiers. Elevation as the basis of a godlike over-view is dramatized at those moments when Prospero is '*on the top*', apparently looking down from the musicians' gallery. Antony, coming down from his vantage-point after the battle or hoisted up to Cleo-patra's Monument in death, acts out the movement of his destiny. The danger of high places, the tragic vertigo, is vividly brought home in Horatio's fear lest Hamlet topple off some dreadful summit, 'That beetles o'er his base into the sea'. And that is all we need to know in order to establish the certainty that Shakespeare never visited Denmark, which is as conspicuous for its summits as Bohemia is for its sea-coasts.

But we must turn back to Dover Cliff. 'Wherefore to Dover?' Three times Gloucester is asked this question by his torturers. Lear was there, of course; and Lear was there because the French Army was there, though the King of France had discreetly withdrawn so that his rescue party would not be mistaken for a foreign invasion. There the gleaming white cliffs, greeting the traveller on his return from the continent, mark a perpetual bourn. 'Within these breakwaters English is spoken,' writes W. H. Auden,

> without
> Is the immense improbable atlas.

Nature in Lear, he has been chastened to learn, 'is on the very verge/ Of her confine'. Just as the tempest in his mind, in the 'little world of man' or microcosm, is a reverberation of the macrocosm, the distur-bance of outer nature; so now Gloucester, led by Edgar, has reached the 'extreme verge', the edge of the precipice. It is like the thin line between life and death, between the known and the unknown, that lies before Tolstoy's heroes in *War and Peace*.

Here Edgar, the assumed madman, addresses his charge, the blind

man—and remember that we are just as blind as Gloucester. Theatrical
convention prescribes that we accept whatever is said on the subject of
immediate place as the setting. We may grow slightly suspicious, when
Gloucester fails to notice the slant of the ground or the sound of the sea;
and we join him in remarking an alteration of tone, since Poor Tom
has shifted to blank verse and soon embarks on his topographical
passage.

> How fearful
> And dizzy 'tis to cast one's eyes so low!

His downward glance proceeds to the half-way point, where it encounters the samphire-gatherer at his precarious business of picking the
herb of Saint-Pierre from the rocks. Thence to the beach, where the
fishermen look like mice, the birds like insects, the ships like their
boats, and the buoys are invisible. Everything suffers a diminution in
scale. 'I'll look no more,' vows Edgar at the end of fifteen lines,

> Lest my brain turn, and the deficient sight

—a relevant phrase, 'deficient sight', which universalizes the blindness
of Gloucester while commenting on the trepidation of heights—

> I'll look no more,
> Lest my brain turn, and the deficient sight
> Topple down headlong.

This may strike the average reader or hearer with a distant, dizzying,
vertiginous impact; Addison remarked that it could hardly be read
without producing giddiness; but Dr. Johnson refused to be impressed.
A precipice in the mind, he argued, should be 'one great and dreadful
image of irresistible destruction'. Here we were too readily diverted by
'the observation of particulars'. Clearly, Johnson's criterion was the
neo-classical grudge against concreteness that prompted him to inveigh
against numbering the streaks of the tulip. In Boswell's account, he
went even further when he discussed Edgar's speech with Garrick and
others: 'It should be all precipice—all vacuum. The crows impede your
fall.' It was the same Miltonic taste that emended Macbeth's 'blanket of
the dark' to 'blank height'. Yet Lessing finds Shakespeare's description
superior to Milton's lines where the angels scan the 'vast immeasurable
abyss' of chaos. In Paradise Lost the declension is out of scale, Lessing
asserted; the distance traversed is too vast to be fathomable in human
dimensions. To jump to the beach from a cliff as high as ten masts is

breath-taking danger, whereas a limitless precipitation through the void is mere astronomy. That vista may be even less thrilling to-day, as traffic increases in outer space.

The sense of immediacy and the sense of remoteness, the sensation of being up here one moment and down there a few seconds later, to-gether with all the other sensations heightened by the hazards of the plunge, these feelings are concentrated into our identification with Gloucester and our prospective detachment from him. He is presum-ably standing at the brink as he lets go Edgar's hand, rewarding him and bidding him farewell. Whereupon Edgar, in a cryptic aside, gives us our first hint that the situation is not precisely what Gloucester believes it to be:

> Why I do trifle thus with his despair
> Is done to cure it.

From this announcement, at least, it is clear that Edgar has a strategem for saving Gloucester; but, on a non-representational stage, it would still be difficult to foresee how the rescue might be effected. On a pro-scenium stage, the whole situation would be impossible; for, depending on realistic scenery, we should be fully aware whether Gloucester was or was not at the top of a hill. The best that nineteenth-century staging could do was to cut the passage heavily, letting Edgar catch Gloucester as he lurches forward into a faint, and quickly shifting to the next phase of the scene with the entrance of Lear. Meanwhile the audience would not be undergoing any throes of suspense, since the scenic arrangements would have indicated that Gloucester was perfectly safe. On occasions, the Dover Cliffs have been painted upon the backdrop; it was to be in-ferred that Edgar had taken Gloucester directly to the beach, where he should not have had any trouble in hearing the waves.

'He falls,' according to the stage-direction, which editors have em-bellished but not improved. Most of them add 'forward'; some add 'and swoons'. He falls, at all events, but not far. Not so far as from the upper stage, I should guess, inasmuch as Romeo needed a rope and—lacking one—Prince Arthur lost his life. There may be a single step or a simple platform; or, again, the business may be enough—enough for Edgar to play his trick upon Gloucester and to lay bare the trick that Shakespeare has played upon ourselves, his audience. Gloucester, having gone through the motions of an ineffectual jump, lies on the ground; Edgar, assuming another character, now rushes up to revive him; and both are changed men. In complementary verses, breathless with polysyllabics, Edgar describes how Gloucester has fallen perpendicularly from a vast altitude and somehow survived: 'Thy life's a miracle.' Vainly, but not without irony, he exhorts him: 'Look up a-height.' And in contrast to all the *hybris*, the giddy exaltation of looking down from the heights, we seem to have plunged into the depths and to have touched bottom; we can fall no lower.

This is the nadir; the worst is over; we seem to be looking up; and the situation is framed by larger perspectives. 'As I stood here below methought,' begins Edgar, as if he were recounting a dream, a bad dream which ends with Tom of Bedlam turning into a fiend and flying away. Edgar's portrayal of his departing self is an exorcism, leaving innocence no longer possessed by guilt. Just as Gloucester utters his cry of despair—comparing the gods to boys and ourselves to flies—on his first encounter with mad Tom, so with Tom's departure Edgar voices his answering affirmation:

> Think that the clearest gods, who make them honours
> Of men's impossibilities, have preserv'd thee.

Providence must be at work, after all; and if we discern the workings of cosmic design in our personal destinies, then no man has a right to take his life; he must bear the slings and arrows of fortune, however outrageous they seem. To the Stoic argument for suicide Edgar would oppose the Christian attitude, in words which reverberate from the Gospel of Luke: 'The things which are impossible with men are possible with God.'

Since our eyes have been opened, we are bound to bear witness that Edgar himself has been fully responsible for the stratagem he now attributes to divine intervention. His intentions were kindly, where Edmund's have been malign; but he has deceived their father quite as much with his imaginary fall as Edmund earlier did with his forged letter. 'Let's see,' said Gloucester, snatching at that device, 'come; if it be nothing, I shall not need spectacles.' He saw; he stumbled; and, now that he is sightless, he is rescued by the victim of the letter. Edgar has proved to be as good a stage-manager as Edmund, and in a better cause. Yet, unless his presence in the vicinity is the result of stage-management on the part of the gods—unless it is providential, that is to say, rather than coincidental—we must admit that his miracle is more truly a pious fraud; and we must conclude that the gods help those who help themselves, or else those who are so fortunate as to be helped by their fellow men.

Man stands on his own feet in *King Lear*. There is no supernatural soliciting; there are no ghosts or witches or oracles; and the only demons are those which Edgar imagines while enacting his demonic role. Man takes his questionings directly to nature. Perhaps the ultimate meaning of Gloucester's fall is its symbolic gesture of expiation, re-enacting his own original sin, as well as the fall of man and his consequent progression toward self-knowledge. Other agonists have undergone it under widely differing conditions: Herman Melville narrates it, in his *White-Jacket*, as a fall from the yardarm of a ship at sea. Because he could not bear his great affliction without cursing the gods, Gloucester has attempted to shake it off 'patiently'. But Edmund's moral, which completes the exercise, redefines patience as the ability to bear one's sufferings, to face and endure them in calm of mind: 'Bear free and patient thoughts.'

Patience has been the greatest need of the King. He has resolved to be 'the pattern of all patience'; whereupon he has run the gamut of passions, from rage through hysteria to delirium and finally lunacy. It is as an escaping lunatic, grotesquely decked with weeds, that he is confronted by Edgar and Gloucester at this strategic moment of the play; and it may well be the shock of this reunion that has obscured the significance of their foregoing scene. From the interchange it would appear that, if Lear stands for reason in madness, Gloucester may stand for vision in blindness. When Lear asks if he sees how the world goes, Gloucester replies: 'I see it feelingly.' His groping pun is heavily fraught with shame and remorse for the figure he has earlier cut: 'the superfluous and lust-dieted man . . . that will not see/Because he does not feel.' This parallels the insight that Lear has acquired on the heath: 'to feel what wretches feel'. Gloucester has immediately recognized Lear's voice; Lear rounds out the recognition-scene by naming Gloucester and preaching, 'Thou must be patient.'

Lear is unquestionably the *persona patiens*, as Coleridge insisted; he is the agonizing figure of this passion play where all the characters suffer. Having committed his rash action, he suffers for it on and on, until he is justified in regarding himself as 'a man/More sinn'd against than sinning'. Edmund is the main agent, in Coleridge's estimation; certainly, he is most active in pulling the strings at the outset. 'The younger rises when the old doth fall.' But the defeated opportunist concedes that, with its last revolution, his wheel comes full circle. Edgar, his polar rival, is passive at first; he suffers, then he acts; and it is his suffering that prepares him for action. When Gloucester thanks and blesses him for his anonymous aid, he characterizes himself as

> A most poor man, made tame to fortune's blows;
> Who, by the art of known and feeling sorrows,
> Am pregnant to good pity.

As such, he is the right instrument for conveying a sense of fellow-feeling, both to Lear in the hovel on the heath and to Gloucester at Dover Cliff.

It is a cruel world where the honest Kent must go incognito, and where the once-naïve Edgar has to run through a protean repertory of roles. After the disappearance of Tom of Bedlam, he is more simply a neutral benefactor, the Good Samaritan. But when he protects Gloucester from Oswald's attack and is called 'bold peasant' by the courtier, he adapts himself to that appellation by replying in a rustic dialect. He disposes of Oswald, thereby saving the life that Gloucester would have thrown away. But he cannot disclose his identity before he has made his appearance as a nameless champion; and even this last masquerade is preceded by another one, that of the messenger delivering the challenge. However, the battle must precede the tournament. *Drums afar off* have terminated the Cliff Scene. They grow louder when the French forces, flying Cordelia's colours, march to meet the British. While the engagement is taking place off-stage, we await the outcome with Gloucester under a tree.

Hard upon the heels of retreating soldiers, Edgar reports the defeat and capture of Lear and Cordelia, and Gloucester reverts to his former mood of self-pity. Why should he let himself be led any farther? 'A man may rot even here.' But just as growth yields to decay, so decay fosters growth, in the biological cycle. What is important, fulfilment, is a matter of timing. Man must reconcile himself to the fact that nature will take its course. Edgar, picking up Gloucester's negative image, transposes it into the most positive statement of the play:

> Men must endure
> Their going hence, even as their coming hither;
> Ripeness is all.

Edgar's aphorism can be traced back to Montaigne's essay, 'That to philosophize is to learn how to die'. Such was the end of knowledge for the tragic playwright, as well as for the sceptical philosopher. It is rather more than a coincidence that the same sentiment is expressed, though not imaged, at the same point in *Hamlet*: 'The readiness is all.' The manner of one's death and the moment of it were ultimate concerns to the Elizabethans.

By averting the suicide and nursing his father's miseries, Edgar has saved him from despair. Could he but live to see his son in his touch, Gloucester has feelingly vowed, 'I'd say I had eyes again.' We do not witness the recognition-scene wherein this yearning is fulfilled at last. But in the final scene, when the explanations come out, Edgar relates the circumstances of Gloucester's happy death, 'Twixt two extremes of passion, joy and grief'. These mixed emotions match the smiles and tears with which Cordelia has received the news of her father: 'Sunshine and rain at once.' Edmund, sincerely moved by his brother's report, resolves to do some good; but retrospective narration prolongs the delay, and his one humane impulse is thwarted; the reprieve of Cordelia comes too late. When the brothers fought and were reconciled, Edgar pronounced upon his brother and father in apocryphal terms:

> The gods are just, and of our pleasant vices
> Make instruments to plague us.

Edmund's existence is at once the consequence of, and the retribution for, Gloucester's sin.

> The dark and vicious place where thee he got
> Cost him his eyes.

Where the inequities of this world have made Gloucester and Lear more and more doubtful as to the justice of heaven, Edgar is wholeheartedly its exponent. Albany, too, can point to the death of Cornwall, fatally wounded in the very act of torturing Gloucester, as an indication that the guilty are punished here below. But so are the innocent. So is Cordelia; and this, more than anything else, I suspect, is why critics have flinched at the notion of performing the play. There is a grim sort of poetic justice in the scene where the King refuses to accept her death; and his own demise, just afterwards, is a deliverance for him. But audiences have frequently shared his and Gloucester's unwillingness to bear an unhappy ending patiently; the chronicle-history ended happily; while the adaptation by Nahum Tate, which all but replaced Shakespeare's tragedy for a hundred and fifty years, managed to marry off Cordelia to Edgar, who thanks the King with these concluding lines:

> Thy bright example shall convince the World
> (Whatever Storms of Fortune are decreed)
> That Truth and Vertue shall at last succeed.

Shakespeare's Edgar repeats to the dying Lear his optimistic counsel to Gloucester: 'Look up, my lord.' But he cannot contrive another miracle. The problem of evil is unresolved at the conclusion, though the prevailing catastrophe is accepted. It is, as Kent says, a presentiment of doomsday, 'the promis'd end'. Edgar, rather than Albany, speaks the final speech in the Folio. Well might he proclaim a farewell to dissembling and a renewal of sincerity. It is high time to 'Speak what we feel, not what we ought to say.' And, in his terminal couplet, our deficient sight is contrasted with the insight painfully achieved through old age:

> The oldest hath borne most: we that are young,
> Shall never see so much, nor live so long.

We leave him looking across the straits, listening to the cadence of human misery in the ebb and flow of the tides, and catching that eternal note of sadness which Sophocles heard long ago and which Matthew Arnold caught in his poem, 'Dover Beach'. As with Oedipus, blind and dying at Colonus, so with Gloucester at Dover. In each case, the passion of a patriarch has met with compassion on the part of a filial survivor, be it Edgar or Antigone. But it is Goethe who puts his finger on the archetype in that relationship: *'Ein alter Mann ist stets ein König Lear.'* May I translate freely, in order to keep the rhyme?

> An aged man is always like King Lear.
> Effort and struggle long have passed him by;
> And love and leadership are pledged elsewhere;
> And youth must work out its own destiny.
> Come on, old fellow, come along with me.

H

7

SHAKESPEARE AND THE DRAMATIC CRITICS

by NORMAN MARSHALL

IN England it has never been disputed that it is the dramatic critics who should be the judges of Shakespeare in the theatre. The professors, the scholars of Shakespeare, have never challenged this right. But in many countries in Europe the university professors have considered it their duty jealously to guard the academic interpretation of the classics against any producer or actor with ideas of his own, and they have had sufficient prestige and authority to demand that when a classic is being performed it is they who should occupy the seats of the dramatic critics. Ernst Stern, in his autobiography, *My Life; My Stage*, describes how Reinhardt, when he sought to interpret Shakespeare's plays afresh, had to battle furiously with the professorial critics who were determined that everything should be done in exactly the same way as it had always been done before. 'The result was that when the classics were performed the audience saw what might be compared with a blackened masterpiece in which all colour and life had been deadened by layer after layer of ancient varnish.' Stern goes on to describe how, when Reinhardt staged his first Shakespearian production, 'the critics howled, "Sacrilege! Reinhardt detracts from the essential! Meretricious superficialities! A debasement of the classical spirit!" And so on. They seem to regard his productions as a personal insult, as an attack on their supreme right to determine what should and what should not be done in the theatre, and they did their best to put him out of business.'

In France Louis Jouvet found himself up against the same sort of opposition when he sought to free the plays of Molière from the weight of tradition which was stifling them on the stage. It was not a genuinely theatrical tradition handed down from the days of Molière. It had been imposed upon the actors by the scholars when they made Molière a 'subject', claimed that he belonged to literature rather than to the theatre, and claimed, too, as their right, that when a Molière play was produced the tickets intended for dramatic critics should be handed over to them. As a result, Jouvet found when he embarked upon his first Molière production that 'the play was choked with opinions, oppressed by explanations, crowded in theories, asphyxiated by controversy, but still green in the sap of the text'.

In England the scholars have never attempted to dictate to the actors and the producers. In fact, until quite recently, in their writings about Shakespeare they so very rarely gave any hint of ever having seen any of the plays on the stage that one felt they were deliberately keeping themselves aloof from the theatre so that their opinions should not be contaminated by seeing the plays in performance. One must admit that there was a good deal of justification for this attitude during the period which lasted for well over two hundred years when the theatre consistently mauled and savaged Shakespeare's texts, ruthlessly cutting them, and extensively rewriting them. Colley Cibber's adaptation of *Richard III*, which was preferred to Shakespeare's for well over a hundred years, was so drastically rewritten that more than half the lines were by Cibber, and a large proportion of those by Shakespeare were taken from his other historical plays. Edward Ravenscroft proudly claimed for his version of *Titus Andronicus* (re-titled *The Rape of Lavinia*) that 'None in all that author's works ever received greater Alterations or Additions.' The prologue to George Granville, Baron Lansdowne's *Jew of Venice*, describes it as 'Shakespeare's play Adorned and Rescued by a Faultless Hand', and goes on to assure the audience that although, 'The first rude sketches Shakespeare's Pencil drew, All the Master-Strokes are new.'

In the later part of the nineteenth century the theatre began to develop a little more respect for Shakespeare's own text and one manager announced, as a great novelty, a Shakespeare play, 'Acted Entirely in Shakespeare's Own Words.' But it was believed that the theatrical public were not really interested in the plays except as a means of providing an exciting star performance and a lavish display of spectacle; drastic surgical operations were therefore performed upon the text to make them fit this theory. Such was Irving's ruthlessness with the texts that Shaw protested in 1898 that 'in a true republic of art Sir Henry Irving would ere this have expiated his acting versions on the scaffold. He does not merely cut plays; he disembowels them.'

In the early days of the present century, as a result of the reforms in Shakespearian acting and production initiated by William Poel and

Granville-Barker, Shakespeare in the theatre began to approximate more nearly to Shakespeare on the printed page: but it took a long time for the scholars to overcome their prejudice against studying Shakespeare on the stage as well as in print. For instance, when Quiller-Couch published his Cambridge lectures under the title of *Shakespeare's Workmanship* he found it necessary to point out that it was 'no disparagement to the erudition and scholarship that have so piously been heaped about Shakespeare to say that we shall sometimes find it salutary to disengage our minds from it all, and recollect that the poet was a playwright'. Nevertheless, in the course of his lecture on *Cymbeline* he casually mentions, without any sort of apology, that he has never seen the play upon the stage, in spite of the fact that during the three years preceding the date when he gave this lecture there were four productions of this rarely produced play given within easy reach of Cambridge. ·

Today there may be university lecturers prepared to lecture on Shakespearian plays they have never seen upon the stage, but they would certainly do their best to conceal the fact from their audience. Most of those who lecture upon Shakespeare in the universities nowadays have not only frequently seen the plays upon the stage but have often themselves produced Shakespeare for their student dramatic societies. Two eminent Shakespearian scholars, Professor Nevill Coghill and Mr. George Rylands, besides staging many productions at their own universities, also produced Shakespeare professionally in London during Sir John Gielgud's season at the Haymarket Theatre in 1944.

As a result of the scholars becoming practitioners in the theatre the gulf between the academic approach to Shakespeare and that of the dramatic critics has been closed. When I was reading English at Oxford in the 'twenties it was never suggested to me that it might be useful to look up what any of the dramatic critics had to say about Shakespeare's plays; but I would be very surprised to-day if any tutor did not advise his pupils to read such books as Herbert Farjeon's *The Shakespeare Scene*, the selection of James Agate's Shakespearian notices published under the title *Brief Chronicles*, and Ivor Brown's Shakespearian criticisms.

I began this lecture by talking about how the academicians in other countries usurped the critics' function. I sometimes wonder ·if in England during recent years the reverse has happened, with the result that some of our leading critics have tended to write about Shakespeare as if they were clad in gown and mortar board. Are they perhaps too coolly scholastic and too unemotional in their reviewing of a Shakespearian performance? For instance, James Agate tended to seize upon a single scene and use it as a starting point from which to launch out upon a scholarly analysis of what he personally considered to have been Shakespeare's intentions. His successor on the *Sunday Times*, Mr. Harold Hobson, a critic with an exceptional gift for recalling in detail his past experiences as a theatregoer, is an exponent of the comparative method of Shakespearian dramatic criticism. For instance, writing about that lovely performance of *Much Ado About Nothing* in which Diana Wynyard was the Beatrice and John Gielgud the Benedick he makes, within the space of a single paragraph, comparisons with Henry Ainley's performance in a radio production twenty years previously, then refers to how Renée Asherson and Robert Donat played the parts, and goes on to describe Peggy Ashcroft and Anthony Quayle as Beatrice and Benedick. Personally, I find an enormous amount of pleasure, information and stimulation in this kind of dramatic criticism, but I wonder if it is not too specialized for the sort of theatregoer whom we—and the critics too, I am sure—want to lure into the theatre to see Shakespeare. It is the sort of comparative criticism I often indulge in myself in the course of conversation. Recently, at a small party after an important Shakespearian first night, I was talking about it rather as Mr. Hobson might have written about it (though not nearly so well, I hasten to add), when I sensed that one or two of the people in the room who had not been to the play that night, and had not seen any of the other productions which I had mentioned, were not particularly interested in what Sir John Gielgud did with the part eleven years ago or how Michael Redgrave played it in its last revival. What they were interested in was how the play had gone that night, how the audience had reacted, what the sets and costumes were like, how some of the lesser parts were played, and so on. I suggest that some of our dramatic critics use up too much space in comparative criticism—space which could be more valuably used in exciting the ordinary theatregoer to see the play.

Mr. Kenneth Tynan, the youngest of our leading dramatic critics, is less apt to indulge in comparative criticism, for the simple reason that he has seen far fewer Shakespearian productions than his colleagues. Consequently he is not, to quote Ivor Brown, 'Shakespeare-sodden and inevitably Bard-weary, mainly interested to see what so-and-so will do with such-and-such a passage'. But he too, I think, as a Shakespeare critic has overmuch scholastic zeal. With him it takes the form of wanting to educate and reform Shakespearian audiences. Writing of the Old Vic audience he once said, 'I find them culpable and in need of stricture.' So do I. I have always been in warm agreement with him when he has reproved 'the loud battalions of ingenuous claqueurs'. About any Shakespearian production he writes, as always, penetratingly, wittily and entertainingly, but often he omits to convey the fact that the performance itself was entertaining; sometimes it may not have been so. But even when writing about productions which were, by general consent, memorable, he fails to convey to his readers any real sense of his own enjoyment as a member of the audience. A fine production stimulates him into making a penetrating analysis of some aspects of the play and its performance, but the sum total of his notice is essentially a highly intellectual dissection rather than an account of his own vivid impressions of the performance.

Today the impressionist critic is out of fashion. A. B. Walkley defined the impressionist critic as one who 'takes a pure natural joy in his own sensations, because they are his own, and declines to be "connoisseured out of his senses" '. Walkley believed that 'perhaps the most fundamental of the critics' tasks is to be the ideal spectator'. Our present-day critics have given abundant proof of their ability to fulfil this role. My complaint against them is that they so rarely assume this role when they write about a Shakespearian production. Remember, for instance, the verve and excitement with which they wrote about the first night of *Oklahoma*, how vividly they reported not only their own pleasures but also the delight and enthusiasm of the audience and how that, in turn, stimulated those on the stage to giving a performance of extraordinary warmth and vivacity. I know that many theatregoers who never normally go to musicals found these notices so exciting that they straightway set about booking seats for *Oklahoma*. But how many theatregoers who have never gone to a Shakespearian play of their own free will have been so enthused by a critic's notice of a Shakespearian first night that they felt they must not on any account miss this play?

For instance, I have been re-reading some of the notices of one of the most exciting Shakespearian first nights I have ever attended—that night at the New Theatre in 1944 when Laurence Olivier appeared as *Richard III* in company with Ralph Richardson, Sybil Thorndike and Margaret Leighton. I found these notices made fascinating reading. They were judicial, erudite, finely phrased, but somehow I was often reminded of a dentist probing in a patient's mouth, spending little time over the teeth which are perfect but meticulously examining those which his probing discovers to be unsound. To take but one example, Agate's notice is largely devoted to pointing out why and where Olivier's interpretation was not, in Mr. Agate's opinion, ideal. The performance stirs him to many comparisons—this time not with other actors as Richard but with actors of the past playing parts as varied as Charles II, Robert Macaire, Alfred Jingle, Iago, Iachimo and Mephistofeles. In the end, in spite of all Mr. Agate's reservations, he admits that Olivier 'carried almost complete conviction' but we get hardly any hint in this notice that it was an enthralling night in the theatre. Some months later I heard Agate speak with warming enthusiasm of the occasion, but the nearest he gets in his notice to conveying any enthusiasm is a rather chilly line which describes how he 'sat attentive at this admirable performance'.

It is interesting to compare his notice with that of a much more impressionist critic, J. C. Trewin. 'In Shakespeare's Saturday night melodrama, Laurence Olivier strode across the contentions of York and Lancaster to give the most theatrically overwhelming performance of the period. This was out-and-out acting from the moment that Olivier entered like a baleful raven. It was no strutting, wicked-uncle affair. Olivier, never a mere Crookback gloating among the fanfares of the verse, united intellect and dramatic force, bravura and cold reason: he was the double Gloucester, thinker and doer, mind and mask. Playgoers, generations on, will be told how the actor, pallid, limping, with long black hair and a long, peering nose, moved like a sable cloud into the opening soliloquy. They will hear of the *diablerie*, the crackling, sardonic humours; of the imperious, regal gesture with which he proclaimed his new-born royalty in its very moment of birth; of the Irvingesque figure, crowned and sceptred, that crouched upon the throne like some emanation from a witches' cauldron; of the swoop back to the throne at the line, "Is the chair empty? Is the sword unsway'd?"; of the darkling cry before Bosworth, "There is no creature loves me," of the wistful-despairing, "Not shine today!" as Richard studied the sky; and of the prolonged spasm of the death-agony at Richmond's feet. Here was a figure truly diabolical: a Red King; one raised in blood and one by blood established.'

The value of this sort of notice is not just that it makes one urgently want to see the play; it is immensely valuable to those who many years hence will want to know how Olivier looked and sounded and moved in the part, what sort of excitement his performance generated in an enthusiastic spectator. Mr. Trewin is far more than just a dramatic reporter, but alone among contemporary critics he has much in common with that greatest of all dramatic reporters, Clement Scott. It is unfashionable in these days to admire Clement Scott. If one regards him seriously as a critic one must admit straightaway that his critical sense was, to put it mildly, unreliable. For instance, his opinions of Ibsen's plays were plain silly. He considered that those critics who approved of Ibsen 'were coquetting with the distorted, the tainted, and the poisonous in life', and he ascribed the fact that anyone who could see good in Ibsen to 'the change of tone and thought at our public schools and universities, to our godless method of education, and to the comparative failure of religion as an influence'. I agree with Alan Dent that his work had neither of the two great antiseptics of criticism, wit and style, but I also agree with Dent that Clement Scott 'became in his time, and has remained ever since, immeasurably the most popular and influential dramatic critic who ever lived'. Why? Because no other critic has ever had the same ability to convey the glamour and the excitement and the sense of occasion of a memorable first night. It is impossible to quote him briefly because he had no gift for the incisive, telling phrase. He needed lots of space for his dramatic reporting—and he got it. For instance, his report on the first night of Irving's Hamlet in the *Daily Telegraph* ran to some three thousand, five hundred words. Nowadays Mr. Darlington, the *Telegraph's* present critic, rarely has as much as even five hundred words with which to describe and criticize a notable first night.

Clement Scott begins his notice of Irving's production of *Hamlet* with a description of the atmosphere of excitement in the auditorium as it filled up, of the growing sense of anticipation, until 'with all on the tiptoe of excitement, the curtain rose. All present longed to see Hamlet. Bernardo and Marcellus, the Ghost, the platform, the grim preliminaries, the prologue or introduction to the wonderful story, were, as usual, tolerated—nothing more. Away go the platform, the green lights, the softly-stepping spirit, the musical-voiced Horatio. The scene changes to a dazzling interior, broken in its artistic lines, and rich with architectural beauty; the harps sound, the procession is commenced, the jewels, and crowns, and sceptres, dazzle, and at the end of the train comes Hamlet. Mark him well, though from this instant the eyes will never be removed from his absorbing figure. How is he dressed, and how does he look? No imitation of the portrait of Sir Thomas

Lawrence, no funeral velvet, no elaborate trappings, no Order of the Danish Elephant, no flaxen wig after the model of M. Fechter, no bugles, no stilted conventionality. We see before us a man and a prince, in thick robed silk and a jacket edged with fur; a tall, imposing figure, so well dressed that nothing distracts the eye from the wonderful face; a costume rich and simple and relieved alone by a heavy chain of gold; but, above and beyond all, a troubled, wearied face displaying the first effects of moral poison. The black disordered hair is carelessly tossed about the forehead, but the fixed and rapt attention of the whole house is directed to the eyes of Hamlet: the eyes which denote the trouble—which tell of the distracted mind. Here are "the windy suspiration of forced breath", "the fruitful river in the eye", the "dejected 'haviour of the visage". So subtle is the actor's art, so intense is his application, and so daring his disregard of conventionality, that the first act ends with comparative disappointment. Those who have seen other Hamlets are aghast. Mr. Irving is missing his point, he is neglecting his opportunities.'

Scott continues his reporting even through the interval, recounting the arguments among the audience, the dismay of some of Irving's most ardent admirers, and the spell he had already cast over those who had been watching him carefully and intelligently enough to understand that they were witnessing an entirely new approach to the part. 'The Second Act ends with nearly the same result. There is not an actor living who on attempting Hamlet has not made his points in the speech, "Oh! what a rogue and peasant slave am I!" But Mr. Irving's intention is not to make points, but to give a consistent reading of a Hamlet who "thinks aloud". For one instant he falls "a-cursing like a very drab, a scullion"; but only to relapse into a deeper despair, into more profound thought. He is not acting, he is not splitting the ears of the groundlings; he is an artist concealing his art; he is talking to himself; he is thinking aloud. Hamlet is suffering from moral poison, and the spell woven about the audience is more mysterious and incomprehensible in the second act than the first. In the third act the artist triumphs. No more doubt, no more hesitation, no more discussion. If Hamlet is to be played like a scholar and a gentleman, and not like an actor, this is the Hamlet. The scene with Ophelia turns the scale, and the success is from this instant complete. But we must insist that it was not the triumph of an actor alone; it was the realization of all that the artist has been foreshadowing. . . . Mr. Irving did not make his success by any theatrical *coup*, but by the expression of the pent-up agony of a harassed and disappointed man. According to Mr. Irving, the very sight of Ophelia is the keynote of the outburst of his moral disturbance. He loves this woman; "forty thousand brothers" could not express his overwhelming passion, and think what might have happened if he had been allowed to love her, if his ambition had been realized. The more he looks at Ophelia, the more he curses the irony of fate. He is surrounded, overwhelmed, and crushed by trouble, annoyance, and spies. They are watching him behind the arras. Ophelia is set on to assist their plot. They are driving him mad, though he is only feigning madness. What a position for a harassed creature to endure! They are all against him. Hamlet alone in the world is born to "set it right". He is in the height and delirium of moral anguish. The distraction of the unhinged mind, swinging and banging about like a door; the infinite love and tenderness of the man who longs to be soft and gentle to the woman he adores; the horror and hatred of being trapped, and watched, and spied upon were all expressed with consummate art. Every voice cheered, and the points Mr. Irving had lost as an actor were amply atoned for by his earnestness as an artist. Fortified with this genuine and heart-stirring applause, he rose to the occasion. He had been understood at last. To have broken down here would have been disheartening; but he had triumphed.'

I would like to be able to read you the whole of Scott's notice but that would take too long. You can read it for yourselves in his collected criticisms published under the title of *The Drama of Yesterday and Today* or in James Agate's anthology, *The English Dramatic Critics*. You will find the entire performance vividly described in detail, scene by scene. Let me quote just one more paragraph telling how Irving acted the play scene. 'He acted it with an impulsive energy beyond all praise. Point after point was made in a whirlwind of excitement. He lured, he tempted, he trapped the King, he drove out his wicked uncle conscience-stricken and baffled and with an hysterical yell of triumph he sank down, "the expectancy and rose of the fair state", in the very throne which ought to have been his, and which his rival had just vacated. It is difficult to describe the excitement occasioned by the acting in this scene. When the King had been frighted, the stage was cleared instantaneously. No one in the house knew how the people got off. All eyes were fixed on Hamlet and the King; all were forgetting the real play and the mock play; following up every move of the antagonists, and from constant watching they were almost as exhausted as Hamlet was when he sank a conqueror into the neglected throne. It was all over now. Hamlet had won. He would take the ghost's word for a thousand pounds. The clouds cleared from his brow. He was no longer in doubt or despair. He was the victor after this mental struggle. The effects of the moral poison had passed away.'

We shall never read the like of Clement Scott again—if only because there is no longer room in our newspapers for dramatic reporting on that scale. Today films, television, radio, the ballet and almost nightly concerts compete with the theatre for the space allotted to entertainments in newspapers which are very much smaller than they were in Clement Scott's day, with print which is very much larger, and with headlines in big type which take away still more of the dramatic critics' space. It is getting on for a hundred years since Clement Scott wrote that report of the first night of Irving's Hamlet. A hundred years hence nobody will be able to find comparable reports on the great Hamlets of our day. They will be able to read, in notices which are miracles of incisiveness and compression, highly intelligent and knowledgeable analyses of the Hamlets of Sir John Gielgud, Sir Laurence Olivier, Mr. Michael Redgrave and the rest. They will be able to read occasional descriptions of how these actors took certain lines and certain scenes. But never will they find a criticism which gives a detailed description, act by act, of how the play was performed, besides conveying the theatrical excitement of the occasion in a way which vividly re-creates for us what it must have been like to have been one of the audience on that night.

Please do not misunderstand me, I am not suggesting that Clement Scott's enthusiastic dramatic reporting is preferable to the cool and considered judgments of dramatic critics of today. What would be ideal is if, on the day after an important Shakespearian first night, we could have a vivid, factual account of the performance; then on the following day the dramatic critics' appraisal of its merits and demerits. When a few years ago I took a production of *Hamlet* on a tour of the German theatres there were several occasions when the newspapers adopted this practice. In England, Shakespeare needs dramatic reporting as well as dramatic criticism more than any other author because, let's face it, he is not a popular dramatist. That may seem an odd statement to make in this town where every year the season grows longer and longer and the seats become more and more difficult to obtain. But most of those who come to Stratford see more than one play, and they are drawn from all over the world. Much the same is true at the Old Vic, which presents a considerable number of plays during the course of a season and relies largely on a repeater audience. The total audience for Shakespeare to-day is very small. Clement Scott brought into the theatre to see Shakespeare's plays thousands of people who would not otherwise have thought of doing so. Today the Shakespeare theatre desperately needs more converts. Our dramatic critics have probably done more than the critics of any other age to enhance the pleasure and understanding of the regular Shakespearian playgoer, but I wonder how many converts they have made from among the unbelievers—from those who have never been persuaded that Shakespeare is a genuine part of theatrical entertainment.

Our critics can on occasions write with uninhibited and infectious enthusiasm about every sort of entertainment apart from Shakespeare. Why is it that they can so seldom send their readers scuttling to the box office when they write about a Shakespearian production? I think Ivor Brown has the explanation when he says that a critic attending a Shakespearian performance cannot hope for 'the delight of innocence' with which he watches a new play. Recalling 'the high pleasure' he enjoyed at a particularly good production here in Stratford he remarks that he found it 'strange and distressing' that so many of the next day's notices 'contained so much melancholy evidence of chilly aloofness'.

I suspect that one of the resons for this 'chilly aloofness' has been the influence which James Agate exerted upon many of his colleagues and his successors. He believed that it was the business of the critic attending a Shakespearian play 'not to wonder but to expound'. Writing of Wolfit's Lear, which he considered 'the greatest piece of Shakespearian acting I have ever seen since I was privileged to write for the *Sunday Times*', he describes the audience's 'amazed and sudden surrender to some stroke of passionate genius', but it troubled him that the audience surrendered to it without quite knowing what it was to which they were surrendering. He describes them leaving the theatre 'conscious of having been swept off their feet and not bothering to wonder why'. He makes it clear that in spite of his intense admiration for this performance, *he* had not been swept off his feet, but had remained aloof from the audience, coolly and analytically examining the performance. So he proceeds to tell the audience exactly why, in his opinion, they were so impressed and to explain just exactly what Wolfit did at the peak moments of his performance and how he did it. In fact one is given an analysis of the actor's mental processes but little or no impression of the emotional impact upon the audience, or upon the critic himself.

Perhaps the fundamental trouble about Shakespearian dramatic criticism today is that the critics have had to write about far too many productions of the same play. Inevitably, the more often one sees a play the more detached one becomes as a spectator and nothing but 'the exquisite experience of seeming to see a masterpiece afresh, anew, with its metal as near to new-minted as may be' can prevent the mind from continually comparing what is happening upon the stage with recollections of numerous other performances. As a critic becomes more and more familiar with a Shakespearian play on the stage he finds his attention concentrating more and more on the minutiae of the performance rather than upon the play as a whole. To those who know their Shakespeare well, each notice reveals fresh and undiscovered aspects of the text, but to the ordinary reader, especially if he is youthful, many of the points which a critic deals with may seem finicky and unimportant. The ordinary everyday theatregoer reads a critic's notice mainly to discover the answer to the question: 'Shall I or shall I not go to see this play?' If only editors would give back to the critics just a little more of the space that they used to have, I have no doubt that within the scope of the same notice we could have criticisms which besides being comparative and analytical would also be impressionist, and thus satisfy both the devotees of Shakespeare and the playgoers who want to know 'whether it's worth going to see'.

8

SHAKESPEARE'S MEN AND THEIR MORALS

by J. I. M. STEWART

I

As the industrious years go by, it becomes increasingly difficult not only to add to the criticism of Shakespeare, but even to report adequately upon a single aspect of it. Today, we find a greater variety of opinions about Shakespeare, and a larger body of controversy about his work, than any previous age has known. I shall try, if very briefly, to place this unrest in Shakespeare studies (as one conservative commentator has disapprovingly called it) by relating it to two central works in the history of Shakespeare criticism: Dr. Johnson's *Preface* to his edition of the plays, published in 1765, and A. C. Bradley's *Shakespearean Tragedy*, published in 1904.

It was Johnson's grand contention—as it had been Dryden's, indeed, immediately before him—that Shakespeare gives us Nature: Shakespeare's world is our world in concentration. The heroes of other playwrights are often only phantoms, but Shakespeare's heroes are men. Shakespeare discerns truly and depicts faithfully. His book is thus a map of life, an epitome of human experience. It is true that the plays are not planned moral fables, contrived to edify and instruct, as is Johnson's own tragedy, *Irene*, or as is Johnson's novel, *Rasselas*. Nevertheless Shakespeare affords knowledge immensely valuable to us as moral beings. And he does this all the way through. Even 'the character of Polonius is serious and useful, and the gravediggers themselves may be heard with applause'. It is important to notice that Johnson sees no great difficulty in the fact that these intensely real people of Shakespeare's are involved in some rather unreal fables. Shakespeare's stories are merely the vehicles on which the characters and their moral life are brought to us. It is from the characters, copiously diversified and justly pursued as they are, that our delight and instruction derive. We need not much labour, then, to rationalize the stories.

Again it is important to notice Johnson's strong sense of these so natural characters as yet being fictions. The plays are not *records* of human transactions. They are 'faithful miniatures' of human transactions. They make us free of Nature only by themselves yielding to the rules of Art.

A good many things happen between Johnson and Bradley. First, the characters march out of the plays, led by Falstaff in Maurice Morgann's famous essay. Presently they are being discussed as if they were historical personages, and on this basis a swelling flood of commentary continues throughout the nineteenth century. I think myself that Shakespeare criticism has been enriched in consequence. But the dangers are obvious. There is an invitation to irrelevant reverie, as upon, say, the girlhood of Shakespeare's heroines. We may also come to feel that with a play, as with a historical action, crucial facts are likely to have perished tantalizingly from the record, so that they are recoverable only by ingenious inference. It is incumbent upon us, we may be brought to feel, to reconstruct the truth on the basis of such fragmentary evidence as the play has preserved for us. How many oddities has this persuasion produced!

A second development, unknown to Johnson and associated with the romantic critics (notably Coleridge) has been towards the dogma that Shakespeare never nods, that his judgment is always equal to his genius, and that the several elements in his plays are with a quite exceptional perfection always fused into an artistic unity. This conviction has been reinforced, I imagine, by the rise to the position of a major literary form of realistic and psychological prose fiction. The effect is to make us feel something mildly shocking in any proposal to be merely light-hearted about Shakespeare's plots and situations.

These, then, were the developing trends before Bradley. Correspondingly, we must notice certain aspects of Shakespeare that were no longer much attended to. Any marked feeling for Shakespeare as an Elizabethan, as a man developing and writing within a certain intellectual atmosphere, had died out. So had any strong sense of him as working for a particular theatre and within particular theatrical conventions. Criticism concerned itself, very confidently, with absolute and not with historical judgments.

Bradley came to crown this situation. He brought to it first his genius (for the writer of the best book on Shakespeare must, I think, be allowed that) and secondly a great interest in the philosophy of tragedy. For Bradley, as for Johnson, Shakespeare's heroes are men. But now they are men realized for us, in the two-hours traffic of the stage, in the richest and most delicate psychological detail. They are men moving through actions at once perfectly realistic and supremely poetic—actions subtly contrived in their every implication and affiliation. But, although they belong to works owning the highest degree of artistic unity, they yet have a life that, mysteriously, extends far beyond the limits of their play. Shakespeare's characters have, as it were, a larger personal history which can be reached from the springboard of the play. And they have, too, this as their final greatness: they embody (triumphantly and—we must say—by a mysterious anachronism) a theory of tragedy to the shaping of which Aristotle, Coleridge and Hegel have all contributed the finest essence of their thought.

Perhaps he is a little too good to be true, this serene and timeless Shakespeare, with Aristotle and Hegel in one pocket, the Oxford of 1904 in the other, and the sacred coal ever at his lips. But only perhaps —for who can tell? Is there anything, then, *demonstrably* wrong with Bradley?

Many people now say, Yes. The plays and characters Bradley offers us are his own creation quite as much as Shakespeare's. Really attend to Shakespeare's plain text, disregard the mass of anachronistic subtlety that has long been projected upon it, and you will find no elaborately developed psychological studies and not many genuine human predicaments. You will find—Robert Bridges announced in 1907 in an essay called *The Influence of the Audience on Shakespeare's Drama*—grossly inconsistent characters being bumped and jockeyed through a variety of sensational incidents by a great poet who was constrained by the barbarity of his audience to work in terms of the crudest melodrama. In 1919 Professor Levin Schücking developed this theme in a book shortly afterwards translated as *Character Problems in Shakespeare's Plays*.[1] Schücking maintained that Shakespeare's dramaturgy is essentially popular and primitive. Shakespeare simply moves from scene to scene seeking immediate theatrical effect. Cleopatra is a harlot at the beginning of her play because plays about harlots were a good draw, and is somebody quite different at the end because her creator became belatedly conscious that he must make some contact with the Cleopatra of Plutarch whose story he is following.

But more important than Schücking was Professor Elmer Edgar Stoll, a trenchant, pertinacious and learned American critic who, in a sense, stands Bridges' contention on its head. The psychological in-

[1] Harrap, 1922.

coherence and the ruthless pursuit of a hodge-podge of emotions which Bridges sees as destroying Shakespeare's art Stoll declares to be, in drama, a splendid artistic strength. For, essentially, we go to the theatre to be thrilled—and to be thrilled by 'another world, not a copy of this.' 'Life,' Stoll says, 'must be . . . piled on life, or we have visited the theatre in vain.' Shakespeare, knowing this, chiefly seeks a kind of 'emotional effect, with which psychology or even simple narrative coherence often considerably interferes'.[1]

You see, then, what a confusion of voices the appraisal of Shakespeare's characters can evoke. Take, for example, Othello. For Bradley, Othello is a marvellous study in depth of an extremely noble and at the same time wholly convincing individual. His conflict with Iago—again a complex and perfectly credible figure—fulfils the strictest laws of tragic causality in that the hero's very nobility is his undoing. He is *too* trustful; 'his trust, where he trusts, is absolute'; and so he is helpless before deception. His fate is plausible, convincing, deeply moving, and consonant with a just and elevating philosophical reading of life. Bridges will have nothing of all this. 'The whole thing is impossible,' he cries. There is nothing elevating about it. Shakespeare's aim was merely to scarify a particularly thick-skinned audience. And for Professor Stoll, too, Othello is an impossible figure. Bradley's crucial contention ('his trust, where he trusts, is absolute') is mere cobweb—since, if trustfulness is the key to the character, then surely Othello should trust his wife and friend at least as fully as he trusts a stranger. 'What is to be made of this heap of contradictions?' Stoll exclaims, when he has analysed the hero—and answers, in effect: 'In terms of actual human psychology, nothing; in terms of the emotional artifice that constitutes a good play, a great deal.'

Now, what we may call the negative or destructive side of Stoll's historical realism was much more effective than the obscure aesthetic of sensation that it throws out as a sort of life-line to Shakespeare's reputation. It is almost possible to say that our faith in Shakespeare's characters was shaken; we were at a loss for a reply to the onslaught; and we turned our attention to other things. Textual research very fascinating to keen minds, re-creatings of the Elizabethan 'climate of opinion', studies (very valuable indeed, the best of them) in Shakespeare's poetic, explorations of a possible symbolical content, conscious or unconscious, in the plays: there are all these approaches and many more available to the inquirer who hesitates before this perplexed

---

[1] Stoll: *Art and Artifice in Shakespeare* (Cambridge, 1933).

matter of the characters. But ought we not to face up to the problem? 'Shakespeare's heroes are men.' Is it true, or was Dr. Johnson wrong?

I suspect that we are apt to be a little intimidated, some of us, by the erudition of these 'realists'. We have not read nearly so many plays as they have, and those that we have read we don't seem to remember nearly so well or be anything like so sure about. Indisputable, too, is their claim to know whatever can be discovered about the Elizabethan theatre and audience, about conventional types and roles and situations, about the views of learned and simple Elizabethans regarding the state, and the solar system, and the human soul; about ghosts and witches and devils and angels. And yet I am not quite confident that all this valuable information is really at the heart of the matter. When I ask myself why I have some confidence in Dr. Johnson and am reluctant to scrap him I find that it is because he is known to have been intensely interested not only in Shakespeare's men but in real men as well. Johnson, so to speak, tackled the problem from both ends. And, in the field we have been considering, I should have more confidence in the judgment of one who sat for months on end in what we should now call a police court, just because men interested him, than I should have in one who sat ever so much longer in a carrel in a library, with any distracting view of his fellow mortals ingeniously cut off by worm-eaten oak or by steel shutters. Again, I should listen to a wise man who had worked long in actual theatres for actual audiences more attentively than I should to a man, equally wise, whose frequentation had been all of the ghost of the Globe. I am interested, then, in what men of the theatre think about our problem—and in what is thought about it, too, by certain comparative newcomers to the game, the depth psychologists.

Is it not significant that the late Harley Granville-Barker, a scholar who was at the same time an experienced Shakespearian actor and a brilliant Shakespearian producer, entirely rejected the notion of Shakespeare's primitivism, sensationalism, psychological incoherence and the like; and that he should have given us in his great series of *Prefaces* character-studies almost in the direct line of Bradley, only informed and (we may say) pruned by a closer knowledge of the stage? And is it not significant, too, that Freud vindicated Shakespeare, whose works he had abundantly studied, as a psychologist of genius? As long ago as 1923 a conservative but acute commentator on the cockpit of Shakespeare criticism, the late Professor C. H. Herford, remarked that modern psychology, by its disclosure of such phenomena as those of dual and multiple personality, might unexpectedly illuminate the vexed problem of apparent inconsistency in Shakespeare.

In point of fact, modern psychology has been rather more ambitious than that. Dr. Johnson, you remember, set little store by Shakespeare's stories; it seemed to him of small consequence whether these were probable or unlikely. Freud and his followers have contended that, where the stories are unlikely, they are unlikely much after the fashion of dreams, and for the same reason.

A tragedy is essentially a symbolical representation of wishes and conflicts urgent in us all, but of which a psychic censorship forbids the direct and undisguised expression. Hence the power of tragedy, when imaginatively received either in the theatre or in reading. It affords tremendous relief. It is just the cathartic or purging instrument that Aristotle long ago declared it to be. Hence too all those irrational and puzzling elements evident in tragedy when *not* imaginatively received. For Shakespeare's stories and his people often follow the logic of myth and the unconscious rather than the logic of waking life. This means that they are, in one sense, less 'realistic' than Bradley was inclined to suppose them. But the psychological critics are inclined to maintain, at the same time, that Shakespeare's major characters, taken simply as very actual men and women, become far more explicable in terms of what is now known about the mechanisms and motives of the human mind. Thus when older critics have maintained that the credulity of Othello, the malignity of Iago, the sudden senseless jealousy of Leontes, the equally sudden depravity of Angelo are implausible and theatrical, these newer critics would say: 'No, men are like that, although you find it more comfortable to believe that they are not. People come into our consulting-rooms who are capable of behaving just like Othello, or Iago or Leontes or Angelo. And we can explain how they come to behave as they do.'

I confess to finding all this of great interest. At the same time I am sure that we should be a little chary of feeling, 'Ah—light at last!' Mr. T. S. Eliot has somewhere made fun of criticism that comes forward as 'revealing for the first time the gospel of some dead sage, which no one has understood before; which owing to the backward and confused state of men's minds has lain unknown to this very moment'. And if we trace out the fascinating history of 'Hamlet' criticism (as an American scholar, Dr. Paul Conklin, has begun to do)[1]

[1] *A History of Hamlet Criticism*, 1601–1821 (King's Crown Press, New York, 1947).

we shall quickly come upon the chastening fact that Shakespeare's Prince of Denmark is a veritable chameleon, who has taken on, century by century and generation by generation, the very form and pressure of the age. What was Hamlet to the Elizabethan audience? A malcontent, Dr. Conklin assures us; a bitterly eloquent and princely avenger on the verge of a lunacy from which the players would sometimes extract a good laugh; but withal a formidable young man and one much admired for his mouth-filling flood of iambic pentameter. Later, when England fell under the influence of Scotsmen and went soft, this young tough went soft too—and softer in the study than on the stage. In the age of Sterne and Mackenzie, Hamlet becomes a man of sentiment, a man of feeling; Goethe finds him closely related to his own Werther; Coleridge announces that Hamlet is in fact Coleridge—an extremely impressive person of vast intellectual powers embarrassed by an unfortunate weakness of will. Prose fiction takes on a new complexity in its presentation of character: just such a complexity is discovered in the Prince. Scholars distil subtle theories of tragedy out of philosophies old and new: Hamlet turns out to be the hero who fits perfectly. Other scholars fall to studying the Elizabethan drama at large: Hamlet loses his uniqueness and becomes less a character than a role, a series of stage dodges. The text of Shakespeare is studied with a new minuteness: it is discovered (as by Dr. Richard Flatter in a most ingenious book)[1] that the text gives tiny indications which must revolutionize our conceptions of Hamlet's disposition. And finally—finally for the present—comes Dr. Ernest Jones, with his deeply interesting psycho-analytic study, *Hamlet and Oedipus*.[2]

What is the lesson of this? The lesson is surely not that all critical interpretation of Shakespeare's characters is ephemeral modish nonsense. We merely learn that we ought not to let one theory, one reading, sweep away all the others. These people of Shakespeare's really are extraordinarily like life, and life is susceptible of many interpretations which do not necessarily invalidate each other. The danger point comes when we persuade ourselves that the characters are *only* this or that: only artifice, only allegory, only theology, only advice to Elizabethan statesmen, only concealed pointers to Sir Francis Bacon or the Earl of Derby, and so on. And there is perhaps one other danger; that of forgetting that all these inquiries are for the satisfaction of the intel-

---

[1] *Shakespeare's Producing Hand: A Study of his marks of expression to be found in the First Folio* (Heinemann, 1948).

[2] Gollancz, 1949.

lect, since Shakespeare has already satisfied the imagination. When our imagination is kindled we do not think to 'interpret' the characters. We know that the characters are interpreting us.

II

So much for the debate on Shakespeare's men; let me now say something about their morals—and about *his* morals, too. And, this time, let our first critic be a lady. It was in 1775 that Mrs. Elizabeth Griffith[1] determined upon 'placing his Ethic merits in a more conspicuous point of view'—and became thereby (I am afraid) one of a good many writers to contrive mainly absurdity in the consideration of this difficult topic. It would appear that Mrs. Griffith proposed (in addition to giving numerous excerpts of an edifying cast from the plays) to offer compendious remarks on the moral intention animating each play in turn. She begins with *The Tempest*—which teaches (she says):

> that the ways, the justice, and the goodness of Providence, are so frequently manifested toward mankind, even in this life, that it should ever encourage an honest and a guiltless mind to form hopes, in the most forlorn situations; and ought also to warn the wicked never to rest assured in the false confidence of wealth or power, against the natural abhorrence of vice, both in God and man.

That is very well, no doubt—but the next play in the Folio is *A Midsummer Night's Dream*. Poor Mrs. Griffith is already stumped. 'I shall not trouble my readers', she says, 'with the Fable of this piece, as I can see no general moral that can be deducted from the argument.' Then comes *The Two Gentlemen of Verona*. 'The Fable', she says, 'of this play has no more moral in it, than the former.' *Measure for Measure* follows and the poor lady becomes desperate: 'I cannot see what moral can be extracted from this Piece.' And with the fifth play, *The Comedy of Errors*, she gives up: 'I shall take no further notice of the want of a moral fable in the rest of these plays.' It is true, indeed, that Mrs. Griffith does not altogether quit the field. In *As You Like It*, for instance, she triumphantly finds 'a very proper hint given . . . to women, not to deviate from the prescribed rules and decorums of their sex'. But on the whole she must be said to discover (what Dr. Johnson could already have told her) that Shakespeare 'is so much more careful to please than to instruct, that he seems to write without any moral purpose'.

[1] *The Morality of Shakespeare's Drama Illustrated.*

Johnson backs up this stricture of Shakespeare by declaring that 'he makes no just distribution of good or evil', thereby ranging himself with those who require of the dramatist the administration of poetical justice. And the conception of poetical justice, indeed, was for a very long time the focal point round which most debate on Shakespeare's morality turned. Eugenius in Dryden's *Essay of Dramatic Poesy* had censured the ancient dramatists for not taking care to punish the wicked; and Dryden's contemporary Thomas Rymer[1] (who seems actually to have coined the phrase *poetical justice*) transferred the censure to Shakespeare. John Dennis[2] argued with great ingenuity for poetical justice. Real people, he said, must face Judgment in a hereafter. But characters in a play have no hereafter; their sole creator is the dramatist; and therefore the dramatist must, so to speak, play deity to them, and reward or punish them while they are yet on the stage and before they escape into nothingness. Dennis in this was partly actuated by his hatred of Addison, in whose *Cato* a virtuous hero is allowed to perish in a just cause. Addison's counter-arguments in *The Spectator* must at first seem very sensible: *good and evil happen alike to all men on this side of the grave*; and poetical justice must entirely vitiate the drama as a mirror of life. Yet Johnson, although working the mirror-of-life idea hard, was unconvinced by Addison, and at least hankered after poetical justice. He could not bear poetry not to vindicate a moral governance of the world; he believed that at the end of plays the evidence should (as it were) be fudged in order to chasten vice and encourage virtue. The dramatist can't go on to show the Last Judgment in operation. He is therefore obliged (if he is to suggest the final and just balance of things) to anticipate, and to show felicity under the figure of prosperity achieved here below. On this ground Johnson preferred Tate's 'happy-ending' *Lear* to Shakespeare's.

The later history of the 'poetical justice' doctrine is more full of curiosity than instruction. Subscribing to it must necessarily lead, in Shakespeare criticism, to one of two conclusions. Either the major tragedies of Shakespeare are extremely faulty performances in which the principle is for the most part flatly contradicted (and this is what Dennis boldly concludes); or the tragedies present a succession of persons only speciously virtuous, who meet a merited doom, intelligible to us if we will only sufficiently reflect. Since the secure establishing of Shakespeare's reputation in the later eighteenth century it is

[1] *The Tragedies of the Last Age* (1678).
[2] *The Genius and Writings of Shakespeare* (1712).

only this second supposition that has appeared tenable. Or if this has not been held tenable it has yet frequently been held possible to argue for that (as it were) modified or attenuated form of poetical justice represented by the Aristotelian *hamartia*—the notion that there is *some* relationship or correspondence between conduct and character on the one hand and earthly destiny on the other. Critics consequently find themselves labouring to create for each victim some *hamartia* or other. Thus Rymer would jeeringly find in Desdemona this tragic flaw: that she was careless about her linen—that the play is the tragedy of a handkerchief. Others with more seriousness have averred that Cordelia was blameworthy in failing of a little harmless and tactful prevarication. Even King Duncan has been held gravely at fault in imperilling not only his own life but that of his chamber grooms by rashly disregarding that *hoarser croak* whereby the sagacious raven would have apprised him of the inadvisability of entering Macbeth's castle.

It is apparent to us nowadays (whether rightly or wrongly) that all this represents a false cast in the interpretation of Shakespeare. Yet when Dr. Johnson puts the thing at its most general, and declares 'it is always a writer's duty to make the world better', we are conscious of a proposition which, at least, must be treated more warily. Has Shakespeare any aim to instruct? Poets in his time were certainly *taught* that they had a duty to do so. Even if he had no didactic intention, did he yet take for granted any religious or ethical system, within the affirmations of which he unquestioningly worked? Answering this is very difficult, for the simple and obvious reason that all in Shakespeare is expressed in dramatic or personative form. Thus much has been written of recent years about Shakespeare's adherence to mediaeval notions of order and degree. A speech by Ulysses in *Troilus and Cressida* (I. iii. 75 ff.), another by the Archbishop of Canterbury in *Henry V* (I. ii 183 ff.), a third by Menenius in *Coriolanus* (I. i. 101 ff.) are constantly cited as vindicating this. Yet we may well ask, as Professor Harbage does in *As They Liked It*,[1] perhaps the best book on our subject yet published, if anything of all this is designed as doctrinal. 'It cannot be ignored that each of the three speeches is delivered by an unscrupulous politician meeting an immediate problem—advocating a practical programme of somewhat debatable merit.' Moreover, Professor Harbage shows, this is only one instance of a pervasive ambiguousness in Shakespeare's dealing with ethical issues. It may almost be said to be the rule that when his characters come hard up against a

[1] The Macmillan Company, New York, 1947.

moral problem proper—a moral dilemma or hard choice—the dramatist finds means to let them off. The issue is suspended, dissolved or dodged; some theatricality, some trick of distraction is brought in. Even in *Measure for Measure*, the play most commonly cited in arguments here, the dramatist is thoroughly evasive in the end. Then again, a somewhat similar phenomenon confronts us in the study of Shakespearian character. Swinburne[1] describes Brutus as the 'very noblest figure of a typical and ideal republican in all the literature of the world'. But when we look hard at Brutus we see something more complicated and less edifying. Morally, indeed, it is surely the prime characteristic of Shakespeare's major characters that they keep us guessing all the time. Are they, perhaps, constructed to that end? Here, once more, is Professor Harbage:

> Claudius, Gertrude, and Hamlet require constant evaluation on our part. We have to keep weighing them on our scales. Always in Shakespeare we perceive that the good might be better and the bad might be worse, and we are excited by our perceptions. The virtuous seem to need our counsel, and the vicious seem capable of understanding our censure. We are linked to the former by sensations of solicitude, and to the latter by moments of sympathy and understanding. We are constantly *involved*.

In all this, Shakespeare's characters are at an opposite remove from, say, Corneille's. They never give the impression of being moral athletes— a sort of ethical Brains Trust knowing all the answers and existing in order to give an exhibition of them. They are not, in fact, the creations of a moralist. They are not even the creations of an artist who is obliged to pretend at all hard to be a moralist. Rather they are the elements in an entertainment of which the stuff and substance is, indeed, the moral nature of man, but the end of which is not moralistic. Shakespeare, in short, sees it as the business of the poet to exhibit, not to pronounce upon, moral behaviour. In one sense he is dealing with morals all the time. There is scarcely a speech, scarcely even a song in all his plays untouched by ethical sentiment. He deals with morals always; but as a moralist, never. He renders us more aware of ourselves as creatures of good and evil; but he seems to do this rather because such awareness is pleasurable than because it conduces to salvation. He does not work out moral problems for us; yet he leaves us, as moral beings, more alert than he found us. This may itself be a moral act, and laudable. But certainly if (as Johnson would have the artist do)

[1] Algernon Charles Swinburne: *A Study of Shakespeare* (1880).

Shakespeare 'makes the world better' it is by exercising our moral interests and perceptions rather than by any deliberate proposal to alter them, to expound patterns of behaviour, or to bend fiction to the support of principle and precept.

It comes down then (I think) to this. Shakespeare is not ambitious to instruct us. He tells us, indeed, in that Epilogue to *The Tempest* which is conceivably his artistic testament, that *his project was to please*. He pleases us as moral beings—in virtue of our being creatures of good and evil, interested in good and evil. But the interest in good and evil for which he caters is the common man's, not the professional's: Shakespeare does not write as a casuist or for casuists. He writes as one good-hearted for the good-hearted. He has perhaps more insight into how human beings do behave than curiosity about how they *ought* to behave.

But to all this it must be added that the plays create for themselves, and exist in, a real and distinguishable moral climate. It is unmistakable! The Victorians were fond of assuring us that Shakespeare, morally, was as sound as a bell; and there can be no doubt that the Victorians were right. Study Shakespeare's silences and avoidances; study the things he dropped as he worked from his sources. The conclusion to which we are bound to come is that he was a thoroughly wholesome person. Some of his plays must strike us as holding shadows dark enough. But the air is clean, the soil sweet, and the plenty (as with Chaucer) distinguishably God's.

9

THE SUCCESS OF 'MUCH ADO ABOUT NOTHING'

by GRAHAM STOREY

MAY I confess that I only added the first words of my title when I was well into preparing this lecture? Do not mistake me: the riches of the play—the sheer exhilaration of the encounters between Benedick and Beatrice and their arabesques of wit; the superb stupidity of Dogberry and Verges and *their* arabesques of misunderstanding; the skilful weaving and disentanglement of the comic imbroglio—all these are a joy to see and hear, and belong to Shakespeare's most assured writing. But it is a commonplace of criticism that a successful play, like any other work of art, must be a unity: what Coleridge called the Imagination's 'esemplastic power' must shape into one its individual forces and beauties. Whether *Much Ado* has this unity was the question that worried me.

It did not worry Shakespeare's contemporaries. The play offered an exciting Italianate melodrama, enlivened by two variegated sets of 'humours': the wit-combats and properly-rewarded over-reachings of Benedick and Beatrice, and the low-life comedy of Dogberry and Verges; and remember that George Chapman and Ben Jonson had just started a run of fashionable 'humour' plays. As in all proper comedies, the story came out all right in the end. 'Strike up, pipers! *Dance.*' The formula ends that other comedy with a similarly riddling title, *As You Like It*; and whatever the differences of tone, the effect does not vary so much from that of the conclusion of *Twelfth Night*, the third of this group of plays written at the turn of the century:

> A great while ago the world begun,
> With hey, ho, the wind and the rain;
> But that's all one, our play is done,
> And we'll strive to please you every day.

The humours were what the contemporary audience remembered the play by. '*Benedicte and Betteris*,' say the Lord Treasurer's accounts for 1613: and *Much Ado* was almost certainly meant. 'Benedick and Beatrice', wrote Charles I in his second Folio, as a second title to the play— exercising a similar Stuart prerogative in renaming *Twelfth Night* 'The Tragedy of Malvolio'. The 'main plot' is clearly being regarded as a kind of serious relief to the much more absorbing comedy. When, with the Restoration, Shakespeare had to face the formidable canons of the neo-Classic critics, this central plot came in for some hard questioning. The criticism was, as we should expect, formal: the *decorum* was at fault. 'The fable is absurd,' writes Charles Gildon, in 1710, in an essay[1] often reprinted during the eighteenth century; 'the charge against Hero is too shocking for tragedy or comedy, and Claudio's conduct is against the nature of love'. He is almost equally concerned that the people of Messina do not act and talk, he says, like natives of a warm country.

But, at the turn of this century, one or two critics began to show a quite new uneasiness about the play. They found, not unity, not the almost unblemished gaiety that they found in *As You Like It* or *Twelfth Night*; but jarring tones, a gratuitous suffering and heartlessness in crisis —the Church Scene—that the rest of the play could not wipe out, and a distressing inconsistency in the characters of Claudio, the Prince and Leonato. The critical approaches were different: but the resultant *uncomfortableness* they generated was much the same. And it has undoubtedly left its mark upon many performances since.

The most frequent cause of uneasiness has been to respond to the play as though the protagonists were psychologically real. It is indeed the most expected response, as the dominant mode of the theatre is still naturalism. But it plays havoc with *Much Ado* as *comedy*. Stopford Brooke, writing in 1913[2] as a Bradleyan, shows what happens. He clearly wants to like the play; yet its very centre, the exposure in church, is, he writes, 'a repulsive scene'. 'In it all the characters will be tried in the fire'; and, as a Victorian clergyman of strong, if sensitive views, he tries them. They emerge—Claudio, Don Pedro and Leonato —shallow, wilful, cruel, inconsistent with what they were before; and the play, its centre contaminated, is virtually handed over to Benedick and Beatrice. That, I am convinced, is not how Shakespeare wrote the play. But the figures of the main plot are bound to appear in this light, if we see them as fully-rounded characters and subject them to the tests

---

[1] *Remarks on the Plays of Shakespeare:* included in *Shakespeare's Poems,* 1710 (supplementary vol. to Rowe's *Works of Shakespeare*).
[2] *Ten More Plays of Shakespeare,* 1913, p. 21.

of psychological consistency. I see them as something much nearer 'masks': as not quite so far removed from the formalized figures of *Love's Labour's Lost*, where most of the play's life resides in the plot-pattern and the dance of verbal wit, as many critics have suggested. I will return to this suggestion later. Meanwhile, I only want to insist that the opposite approach—that of naturalistic realism—stretches the play much further than a comedy can go, and makes almost impossible demands of the actors for the last two Acts. It can also lead to a quite ludicrous literalism, as where Stopford Brooke, quoting the magnificent, absurd *finale* of Beatrice's outburst against Claudio after the Church Scene—'O God, that I were a man! I would eat his heart in the market-place'—solemnly comments, 'Of course, she would not have done it.'[1]

Others though, besides the 'naturalist' critics, have found *Much Ado* disturbing: and disturbing because they do not discover in it the unity that I have made my main question. Sir Edmund Chambers,[2] writing fifty years ago, was probably the first to note what he called its 'clashing of dramatic planes'. 'Elements,' he wrote, 'of tragedy, comedy, tragi-comedy, and farce are thrust together;' and the result is not unity, but 'an unco-ordinated welter', a dramatic impressionism that sacrifices the whole to the brilliance of individual scenes or passages of dialogue or even individual lines. Other writers have more recently said much the same: the play's elements are incompatible; the plot too harsh for the characters; it is the wrong kind of romantic story to blend with comedy. 'This happy play,' as 'Q.' called it in his Introduction to the *New Cambridge Shakespeare*, 1923, seems, in fact, to be in danger of losing its central place in the canon of Shakespeare's comedies (or it would be, if critics were taken too seriously).

I think that all these critics have seriously underrated the *comic* capacity of both Shakespeare and his audience: the capacity to create, and to respond to, varying and often contradictory experiences simultaneously; to create a pattern of human behaviour from their blendings and juxtapositions; and to obtain a keen enjoyment from seeing that pattern equally true at all levels. I will try to apply this claim to *Much Ado*.

'For man is a giddy thing, and this is my conclusion,' says Benedick

---

[1] Op. cit., p. 27: quoted by T. W. Craik in *Much Ado About Nothing* (*Scrutiny*, October 1953).

[2] Introduction to *Much Ado* (Red Letter Shakespeare, 1904–8). Reprinted in *Shakespeare: A Survey*, 1925.

in the last scene; and this is surely the play's 'cause' or ruling theme. 'Giddy', a favourite Elizabethan word: 'light-headed, frivolous, flighty, inconstant', it meant by 1547; 'whirling or circling round with bewildering rapidity' (1593); mentally intoxicated, 'elated to thoughtlessness' (in Dr. Johnson's *Dictionary*). *Much Ado* has all these meanings in abundance. And Benedick's dictum, placed where it is, followed by the dance (reminiscent perhaps of the *La Ronde*-like Masked Ball of Act II), suggests eternal recurrence: 'Man is a giddy thing'—and ever more will be so. The impetus to two of the play's three plots is the impetus to all the comedies, the propensity to love-making: one plot begins and ends with it; the other ends with it. And the impetus to the third plot, the antics of the Watch ('the vulgar humours of the play,' said Gildon,[1] 'are remarkably varied and distinguished'), is self-love: the innocent, thoughtless, outrageous love of Dogberry for himself and his position.

Inconstancy, mental intoxication, elation to thoughtlessness: the accompaniment of all these states is deception, self-deception, miscomprehension. And deception, the prelude to 'giddiness', operates at every level of *Much Ado*. It is the common denominator of the three plots, and its mechanisms—eavesdroppings, mistakes of identity, disguises and maskings, exploited hearsay—are the major stuff of the play.

In the main plot—the Italian melodrama that Shakespeare took from Matteo Bandello, Bishop of Agen—the deception-theme is, of course, the most harshly obvious. Don John's instrument, Borachio, deceives 'even the very eyes' of Claudio and the Prince; Claudio, the Prince and Leonato are all convinced that Hero has deceived them; Hero is violently deceived in her expectations of marriage, stunned by the slander; the Friar's plan to give her out as dead deceives everyone it is meant to.

The deceptions of Benedick and Beatrice in Leonato's garden-bower serve a function as a comic echo of all this. They are also beautifully-managed examples of a favourite Elizabethan device: the over-reacher over-reached, the 'enginer hoist with his own petar', the marriage-mocker and husband-scorner taken in by—to us—a transparently obvious trick. (It is a major part of the play's delight that the audience always knows more than the actors: hints are dropped throughout; a Sophoclean comic irony pervades every incident.) Here, the metaphors of stalking and fishing are both deliberately overdone; and the effect is to emphasize that each of these eavesdroppings is a piece of play-acting, a mock-ceremonious game:

[1] Op. cit.

DON PEDRO: Come hither, Leonato: what was it you told me of to-day,
    that your niece Beatrice was in love with Signior Benedick?
CLAUDIO: O! ay: (Stalk on, stalk on; the fowl sits.) I did never think that
    lady would have loved any man.[1]

And in the next scene:

URSULA: The pleasant'st angling is to see the fish
                   Cut with her golden oars the silver stream,
                   And greedily devour the treacherous bait:
                   So angle we for Beatrice. . . .
HERO: No, truly, Ursula, she is too disdainful;
                   I know her spirits are as coy and wild
                   As haggards of the rock.[2]

The contrast between prose and a delicate, artful blank verse
makes sharper the difference of the fantasy each of them is offered.
Benedick is given a superbly ludicrous caricature of a love-sick
Beatrice, which only his own vanity could believe:

CLAUDIO: Then down upon her knees she falls, weeps, sobs, beats her heart,
    tears her hair, prays, curses: 'O sweet Benedick! God give me
    patience! . . .' Hero thinks surely she will die.[3]

And his own response, a mixture of comically solemn resolutions and
illogical reasoning, is equally exaggerated:

I must not seem proud: happy are they that hear their detractions, and can
put them to mending. . . . No; the world must be peopled.[4]

Beatrice has her feminine vanity played on more delicately, but just
as directly: she is given a not-too-exaggerated picture of herself as Lady
Disdain, spiced with the praises of the man she is missing. And her
response, in formal verse, clinches the success of the manoeuvre:

                   What fire is in mine ears? Can this be true?
                   Stand I condemn'd for pride and scorn so much?
                   Contempt, farewell! and maiden pride, adieu!
                   No glory lives behind the back of such. . . .[5]

'Elated to thoughtlessness' indeed (and particularly after all their
earlier wit): but not only by a trick. Benedick and Beatrice are both, of

---

[1] II. iii. 98–103.   [2] III. i. 26 ff.   [3] II. iii. 162–5 and 191.
[4] Ibid., 248 ff.   [5] III. i. 107 ff.

course, perfect examples of self-deception: about their own natures, about the vanity their railing hides (and none the less vanity for its charm and wit), about the affection they are capable of—in need of— when the aggression is dropped, about their real relations to each other. This gives the theme of deception in their plot the higher, more permanent status of revelation. Hence much of its delight.

But no one in the play is more mentally intoxicated than Dogberry. He is king of all he surveys: of Verges, his perfect foil; of the Watch; of the peace of Messina at night. Only words—engines of deception— constantly trip him up; though, like Mrs. Malaprop, he sails on magnificently unaware:

> Dost thou not suspect my place? Dost thou not suspect my years? O that he were here to write me down an ass! . . . I am a wise fellow; and, which is more, an officer; and, which is more, a householder; and, which is more, as pretty a piece of flesh as any in Messina. . . .[1]

With Dogberry, the theme of giddiness, of self-deception, of revelling in the appearances that limitless vanity has made true for him, reaches miraculous proportions.

There is, though, the further meaning of 'giddy', also, I suggested, warranted by Benedick's conclusion: 'whirling or circling round'. The structure of *Much Ado*—the melodramatic Italian love-story, enlivened by two humour-plots of Shakespeare's own invention—follows an established Elizabethan comedy-pattern: Chapman was to use it in *The Gentleman Usher* and *Monsieur d'Olive*; *Twelfth Night*—allowing for obvious differences in the tone of the central plot—is the obvious successor. Musically, we could call it a theme and variations. But you have merely to consider the Chapman comedies, where the two plots only arbitrarily meet—or Thomas Middleton, who brought in a collaborator to help him with the 'echoing sub-plot' of his tragedy, *The Changeling* —to see Shakespeare's extraordinary structural skill here. 'Faultless balance, blameless rectitude of design,' said Swinburne: he is right, and it was not what most of his contemporaries recognized in *Much Ado*. But it still does not strongly enough suggest the grasp, the intellectual energy, that holds the play together and makes the kind of suggestions about reality in which the Elizabethan audience delighted. Here, again, Benedick's conclusion says more. Not only the play's wit—a microcosm of its total life—whirls and circles, with often deadly effect ('Thou hast frighted the word out of his right sense, so forcible is thy

[1] IV. 2. 79 ff.

wit,' cries Benedick to Beatrice in the last Act: it suggests that wit—
and wit's author—can destroy or create at will) one of man's main
instruments of living; but, in their vibrations and juxtapositions, the
three plots do much the same.

Twice the plots fuse—once to advance the story, once to deepen it—
and the achievement gives a peculiar exhilaration. Each time it is something of a shock; and then we see that, within the rules of probability
laid down by Aristotle for writers of tragedy (we can validly apply
them to comedy too), it is wonderfully right that it should have
happened like that.

The first occasion is the discovery by the Watch of the plot
against Hero. When they line up to receive their instructions from
Dogberry and Verges—on the principle of peace at all costs—it seems
incredible that they should ever discover anything. But they do:
though, admittedly, Shakespeare has to make Borachio drunk to make
it possible. The Watch and their Officers are now locked firmly into
the main plot, with all their ripples of absurdity; and the final dénouement is theirs. The innocent saved by the innocent, we may say; or,
more likely (and certainly more Elizabethanly), the knaves caught out
by the fools. 'Is our whole dissembly appeared?' asks Dogberry, as he
looks round for the rest of the Court. 'Which be the malefactors?'
asks the Sexton. 'Marry, that am I and my partner,' answers Dogberry,
with pride.

However we look at it, the impact has clearly changed the status of
the villains. 'Ducdame, ducdame, ducdame,' sings Jaques (it is his own
verse) to his banished companions in the Forest of Arden. 'What's that
"*ducdame*"?' asks Amiens. ' 'Tis a Greek invocation to call fools into a
circle.' Here in *Much Ado*, the knaves have been thrust in with the
fools: if it makes the fools feel much more important than they are, it
makes the villains much less villainous; or villainous in a way that
disturbs us less. This is one device by which the interlocking of plots
establishes the play's unity, and, in doing so, creates a new, more inclusive tone.

The entry of the Watch into the centre of the play advances the
story. The entry of Benedick and Beatrice, in that short packed dialogue after the Church Scene, where they declare their belief in Hero
and their love for each other, seems as though it must do so too; but in
fact it does not. Rather, it does not if we see the heart of the play now
as Hero's vindication. That is brought about without help from
Benedick; and, indeed, Benedick's challenge to Claudio, vehemently

undertaken and dramatically presented, is, by the end of the play, treated very casually: only perfunctorily recalled, and easily brushed aside in the general mirth and reconciliation of the ending. Perhaps, then, this scene *removes* the play's centre, puts it squarely in the Benedick and Beatrice plot? That is how many critics have taken it; and what, for example, was in 'Q.'s' mind when he wrote of the scene's climax: ' "Kill Claudio!" These two words nail the play'; and again, '. . . at this point undoubtedly Shakespeare transfers [the play] from *novella* to drama—to a real spiritual conflict'.[1] It is certainly how many producers and actors—with understandable temptation—have interpreted the scene.

Much Ado demands, of course, a continual switching of interest. We focus it in turn on Benedick and Beatrice, on Hero and Claudio, on Don John and Borachio, on Dogberry and Verges, back to Hero and Claudio, and so on. This gives something of the controlled whirl and circling motion I have commented on. It is also true that this scene between Benedick and Beatrice has a new seriousness; that their shared, intuitive belief in Hero's innocence has deepened their relations with each other, and our attitude towards them. But that is not the same as saying that the play has become something different, or that its centre has shifted. That would seriously jeopardize its design; and, although there *are* flaws in the play, I am sure that its design is what Shakespeare intended it to be.

The play's true centre is in fact neither a plot nor a group of characters, but a theme: Benedick's conclusion about man's giddiness, his irresistible propensity to be taken in by appearances. It is a theme that must embody an *attitude*; and it is the attitude here that provides *Much Ado*'s complexity: its disturbingness (where it does disturb); its ambiguities, where the expected response seems far from certain; but its inclusiveness too, where it is assured. For Shakespeare's approach to this theme at the turn of the century (one could call it the major theme of his whole writing-life, probed at endlessly varying levels) was far from simple. The riddling titles of the group of comedies written within these two years, 1598–1600, are deceptive, or at any rate ambiguous. *Much Ado About Nothing, As You Like It, Twelfth Night; or, What You Will*: these can all, as titles, be interpreted lightly, all but cynically, as leaving it to the audience how to take them with a disarming, amused casualness. Or, equally, they can leave room for manœuvre, include several attitudes, without committing themselves to any. This blending or jostling

[1] Op. cit., pp. xiii and xv.

K

of sympathies is sufficiently evident in these comedies to have won for itself the status of a convention. Dr. M. C. Bradbrook, who has lovingly pursued all the conventions of the Elizabethan theatre, has called it 'polyphonic music';[1] Mr. S. L. Bethell, more directly concerned with the Elizabethan audience, calls their capacity to respond to difficult aspects of the same situation, simultaneously, but in often contradictory ways, 'multi-consciousness'.[2] *Much Ado* exhibits the one and demands the other in the highest degree.

We must, I think, respond in much the same way as the Elizabethan audience did, if we are to appreciate to the full the scene between Benedick and Beatrice in the church; and that oddly-tempered, but still powerful scene of Leonato's outbursts to Antonio at the beginning of Act V. For both these scenes, however different—the first is set in a half-comic key, the second employs a rhetoric that is nearer the formally 'tragic'—employ deliberate ambiguities of tone and demand a double response.

I will examine the Benedick and Beatrice scene first. Here, Shakespeare clearly means us to sympathize with Beatrice's vehement attacks on Claudio on Hero's behalf, and with the mounting strength of Benedick's allegiance to her. At the same time, he overdoes the vehemence, exposes it to the comedy of his wry appraisal, brings both characters to the edge of delicate caricature. The scene's climax (I have quoted 'Q.'s' remarks on it) has been taken to show the maximum deployment of Shakespeare's sympathy. It also exhibits perfectly his comedy. Benedick and Beatrice have just protested they love each other with all their heart:

> BENEDICK: Come, bid me do anything for thee.
> BEATRICE: Kill Claudio.
> BENEDICK: Ha! not for the wide world.
> BEATRICE: You kill me to deny it. Farewell.[3]

Superbly dramatic: three fresh shocks in three lines, and, with each, a new insight into human nature; but also highly ironical. To demand the killing of Claudio, in the world established by the play, is ridiculous. To refuse it at once, after the avowal to do *anything*, equally so, however right Benedick may be ethically (and the irony demands that he refuse *at once*: I am sure Dr. Bradbrook[4] is wrong in saying that he

---

[1] In *Shakespeare and Elizabethan Poetry*, 1951: the title of Chapter X.
[2] In *Shakespeare and the Popular Dramatic Tradition*, 1948, *passim*.
[3] IV. i. 293–296.
[4] Op. cit., p. 183.

hesitates). And for Beatrice, upon this refusal, to take back her heart, having given it a moment before, completes the picture: passionately generous to her wronged cousin, if we isolate the exchange and treat it as a piece of magnificent impressionism; heroic, absurd and a victim to passion's deception, if we see it—as we surely must—within the context of the whole play.

Mr. T. W. Craik, in an admirably close analysis of *Much Ado* in *Scrutiny*,[1] makes this scene between Benedick and Beatrice a pivot of the play's values. It is, he says, ' "placed" by the scene's beginning [i.e. the earlier events in the church]. Putting the point crudely, it represents the triumph of emotion over reason; the reasonableness of Friar Francis's plan for Claudio and Hero. . . .'[2] I agree with him when he goes on to say that 'emotion's triumph' is laughable in Benedick (though I think he exaggerates its extent). But surely it is an over-simplification to identify Shakespeare's attitude—as he seems to do more explicitly later in his essay[3]—with the Friar's common sense. The Friar is essential to the plot (and much more competent in guiding it than his brother of *Romeo and Juliet*); and his calm sanity admirably 'places' Leonato's hysteria in the Church Scene. But the whole spirit of the play seems to me antagonistic to any *one* attitude's dominating it. And the second scene I want to examine—Leonato and Antonio in v. i.—appears to bear this out.

For here Antonio begins as the repository of the Friar's wisdom, as the Stoic, calming Leonato down. Yet, as experience floods in on him—the memory of wrong in the shape of Don Pedro and Claudio—he too becomes 'flesh and blood', and ends up by out-doing Leonato:

> What, man! I know them, yea,
> And what they weigh, even to the utmost scruple,
> Scrambling, out-facing, fashion-monging boys,
> That lie and cog and flout, deprave and slander,
> Go antickly, show outward hideousness,
> And speak off half a dozen dangerous words,
> How they might hurt their enemies, if they durst;
> And this is all!

LEONATO: But, brother Antony,—[4]

The roles are neatly reversed. But the invective is too exuberantly

---

[1] October 1953, op. cit.   [3] p. 308.
[3] p. 314.   [4] v. i. 92–9.

Shakespearian to be merely—or even mainly—caricature. Can we say the same of Leonato's outburst that begins the scene?

> I pray thee, cease thy counsel,
> which falls into mine ears as profitless
> As water in a sieve: Give not me counsel; . . .[1]

Considered realistically, it must make us uneasy. Leonato knows (Antonio does not) that Hero is in fact alive: to that extent, most of his emotion is counterfeit. Again, we remember his hysterical self-pity of the Act before, when his attitude to his daughter was very different:

> Do not live, Hero; do not ope thine eyes;
> . . . Griev'd I, I had but one?
> Chid I for that at frugal nature's frame?
> O! one too much by thee. Why had I one?
> Why ever wast thou lovely in mine eyes?[2]

To some extent, he is still dramatizing himself in this scene, still enjoying his grief. But his language is no longer grotesque or self-convicting, as that was. He echoes a theme—'experience against auctoritee', the Middle Ages called it—which in *Romeo and Juliet* had been nearer a set piece:

> FRIAR LAURENCE: Let me dispute with thee of thy estate.
> ROMEO: Thou canst not speak of that thou dost not feel. . . .[3]

but here it has a new authenticity in movement and image:

> for, brother, men
> Can counsel and speak comfort to that grief
> Which they themselves not feel; but, tasting it,
> Their counsel turns to passion, which before
> Would give preceptial medicine to rage,
> Fetter strong madness in a silken thread,
> Charm ache with air and agony with words.[4]

Again, as with Benedick and Beatrice, the whole scene, ending with the challenge of Claudio and the Prince to a duel, presents a mixture of tones: appeal to our sympathy, exaggeration which is on or over the edge of comedy.

Both these scenes, peripheral to the main plot, but of the essence of the play's art, demand, if they are to be fully appreciated, a complex

[1] v. i. 3-5.   [2] IV. i. 125, 129-32.   [3] III. iii. 62-3.   [4] v, i. 20-6.

response. What, then, of the crux of *Much Ado*, the shaming of Hero in church? On any realistic view it must, as has been said, be a repulsive scene: an innocent girl slandered and shamed by her betrothed, with apparently deliberate calculation, during her marriage-service, and in front of her father—the city's Governor—and the whole congregation. However we see it, Shakespeare's writing here is sufficiently powerful to give us some wincing moments. No interpretation can take away the shock of Claudio's brutal

> There, Leonato, take her back again:
> Give not this rotten orange to your friend;[1]

or of the Prince's heartless echo:

> What should I speak?
> I stand dishonour'd, that have gone about
> To link my dear friend to a common stale.

The clipped exchange between Leonato and Don John that follows seems to give the lie the ring of finality, to make false true in front of our eyes:

> LEONATO: Are these things spoken, or do I but dream?
> DON JOHN: Sir, they are spoken, and these things are true.

The generalizing assent, helped by the closed-circle form of question and answer, has a claustrophobic effect on both Hero and us (I think of the nightmare world of 'double-think' closing in in Orwell's *Nineteen Eighty-Four*: this is a verbal nightmare too). Momentarily, we have left Messina and might well be in the meaner, darker world of that later play of similarly quibbling title, but much less pleasant implications, *All's Well That Ends Well*. There 'these things' are commented on by a Second French Lord, who knows human nature; knows Parolles and his hollowness: 'Is it possible he should know what he is, and be that he is?'; and Bertram and his meanness: 'As we are ourselves, what things are we!' ('Merely our own traitors,' adds the First Lord, almost redundantly.)

Then, with a jolt, we remember that 'these things' are *not* true. They are not true *in* the play, which is the first thing to remind our-selves of, if we wish to preserve the play's balance as comedy. For in the later and so-called 'Problem Comedies' (tragi-comedies, I prefer to follow A. P. Rossiter in calling them)—*All's Well, Troilus and Cressida*,

[1] IV. i. 31–2.

Measure for Measure—such accusations *are* true, or would be true if those accused of them had had their way—had not been tricked into doing something quite different from what they thought they were doing (Cressida comes into the first category; Bertram and Angelo into the second). But here the characters are playing out an act of deception, each of them (except Don John) unaware in fact of what the truth is. To that extent, they are all innocent, Claudio and the Prince as well as Hero: played on by the plot, not (as we sense wherever tragic feeling enters) playing it, willing it. The *situation* is in control.

Secondly, they are not true *outside* the play. To state that at all probably sounds absurd. But genuine tragic feeling in Shakespeare forces its extra-theatrical truth on us: continuously in the tragedies, spasmodically —but still disturbingly—in the tragi-comedies. We know only too well how permanently true are *Hamlet, Othello, Macbeth*. But the exposures of the tragi-comedies (Hero's shaming by no means exhausts the *genre*) inflict on us truths about human nature—we may prefer to call them half-truths. 'But man, proud man,' cries out Isabella (and she has every justification),

> Drest in a little brief authority,
> Most ignorant of what he's most assur'd,
> His glassy essence, like an angry ape,
> Plays such fantastic tricks before high heaven
> As make the angels weep; who, with our spleens,
> Would all themselves laugh mortal.[1]

Here, all the possibilities of human nature are on the stage. We are *involved with* the people who are hurt or betrayed or even exposed (Angelo, as he cries out on the 'blood' that has betrayed him, is potentially a tragic figure); we are involved too in the language and its searing comments on human frailty or baseness.

But go back to the scene in *Much Ado*, and, after the first shock, we are no longer fully involved. First, because the identities of Hero and Claudio have been kept to an irreducible minimum. That is why I earlier called them 'masks'. They have a part to play in a situation that is the climax to the whole play's theme; but they have not the core of being—or of dramatic being—which suffers or deliberately causes suffering. It would be quite different—ghastly and impossible—to imagine Beatrice in Hero's position.

And, secondly, the whole scene's deliberate *theatricality* lessens our

---

[1] *Measure for Measure*, II. ii. 117–23.

involvement and distances our emotions. It emphasizes that it is, after all, only a play and intended for our entertainment;[1] we know that the accusation of Hero is false and—as this is a comedy—is bound to be put right by the end. First Claudio, then Leonato, takes the centre of the stage: the effect is to diminish any exclusively tragic concern for Hero, as we appraise the responses of the other two. There can be no doubt about Leonato's: it is highly exaggerated and hovers on the edge of caricature. We recognize the tones from *Romeo and Juliet*. There, vindictive, absurd old Capulet hustles Juliet on to a marriage she abhors; and then, in a stylized, cruelly comic scene, is shown (with his wife and the Nurse) over-lamenting her when she feigns death to avoid it. Shakespeare has little pity for this kind of selfishness. Here, as Leonato inveighs against his daughter—now in a swoon—we have self-pity masking itself as righteous indignation: the repetitions show where his real interest lies:

> But mine, and mine I lov'd, and mine I prais'd,
> And mine that I was proud on, mine so much
> That I myself was to myself not mine,
> Valuing of her . . .[2]

Yet, as he goes on, the tone alters, as so often in this volatile, quick-changing play:

> . . . why, she—O! she is fallen
> Into a pit of ink, that the wide sea
> Hath drops too few to wash her clean again,
> And salt too little which may season give
> To her foul tainted flesh.[3]

That is still over-violent, but the images of Hero's stain and of the sea failing to make her clean introduce a different note. We have heard it in Claudio's accusation:

> Behold! how like a maid she blushes here.
> O! what authority and show of truth
> Can cunning sin cover itself withal. . . .[4]

and in his outburst against seeming: 'Out on thee! Seeming! I will write against it. . . .'

---

[1] S. L. Bethell makes the same point about the ill-treatment of Malvolio: op. cit., pp. 33–4.
[2] IV. i. 138–41.
[3] Ibid., 141–5.
[4] IV. i. 34–6.

Again, there is more here than his earlier, calculated stage-management of the scene. It is as though the situation has suddenly taken charge, become horribly true for a moment; and as if Shakespeare has injected into it some of the disgust at sexual betrayal we know from the dark Sonnets and from the crises of a host of later plays: *Measure for Measure, Troilus and Cressida, Hamlet, Othello, Cymbeline.*

This apparent intrusion of something alien—seemingly personal—into the very centre of the play was what had led me to doubt its success. I was wrong, I think (and it follows that I think other doubters are wrong), for three reasons. First, the intrusion, the cold music, is only a touch; one of several themes that make up the scene. Its language is harsh, but chimes in with nothing else in the play: no deadly vibrations or echoes are set up. Compare Claudio and Leonato with Troilus or Isabella, or, even more, with Hamlet or Othello, in whose words we feel a wrenching, an almost physical dislocation of set attitudes and beliefs: and the outbursts here have something of the isolated, artificial effect of set speeches.

Secondly, the play's central theme—of deception, miscomprehension, man's 'giddiness' at every level—is dominant enough to claim much of our response in *every* scene: including this climax in the church that embodies it most harshly, but most fully. And, in its many-sidedness and 'many-tonedness', this theme is, as I have tried to show, one well within the tradition of Elizabethan comedy.

Thirdly, and lastly, the *tone* of *Much Ado*—animated, brittle, observant, delighting in the ado men make—does not have to stretch itself much to accommodate the moments of questioning in the church. And this tone is ultimately, I think, what we most remember of the play: what gives it its genuine difference from *As You Like It* and *Twelfth Night.* Although two of its most loved figures are Warwickshire yokels (and nothing could change them), the aura of Bandello's Italian plot pervades the rest. The love of sharp wit and the love of melodrama belong there; so do the sophisticated, unsentimental tone, and the ubiquitous, passed-off classical references: to Cupid and Hercules, Leander and Troilus. Gildon was wrong: in essentials, the people of Messina *do* act and talk like natives of a warm country.

The tone I mean is most apparent—most exhilarating and most exacting—in the wit-flytings between Benedick and Beatrice; but it dominates the word-play throughout: and this is one of the most word-conscious and wittiest of all Shakespeare's comedies. If I have said little about the words and the wit, this is because no one was more at home there, and could better communicate his enjoyment of them, than the late A. P. Rossiter: and you can read his lecture[1] on the play from one of the last of his memorable Shakespeare courses at Cambridge. My own debt to him will be very clear to all of you who heard his many lectures here at Stratford.

[1] One of twelve lectures given at Stratford and Cambridge, to be published in 1959 by Longmans.

IO

THE LANGUAGE OF THE LAST PLAYS

by JAMES SUTHERLAND

ALL, or nearly all, the most respected criticism of Shakespeare nowadays is addressed to the elucidation of particular plays; and when the critic is more particularly concerned with Shakespeare's mode of expression we shall probably find him inquiring into the dominant imagery of the play in question, to the virtual exclusion of all other aspects of Shakespeare's style. Yet imagery, however important, is only part of the total impact of language on a reader or listener; and I hope, too, that it is still a legitimate critical activity to interest oneself in Shakespeare's mode of composition without necessarily relating it closely to its dramatic context. What I wish to discuss is a particular kind of writing that seems to be almost peculiar to the later plays, and that appears in them only sporadically. Such passages, when they occur, do not always seem to have any specially dramatic significance, nor to offer, as the imagery so often does, a clue to the way in which Shakespeare apprehended a total situation: the evidence they provide is rather of the way in which Shakespeare's mind worked, and of how its working varied under different pressures.

If this approach to Shakespeare is at present unfashionable, and may even appear to be misguided, it still seems to me that any light that can be thrown on Shakespeare's mode of composition is worth having. Some years ago, in a notable book called *Shakespeare's Imagination*,[1] Dr. E. A. Armstrong drew our attention to the strange and wayward thoughts that will sometimes slide into Shakespeare's head, and he gave us some valuable clues to understanding how the apparently fortuitous and unpredictable in Shakespeare often follows a recurring pattern of association. But Dr. Armstrong's book, though it was by no means neglected, has not perhaps made the impression that might have been expected; and I can only suppose that his truths are not the ones that

[1] Lindsay Drummond, 1946.

144

the contemporary reader wants to hear. I doubt, therefore, if he will wish to hear mine either; but I have thought it right to warn him at the outset of what I am up to, and to repeat that in what follows I shall be concerned with a mode of composition that appears most frequently in the later plays, that seems to be peculiarly Shakespearian, and that is so odd and idiosyncratic that it asks for some explanation.

If I were to look for examples of this mode of composition in a single play I could find all that I need in *Cymbeline*, and I could begin with the opening lines of that play. Here, as often happens, the dramatist has some necessary information to impart to his audience; but he sets about it in a fashion that must have puzzled nine playgoers out of ten.

1ST GENT: You do not meet a man but frowns; our bloods
No more obey the heavens than our courtiers
Still seem as does the king.

2ND GENT: But what's the matter?

1ST GENT: His daughter, and the heir of's kingdom, whom
He purpos'd to his wife's sole son—a widow
That late he married,—hath referr'd herself
Unto a poor but worthy gentleman. She's wedded;
Her husband banish'd, she imprison'd: all
Is outward sorrow, though I think the king
Be touch'd at very heart.

2ND GENT: None but the king?

1ST GENT: He that hath lost her too; so is the queen,
That most desir'd the match; but not a courtier,
Although they wear their faces to the bent
Of the king's looks, hath a heart that is not
Glad at the thing they scowl at.

2ND GENT: And why so?

1ST GENT: He that hath miss'd the princess is a thing
Too bad for bad report: and he that hath her,—
I mean, that married her,—alack! good man!
And therefore banish'd—is a creature such
As, to seek through the regions of the earth
For one his like, there would be something failing
In him that should compare. I do not think
So fair an outward and such stuff within
Endows a man but he.

2ND GENT: You speak him fair.

1ST GENT: I do extend him, sir, within himself,
Crush him together rather than unfold
His measure duly.

2ND GENT: What's his name and birth?
1ST GENT: I cannot delve him to the root: his father
          Was call'd Sicilius. . . .

Of the first two and a half lines of the play Johnson remarked, 'This
passage is so difficult, that commentators may differ concerning it without animosity or shame'; but as Johnson was struggling with a corrupt
text we should not, perhaps, make too much of his difficulties. It is the
speech of the First Gentleman, 'He that hath miss'd the princess . . .',
that is most characteristic of the kind of writing I have in mind. In the
first place, it is obviously written at speed. It contains a parenthesis
(this in itself becomes a stylistic feature of the last plays): a parenthesis,
too, including the elliptical phrase, 'and therefore banish'd'. But the
lines that follow are still more characteristic of this late style: Shakespeare suddenly changes direction in the middle of a sentence, and then
completes the movement by going off on another foot. After 'and he
that hath her . . . is a creature such as', we expect some such phrase as
'cannot be surpassed' or 'would be hard to parallel'; but the dramatist
wants something much more emphatic than that, and rather than
cancel what he has already written and begin the speech all over again
(he 'never blotted a line') he brushes past the syntactical obstacle, and
the meaning comes through by reason of its force and with the help of
the speech rhythms rather than by any clearness of statement.

Parenthesis, it is true, helps to give an air of spontaneity to dialogue;
it suggests a man thinking rapidly as he goes along, correcting himself,
modifying his original statement, and so on. It might therefore be
argued that Shakespeare is carefully and artfully inserting parentheses
in the long speeches of his characters in order to give them a natural
turn. I cannot, of course, disprove this, but in the lines I have quoted
Shakespeare cannot be said to be trying very hard to give a naturalistic
turn to his dialogue, and I suspect that the person who is thinking
rapidly, breaking off, making fresh starts, and so on, is not the character,
but Shakespeare himself.

Parentheses occur again frequently in the long second scene in *The
Tempest* where Prospero is unfolding to Miranda the story of his past
misfortunes (again a passage giving some necessary information to his
audience), and more than once we shall find the same dislocation of the
syntax, when a new idea makes Shakespeare—and therefore Prospero
—swerve from his original intention.

PROSPERO: The direful spectacle of the wrack, which touch'd

> The very virtue of compassion in thee,
> I have with such provision in mine art
> So safely order'd, that there is no soul—
> No, not so much perdition as an hair,
> Betid to any creature in the vessel
> Which thou heard'st cry, which thou saw'st sink. . . .[1]

There again Shakespeare begins by intending to say something like
'there is no soul lost', and then immediately begins groping his way to
something stronger. The idea of 'loss' survives in the word 'perdition'
(a much more powerful word), but by that time he has struck out in a
new direction and has to finish in a way that leaves 'there is no soul'
hanging in the air. Some commentators are so anxious to have Shakespeare writing correctly that they propose to read 'soil' for 'soul'. But
the point is that Shakespeare is *not* writing correctly: he is writing at
speed. So far is he indeed from slowing up as he grows older that he
seems at times in his last plays to be driving himself harder than ever.
When Heminge and Condell tell us that 'his mind and hand went together, and what he thought, he uttered with that easiness, that we have
scarce received from him a blot in his papers', it may well be that the
papers they had in mind were the manuscripts of his *latest* plays, rather
than those that had been written twenty or thirty years before the
publication of the First Folio. Speed, therefore, an increasing impatience
to get the thing down on the paper, with a consequent danger of confusion, and an interesting tendency to be satisfied with a sort of impressionism—those are some of the factors that we have to take into
account in the last plays. In the words of Charles Lamb, 'Shakespeare
mingles everything, he runs line into line, embarrasses sentences and
metaphors: before one idea has burst its shell, another is hatched and
clamorous for disclosure.'

To return for the moment to the *Cymbeline* passage: if we are looking
for evidence of hurry and impatience in Shakespeare, we may perhaps
find it again in the phrase 'so fair an outward and such stuff within',
where the dramatist grabs at the comprehensive but undeniably vague
words, 'outward' and 'stuff within', to sum up the appearance and
character of Posthumus. This has something of the impressionism I
have mentioned, but perhaps a better example is to be found in an
earlier (though still a comparatively late) play. When the sycophantic
Regan and Goneril are expressing their love for their father, Regan
seeks to go one better than her sister:

[1] I. ii. 26 ff.

> In my true heart
> I find she names my very deed of love;
> Only she comes too short: that I profess
> Myself an enemy to all other joys
> Which the most precious square of sense possesses. . . .[1]

The commentators have made lame work of 'the most precious square of sense', and one is tempted to suppose that if the matter had been referred to Shakespeare himself he might have given the same answer as Fielding's Shakespeare gave in Elysium when he was questioned about the right reading of a line in *Othello*: 'Faith, gentlemen, it is so long since I wrote the line, I have forgot my meaning.' What Shakespeare seems to be looking for in this passage is something emphatic to put in the mouth of Regan; it would not serve his purpose if Regan merely said 'all other joys that sense possesses', but if she says 'all other joys the square of sense possesses' the statement is considerably heightened, and if she calls it 'the most precious square of sense' it becomes more emphatic still. We have here an example of Burke's distinction between a strong expression and a clear expression. Shakespeare's desire, then, for something emphatic to suit the needs of the context undoubtedly accounts on at least some occasions for the sort of language that I am trying to define. When the First Gentleman in *Cymbeline* says, 'I do extend him, sir, within himself,' that is an odd, and even awkward, way of saying (presumably): 'I do not stretch my commendation further than his character will bear'; and, 'Crush him together,' seems to indicate again an urgent need on Shakespeare's part, rather than the First Gentleman's, for something resoundingly emphatic, although perhaps he is moved to this antithesis ('extend' . . . 'crush') by a feeling that 'I do extend him, sir, within himself' badly needs amplification for the sake of clarification.

I turn now to a later passage in *Cymbeline* from which we get an even stronger impression of hurry and impatience, and of an almost violent forcing of the expression. Guiderius and Arviragus are both strangely attracted by Imogen, who has come among them disguised as a boy. Guiderius expresses his feeling by asserting that he loves this boy 'as I do love my father'. At which Belisarius cries, 'What! how! how!' Whereupon Arviragus, not to be outdone, exclaims:

> If it be sin to say so, sir, I yoke me
> In my good brother's fault: I know not why
> I love this youth; and I have heard you say,

[1] *Lear*, I. i. 72 ff.

> Love's reason's without reason: the bier at door,
> And a demand who is't shall die, I'd say
> 'My father, not this youth.'[1]

This is surely an astonishingly and improbable way of saying what has to be said. The rapidity of composition is again noticeable, but there is a new recklessness of expression. Undertakers do not come round to the door like dustmen to demand a corpse—a corpse, too, that is not yet dead when they arrive. What Shakespeare has to express is an avowal of love that will go a stage further than that just made by Guiderius: if Guiderius loves the boy *as much as* he loves his own father, Arviragus is going to go one better and claim that he loves him *more* than he loves his father. Clutching at some means to express this thought powerfully, Shakespeare moves naturally enough to a choice between life and death, a choice involving the (supposed) father of Guiderius on the one hand and the boy on the other. But the simple expression of that idea will not do for Shakespeare, or perhaps it never gets the chance to assert itself. Driven on by some compelling urge for the immediate and the emphatic—perhaps visualizing the death situation in a sudden flash—he never pauses to get it into perspective, but suddenly writes down the elliptical and startling phrase, 'the bier at door', and the rest inevitably follows. It is true that the context, which bears a general resemblance to that in *King Lear* when Regan seeks to outdo her sister in protestations of love, demands an abnormal emphasis of expression. But the question is, how does Shakespeare meet that demand? He meets it—or so it seems to me—by forcing the pace.

It is probably the desire for emphasis again which accounts for the strange speech of Ross to Macbeth,[2] when he is describing Duncan's reactions to the news of Macbeth's victory over the rebels:

> The king hath happily receiv'd, Macbeth,
> The news of thy success; and when he reads
> Thy personal venture in the rebels' fight,
> His wonders and his praises do contend
> Which should be thine or his. . . .

Once more Shakespeare seems to have made a rush at it. When Duncan listens to the news, he is lost in wonder at Macbeth's achievements, and he is moved to praise him. But Shakespeare wants something more compelling than that, and he gets it by suggesting a struggle taking place in the mind of Duncan between two simultaneous emotions: his

[1] IV. ii. 19 ff.   [2] I. iii. 89 ff.

astonishment is contending with his admiration, the astonishment ('wonder') being Duncan's, and the praise which he feels moved to give being Macbeth's ('thine'). Shakespeare has succeeded at once in suggesting a confused and turbulent state of mind, but he has done so, characteristically, by jumping his fences rather than by taking us more normally through the gate.

I have suggested that the man who wrote the passages I have quoted was writing at speed, and I now suggest that this very speed leads to— or, alternatively, perhaps is caused by—some element of intellectual strain. It will not dispose of this suggestion to argue that in those passages the violence or abruptness or obscurity is appropriate to the character or the situation; even if this were so, as it sometimes is, it is not so on every occasion. And even on those occasions which require unusual emphasis, Shakespeare is capable of giving us that with a much quieter and more controlled, and yet completely effective, form of expression. When Imogen cries:

> . . . but if there be
> Yet left in heaven as small a drop of pity
> As a wren's eye . . .[1]

we have an exquisite distillation of the thought into a precise, if still surprising, image. Nothing could be more compelling, and nothing could be more delicately controlled. Nor could anything be less like the violent hyperbole and rough impressionism that we get on other occasions, and that seem to be due to some kind of super-charging in the mind of the dramatist, some conscious effort that causes him to expend more force on the expression than the occasion requires. Near the end of *Cymbeline*, when Iachimo is confessing his crimes, he suddenly exclaims:

> . . . 'twas at a feast—O, would
> Our viands had been poison'd, or at least
> Those which I heav'd to head![2]

The arresting phrase 'heav'd to head' has both the violence and the impressionistic effect to which I have already drawn attention; it gives in words something of the huge and powerful impression of a piece of sculpture by, say, Henry Moore. I will freely admit that Iachimo's emphatic outburst is in character; the man is at last filled with remorse for what he has done, and Shakespeare has to make us feel this. But

[1] IV. ii. 303 ff.   [2] V. v. 156 ff.

again it is the *kind* of emphasis that Shakespeare obtains that is significant, an emphasis which the dramatist seems to have achieved through
the expenditure of a tremendous and consciously-induced intellectual
energy.

The Shakespeare, then, that I am offering for contemplation is a
writer who, in those last plays, sometimes appears to be swept along by
some inner compulsion, and whose mind seems at times to be generat-
ing an immense energy which he is applying, as a man might apply a
pneumatic drill, to the immediate problems of composition. It may
therefore come as a surprise to find Professor W. H. Clemen asserting
that, 'Generally it may be said of the romances that the tempo of the
speech and action has slowed down';[1] and Sir Ifor Evans remarking
of *Cymbeline* that, 'if one looks for highly metaphorical language,
crowded phrase, and bold personification . . . one will suffer inevitable
disappointment'.[2] Are those two distinguished critics right, and am I
therefore wrong? Without trying to discover a face-saving formula,
we may all be said to be right, in the sense that what we say we discover
is in fact there. The last plays are curiously mixed in their style of
composition. (If my title suggests that I am dealing comprehensively
with the language of those plays I must make it clear that I am concerned with only one significant aspect of it.) In all of them there are
passages of apparently leisurely, deliberate, and even artificial writing,
marked by what Granville-Barker called 'a new euphuism of imagination'. There is at times a return to an earlier, formal, decorative or
rhetorical style of writing, and where we have that we often get with it
a pleasing ingenuity of concepts and expressions, without, however,
much pressure of thought behind them. It is obviously this kind of
writing that Clemen and Evans had chiefly in mind; it is certainly
there, and it constitutes an important element in the total impression
made by the romances. If anyone is looking for evidence of a serene
and mellow Shakespeare, with his eyes already fixed on retirement to
Stratford, it is there that he will find it. But it is equally true that there
is frequent evidence of that other and very different mode of thought
and expression—impetuous, violent, straining after the maximum of
intensity. How are we to account fo this variety? Startling divergences
of style within the same play have, of course, been used by textual
critics to demonstrate multiple authorship, or at any rate revision by
the author; it is felt that the man who wrote Act I, Scene 1 couldn't

[1] *The Development of Shakespeare's Imagery* (Methuen, 1951), p. 179.
[2] *The Language of Shakespeare's Plays* (Methuen, 1952), p. 176.

possibly be the same man as the one who wrote Act I, Scene 2. It is certainly difficult to reconcile some parts of *Timon of Athens* or *Henry VIII* with others; but we may be too willing to underestimate Shakespeare's capacity for varying his style within the same play. At all events, there is perhaps a special reason why the variety should be more marked in the later plays.

Some thirty years ago Lytton Strachey published an opinion on the last plays that has had the distinction of provoking almost universal disagreement. 'It is difficult to resist the conclusion,' he observed, 'that [Shakespeare] was getting bored himself. Bored with people, bored with real life, bored with drama; bored in fact with everything except poetry and poetical dreams. He is no longer interested, one often feels, in what happens, or who says what, so long as he can find place for a faultless lyric, or a new, unimagined rhythmical effect, or a grand mystic speech.'[1] In view of the critical wrath that this statement aroused at the time and later, it may seem rash to suggest that Strachey is not so wide of the mark as he has been generally held to be. The word that probably annoyed the critics most was 'bored', and I offer no defence of it. The creator of Imogen and Miranda and Perdita, not to mention Autolycus and Caliban, can hardly be said to have been bored. But if Strachey had said, 'It is difficult to resist the conclusion that Shakespeare was getting tired,' he would have said no more than what may sometimes have been true, and what may well account for at least some of the characteristic features of the passages to which I have drawn attention—passages in which, I have suggested, Shakespeare seems to be driving himself hard and to be consciously using a spur 'to prick the sides of his intent'. In the last plays he appears to be writing much more by fits and starts. Sometimes, for a whole scene, the ideas will be flowing in upon his mind as naturally as ever, and finding the old apparently spontaneous expression. But then, perhaps, the inspiration fades; the play goes dead on his hands, the dramatist who has written so many plays, such an infinitive number of speeches for his characters, is beginning to tire. The tiredness, however, is still the tiredness of Shakespeare. He responds to it, not by a collapse into mediocrity, but by putting forth a conscious effort, sometimes a gigantic effort, by seeking (as I have said) to force the pace. What once came almost unsought can still be found by an effort of will, but what is found in that way will carry unmistakable marks of its origin. I do not know of any other explanation which will account so satisfactorily

[1] 'Shakespeare's Final Period', *Books and Characters* (Chatto, 1924), p. 52.

for those sudden transitions from natural, easy, and unforced expression
to difficult and even tortured writing. We might indeed apply to those
two different modes of expression the words of Hermione to Leontes:

> You may ride's
> With one soft kiss a thousand furlongs ere
> With spur we heat an acre.[1]

In the early plays and the plays of his maturity, it seems usually to have
been the curb rather than the spur that Shakespeare found most necessary.

Our problem, however, is complicated by the fact that even in the
earlier plays we may come upon passages in which Shakespeare is
already forcing the pace; and though we can still look for an explanation in the habitual rapidity of his writing, we can hardly postulate
fatigue. An interesting early example of Shakespeare's helter-skelter,
hit-or-miss mode of expression occurs in *Love's Labour's Lost*:

> The extreme part of time extremely forms
> All causes to the purpose of his speed,
> And often, at his very loose, decides
> That which long process could not arbitrate.[2]

Here, as usual, the meaning comes through; but in the first two lines
it has to some extent been *pushed* through by the vigour and deter-
mination of the writer. When we meet with such writing in the plays
before the last period, it will often be found at the very beginning of
the play. On such occasions the dramatist sometimes appears to be
'revving up the engine' before it has warmed to its work, and the effect
is very similar to that which I have been trying to isolate and define in
the last plays—a conscious expenditure of intellectual effort, with a
resulting impression of labour and strain. No doubt the bombastic
speech of the bleeding sergeant at the beginning of *Macbeth* may be
accounted for in various ways, but his flamboyant and orgulous
utterance may be partly due to the fact that Shakespeare has not yet
got going, and is having to put too much conscious will-power into the
writing. In a different fashion the opening speeches of *The Merchant of
Venice* have an air of being thought up for the occasion; the mind of
the dramatist is not yet fully engaged by his theme, but is still circling
over it. To return to a later play, we may hear again the characteristic
sound of Shakespeare putting forth a mighty effort in the opening

---

[1] *The Winter's Tale.* I, ii. 94–6.   [2] v. ii. 748 ff.

scene of *Henry VIII*. The Duke of Buckingham tells the company that
he has been ill, and consequently unable to attend the meeting between
Henry and the King of France. The Duke of Norfolk then proceeds to
describe the pageantry.

DUKE OF BUCKINGHAM: All the whole time
   I was my chamber's prisoner.
DUKE OF NORFOLK: Then you lost
   The view of earthly glory: men might say,
   Till this time, pomp was single, but now married
   To one above itself. Each following day
   Became the next day's master, till the last
   Made former wonders its. . . .
          The madams, too,
   Not us'd to toil, did almost sweat to bear
   The pride upon them, that their very labour
   Was to them as a painting. Now this masque
   Was cried incomparable; and the ensuing night
   Made it a fool, and beggar. The two kings,
   Equal in lustre, were now best, now worst,
   As presence did present them; him in eye,
   Still him in praise; and, being present both,
   'Twas said they saw but one; and no discerner
   Durst wag his tongue in censure. . . .[1]

Shakespeare has braced himself here for a magnificent effort, but it *is*
an effort. The old eagle is soaring with his mighty spread of wings, but
he is toiling upwards where once he sailed along the wind.

  There is a passage in *Cymbeline* where, I fancy, we can see Shakespeare casting back over his manuscript when the inspiration has
flagged. The Queen is trying to get rid of the faithful Pisanio by giving
him a box containing poison, which she tells him is a sovereign remedy
against disease. The whole episode is rather ineffective, and Shakespeare
may well have grown tired of it—even, I will dare to say, bored. The
speech that he has been writing for the Queen is certainly rather flat;
and then suddenly she refers to Posthumus in a rather surprising
metaphor. 'What shalt thou expect,' she asks Pisanio,

   To be depender on a thing that leans,
   Who cannot be new built, nor has no friends,
   So much as but to prop him.[2]

Posthumus, the man whose fortunes are tottering, is seen as 'a thing

     [1] I. i. 12 ff.   [2] I. v. 57.

that leans', a building that is leaning over. I have never had the courage to put into print what I am now going to say; but my guess is that Shakespeare had come to a full stop in the middle of the Queen's speech, and, as he was wondering what should follow, his eye wandered idly over his manuscript, and he saw the words that he had written for Pisanio's entrance—'Enter *Pisa*.'—and the leaning tower came into his head.

If anyone is inclined to resist my thesis that Shakespeare was growing tired I will not press it too far. In any case, as an explanation of what was happening in the last plays it is apt to break down at any moment; for Shakespeare, beginning perhaps with a conscious effort, is always apt to pass on to something more spontaneous, as the wheels (in Coleridge's phrase) take fire from the mere rapidity of their motion. Something, too, must be allowed (and this would tell against my general thesis) for Shakespeare's tendency to use an exaggerated and strained language in those contexts where a character is speaking insincerely or craftily (e.g. the protestation of Goneril and Regan in *Lear*, I. i. or Iachimo's, 'It cannot be i' the eye,' *Cymbeline*, I. vi. 39, quoted below). Still more relevant to our problem is Shakespeare's tendency to put forth the sort of effort that we have been considering when he is writing a piece of retrospective narrative. The bleeding sergeant in *Macbeth* is describing events that have occurred off stage, and his words are a sort of substitute for action. As such, they do suggest with a rough effectiveness a violent and bloody struggle on the battlefield. It will have been noticed that most of my quotations come from passages of narrative. It may be that Shakespeare was afraid on such occasions that the attention of the audience might begin to wander, and therefore consciously wrote up his narrative passages to prevent any danger of flatness. On the other hand he was quite capable of writing a long narrative passage, such as Hotspur's speech beginning, 'My liege, I did deny no prisoners,' (I *Henry IV*, I. iii. 29 ff.), in which the language is so natural and so vivid that the blank verse melts into the rhythms of colloquial speech.

It would be reasonable, again, to account for at least some of the recklessness of Shakespeare's later style by saying that he had now reached that point of assured mastery in his profession where he felt that he could let himself do whatever he liked. Expression is always a compromise between how one would put it if one were perfectly free, or if one were sure of having a perfectly sympathetic listener who could be trusted to get one's meaning from half hints and broken phrases, and, on the other hand, how it is normally put. Even in the earlier plays there are fairly frequent signs of Shakespeare being willing to take short cuts, to indulge his idiosyncrasies, to coin words, to rely on the sound helping to carry the sense to the audience; but there is also a corresponding centripetal force that keeps him from flying out too far from the normal. In the last plays he seems to be much less concerned to remain within the bounds of the normal and the expected—less concerned with communication, less careful to make his characters speak *as you like it*, and more ready to make them speak *as he likes it*. This Shakespeare would not be the bored elderly playwright, bored because he had played all the old tricks over and over again, but the acknowledged master of the theatre, who knew, as Dickens came to know, that his public would take anything that he cared to give them. He did not have to trouble about being *easily* intelligible; he could afford to take chances, and he took them. He had reached the point where he could say with Ben Jonson, 'By God! 'tis good, and if you like't, you may.'

There is one other alternative to the diagnosis I have offered. In the last plays we constantly meet with natural human thoughts and feelings which seem somehow to have been rethought, so that they emerge in the most tortured and unlikely expression. When Imogen is told that Cloten has drawn his sword upon her husband, and that Posthumus, who could have killed him with ease, was content merely to parry his thrusts, she exclaims:

> To draw upon an exile! O brave sir!
> I would they were in Afric both together,
> Myself by with a needle, that I might prick
> The goer-back.[1]

How that needle came into Shakespeare's head it would be hard to say. The context, of course, implies sharp pointed swords, and from them Shakespeare's vision may have narrowed to a needle-point. Or the needle may give us a clue to Shakespeare's conception of Imogen: gentle, womanly, the housewife.[2] But either way, the idea of Imogen

---

[1] I. i. 166 ff.

[2] Imogen mentions her needle again in I. iii. 17ff, when she has been listening to Pisanio's account of how he watched the ship that carried Posthumus from Britain:

> I would have broke mine eye-strings, crack'd them, but
> To look upon him, till the diminution
> Of space had pointed him sharp as my needle. . . .

dancing round the angry swordsmen pricking with her needle the buttocks of the retreating Cloten is a highly recondite one.

Again, when Iachimo is making his diabolical suggestions that Posthumus has forgotten his wife, and is amusing himself at Rome with whores, Shakespeare conveys this to us in at least one quite extraordinary image. 'What makes your admiration?' Imogen asks. What Iachimo has to say in reply is that it passes all comprehension how Posthumus, with such a lovely wife, could even look at other women. His eye and his judgment must tell him that Imogen is infinitely more desirable; and even if Posthumus were moved by mere lust, the memory of Imogen's 'neat excellence' would surely make those other women seem nauseating. But how oddly Shakespeare says it:

> It cannot be i' the eye; for apes and monkeys
> 'Twixt two such shes would chatter this way and
> Contemn with mows the other; nor i' the judgment,
> For idiots in this case of favour would
> Be wisely definite; nor i' the appetite;
> Sluttery to such neat excellence oppos'd
> Should make desire vomit emptiness,
> Not so allur'd to feed.[1]

This kind of writing, with its remote and far-fetched ideas, is what we normally associate with metaphysical poetry. Was Shakespeare, then, turning into a metaphysical poet in his middle age, and if so, why? When this sort of question is asked there are always two possible ways of answering it. You can either say that Shakespeare was following a fashion, or you can say that this development in his style was due to some change in himself. As for following a fashion, it has been suggested that the tragi-comical romances which he wrote at the close of his career—with their tyrannical and unpredictable characters like Leontes, their unexpected and fantastic events, and much else—were influenced by the early work of Beaumont and Fletcher. But even if the plays could be dated precisely enough to make this suggestion plausible, the writing of Beaumont and Fletcher is in general so diffuse that Shakespeare could never have learnt to write like a metaphysical poet by imitating them. Nor is it easy to point to any other contemporary who could have influenced him in that way.

Was there, then, a change in Shakespeare himself? That he had come round to writing at times in the manner of a metaphysical poet would

---

[1] I. vi. 39ff.

not be—to me—incompatible with my thesis that in the last plays there are signs of mental fatigue. Without wishing to revive the notion of the Romantics that there is a poetry which is conceived in the wits and another kind of poetry which is conceived in the soul, I would still hold that metaphysical poetry is, to an unusual degree, the product of cerebration. *Good* metaphysical poetry is, no doubt, the result of a predominantly unconscious cerebration; yet there is always about it a suggestion of the poet putting his mind to work, chasing his thoughts, pursuing them into all sorts of remote and unlikely places. In that sense, in the sense that he is often going out of his way in the last plays to *look for* his ideas, Shakespeare may be said to be writing in the manner of a metaphysical poet. The process had not gone very far when he stopped writing plays altogether. I doubt if he could have continued to write plays for successful performance on the stage if he had carried it much further.

In what I have written I have been more concerned to draw attention to a mode of writing in Shakespeare than to account for it. I have, it is true, tried to explain it in various ways, but if none of my explanations should commend themselves to the reader, the phenomenon itself still remains—awaiting explanation.

II

THE MIND OF SHAKESPEARE

by JOHN WAIN

My title, I realize, might be felt to need a word of explanation. It so happened, a few weeks before I gave my Stratford lecture, that one of our young literary lions had described Shakespeare as having a 'second-rate mind'. Challenged to say more precisely what he meant, he obliged in a letter to *The Times Literary Supplement*. Shakespeare (he explained) had a great sensibility; he was a great poet; but as a speculative instrument, able to *do* things, his mind was second-rate compared with that of a philosopher (Kant, I remember, was the example given). This being in the air at the moment, it seemed reasonable to lecture on the mind of Shakespeare, one's object being to show that this postulated 'great poet' with a 'second-rate mind' was a mere contradiction in terms; that such an idea can only spring from a misunderstanding of the nature of great poetry and also a too *naïf* view of the psychology of literary creation; and that Shakespeare's work, attentively read, offers abundant proof of all this. Concluding, perhaps, with Coleridge's prayer, 'From a popular philosophy and a philosophic populace, Good Sense deliver us!'

Coleridge comes in well here, because he spoke of the 'esemplastic' power of the imagination, meaning its power of creating new organic wholes out of disparate elements. This is something that no one has ever failed to notice who has looked at the nature of the imagination at all closely; it is part of all the definitions that try to say what the imaginative writer is really doing, from Johnson's description of wit as 'the unexpected copulation of ideas', to Shelley's 'metaphorical language ... marks the before unapprehended relations of things'. If we want to see this power demonstrated at its highest pitch, we turn to Shakespeare before any other great writer; because he, more than anyone, made it the governing principle of his work. He had the kind of mind that seeks always to reduce multiplicity to unity, to take the widest possible

159

spread of material and weld it together into a whole. The resultant whole is often of a rather sophisticated kind, not at all apparent to the casual glance; Shakespeare's original audience were at an advantage in this respect, because their civilization had more of a gift for making unity out of diversity than ours has; certainly no one in his own time seems to have considered him primitive, even rustic, a native genius working entirely by intuition, as the criticism of the eighteenth and nineteenth centuries would have it. We have not quite got rid of this bad tradition of criticism yet; the new Shakespearian criticism, that takes it for granted that he was as intelligent as we can possibly be, and works by means of perceiving structures, counting images, and what not, is firmly entrenched in the universities, but there is still (in the theatre, for instance) a tendency to think of Shakespeare's work as so much raw material, deposited by some kind of process in nature, and lying about in heaps asking to be worked on. Actually the only 'working' that is necessary, or indeed permissible, is the effort to see the relationships that are already there in the plays, to perceive them as wholes bearing on a single focus: to accept, in short, what Shakespeare gives us, rather than in trying to make his work interesting in some other idiom—as nineteenth-century criticism tries to make them sound like novels, and the modern stage turns them into vaudeville.

To Shakespeare's contemporaries, as I say, the impulse to make unity out of complexity was nothing strange. In the pre-scientific world, unity was prized just as particularity is prized in our world. Our civilization proceeds on the assumption that if we want to know the *truth* about a thing, we take it into a laboratory, break it down into its constituent parts, and then proceed to weigh and measure these parts, and to observe their properties. And this procedure, carried out literally in the physical sciences, is carried out figuratively—the same *method* is applied, though naturally with different techniques—in other departments of life. In fact it is a mark of this same mind that the phrase 'departments of life', comes so naturally to my pen. In the pre-scientific world, life was not divided this way. Everything bore on everything else. Hence the encyclopœdic tradition of medieval and renaissance learning was not so quaint as it seems to the modern novice. It really was not impossible to take, say, a chapter of Scripture and proceed to build round it an elaborate commentary which said, quite literally, everything worth saying. After all, the Bible contained the word of God, and it was surely not straining one's piety, or one's ingenuity, to try to bring everything into a direct relevance to that word. Knowledge had to hang together, or they had no use for it.

For us, of course, the pendulum has swung far enough, and we are already aware of a gathering swing back. Everywhere, people are tired of the old compartmented, cut-into-strips thinking. The characteristic modern prophet—D. H. Lawrence, for example—always begins by insisting on the basic unity of life. And that insistence ripples out, having its effect on everything. Literary criticism, for instance, is slowly getting over the withering effect of an attitude that could separate scholarship—the acquisition of facts *about* literature—from aesthetic 'appreciation', and then go further and cut that same appreciation off from its roots in day-to-day living; so that the critic, as well as the artist, was left in the echoing cul-de-sac of 'art for art's sake'. Today, even quite minor critics, men who have no claim to originality but merely implement the policies handed down from above, show an impressive willingness to allow literature its full set of ramifications. And Shakespeare is bound to be seen more clearly by such a criticism, just as the music of Byrd and the theology of Hooker will also lose their quaintness and appear more natural to us than our fathers would have thought possible.

To labour the point a little more—for, if I do not make this clear, I make nothing clear—let us imagine ourselves explaining to a Victorian audience (in, say, the period of early H. G. Wells) that Elizabethan medical science could seriously discuss such a question as: what is the relationship between the number of planets in the sky and the number of diseases to which the human body is subject? Our audience would have smiled, confident that their frock-coats, the railway shares in their pockets, the whole rational and institutional life they were building up, put them far above such superstitious fancies. To them, a disease was a disease, which could be isolated, studied, and attacked with drugs or surgery. But to us—though a disease is still all these things—the notion of a correspondence is one that wins far more respect. There may well be no relation between the diseases and the planets, for that notion depends on a doctrine of 'influences' which did not survive the Middle Ages. But a relation between the diseases and *something* there certainly is; if a man falls ill, he does so because of some disturbance which may have no local cause, but a cause it has; and this cause can be philosophical, metaphysical, moral. The individual is at the centre of a web of contacts with life; let something get tangled in the most distant part of that web, and there is a tremor at the centre.

Yeats knew this instinctively, when he turned from the dismembering scientific rationalism of his day to crystal-gazing and secret brotherhoods; the subject-matter was absurd, but the attitudes which informed them were valuable. He knew, with a poet's intuition, that life cannot be separated into its individual grains, even for the purpose of examination. For, if we do so, what we are examining is not life.

What this means in terms of our appreciation of Shakespeare is, clearly, nothing less than a revolution. It means that at last we can heed what Shakespeare is telling us. Instead of concentrating our entire energy on irrelevances (from character-study to source-hunting) we can, for the first time since the Civil War closed the theatres, hush our wearisome clatter and let Shakespeare speak to us; simply, naturally, and quite clearly.

Clearly? A strange word to use of Shakespeare, surely—Shakespeare who is known for his riddling, his multiple significances, his complicated superimposition of plot on plot. 'The style of Shakespeare is itself perplexed, ungrammatical and obscure.' And Johnson was right; it is all those things. But it is clear too. Even the most flagrantly ungrammatical and illogical sentence-constructions, such as:

> like one,
> Who having, into truth, by telling of it,
> Made such a sinner of his memory,
> To credit his own lie—he did believe
> He was himself the duke

even a sentence like that is not, in fact, difficult to understand; it is put together in a way that would be obscure in a prose writer, but then one of the things Shakespeare so magnificently exemplifies is that the verse-writer can get away with a much looser syntax, provided he is able to use his verse to hold up the sagging edges of what he has to say. The verse-rhythms will present the words in their most effective order, and they will enter the hearer's mind clearly; it will not puzzle him to construe the sentence until he gets it down on paper and begins to look for the grammar.

Shakespeare's mind, then, lends itself to clarity; all the famous riddling and quibbling, the density of construction, is in the interests of richness, but it is not against those of clarity. If we are interested in knowing what he has to say, rather than merely appreciating him for incidental beauties, we shall understand fast enough.

Not, of course, that Shakespeare is preaching. His fundamental atti-

tude, which the plays very strongly convey, is not so much a doctrine,
to be taught, as an opinion which, since he held it naturally, formed a
natural base for his imaginative work. That opinion can be stated
baldly as follows: there is a natural order, or *pietas*, which must not be
violated; certain emotions, certain observances and attitudes, are right
and necessary; to reject them is unnatural, rather like trying to make
crops grow in the snow, and equally futile; it will result in failure, and,
if done on a large enough scale, it will unleash 'chaos', the state in
which:

> Strength should be lord of imbecility,
> And the rude son should strike his father dead;
>
> Force should be right; or rather, right and wrong,
> Between whose endless jar justice resides,
> Should lose their names, and so should justice too.
> Then everything includes itself in power. . . .

This is, of course, an attitude Shakespeare shared with most people at
that time; Elizabethan minds naturally pivoted on the metaphors of
music, on the one hand, and chaos on the other. Shakespeare's characters nearly always begin to talk about music as soon as a state of peace
and happiness is attained or glimpsed—as they do, for instance in the
fifth act of *The Merchant of Venice*, when the disruptive element, Shylock, has been expelled, leaving the young people to get on with their
natural business of loving each other.

This is no idiosyncrasy of Shakespeare's; Milton, only a few years
later, cannot write a poem about music without bringing in the idea:

> That we on Earth with undiscording voice
> May rightly answer that melodious noise;
> As once we did, till disproportion'd sin
> Jarr'd against nature's chime, and with harsh din
> Broke the fair music that all creatures made
> To their great Lord, whose love their motion sway'd
> In perfect Diapason, whilst they stood
> In first obedience, and their state of good.

For an illustration of the companion metaphor, 'chaos', we might turn
to Hooker (*Ecclesiastical Polity*, Book I):

His commanding those things to be which are, and to be in such sort as they
are; to keep that tenure and course which they do, importeth the establishment of nature's law. This world's first creation, and the preservation since

of things created, what is it but only so far forth a manifestation by execution,
what the eternal law of God is concerning things natural? And as it cometh
to pass in a kingdom rightly ordered, that after a law is once published, it
presently takes effect far and wide, all states framing themselves thereunto;
even so let us think it fareth in the natural course of the world: since the time
that God did first proclaim the edicts of his law upon it, heaven and earth
have hearkened unto his voice, and their labour hath been to do his will: He
'made a law for the rain'; He gave his 'decree unto the sea, that the waters
should not pass his commandment'. Now if nature should intermit her course,
and leave altogether though it were but for a while the observation of her
own laws; if those principal and mother elements of the world, whereof all
things in this lower world are made, should lose the qualities which now they
have; if the frame of that heavenly arch erected over our heads should loosen
and dissolve itself; if celestial spheres should forget their wonted motions, and
by irregular volubility turn themselves any way as it might happen; if the
prince of the lights of heaven, which now as a giant doth run his unwearied
course, should as it were through a languishing faintness begin to stand and
to rest himself; if the moon should wander from her beaten way, the times
and seasons of the year blend themselves by disordered and confused mixture,
the winds breathe out their last gasp, the clouds yield no rain, the earth be
defeated of heavenly influence, the fruits of the earth pine away as children
at the withered breasts of their mother no longer able to yield them relief:
what would become of man himself, whom these things now do all serve?
See we not plainly that obedience of creatures unto the law of nature is the
stay of the whole world?

The polarity was in everyone's mind, and no one doubted that a
wholesome unity was what we had to preserve. (It was this attitude
that made Pride a deadly sin, since Pride will brook no one higher than
himself.) And Shakespeare would have been astonished to have any
originality claimed on his behalf, for holding such an attitude. What he
understood best was how to give this concept the strength and concreteness of great art; in that, he unquestionably led the way; as an
artist, there can be no doubt, he would be perfectly well aware of the
extent of his own originality.
    The more closely one looks at Shakespeare, the more one finds that
the key to his work lies in this combination of a world-view that called
for unity and correspondence with a natural turn of mind that sought
always to resolve discord into harmony and multiplicity into singleness.
Certainly a criticism that puts anything else at the centre is bound to
find itself with some awkward explaining to do. If—for instance—
Macbeth is primarily a character-study, what pitiful mumbo-jumbo are

the two prodigies that come in at the *dénouement*, the 'Birnam Wood coming to Dunsinane' business and the appearance of an adversary owing his birth to a Caesarian operation. What can such things have to do with character, or the drawing of a political moral? But as soon as we see that the main thread of the play is the description of *pietas*, causing a widening circle of further disruptions, it becomes plain that such an open defiance of Nature is bound to involve prodigies— horses that turn cannibal, a hawk killed by an owl, a woman who cries out to be unsexed, and a man who wishes it would go dark in the day-time. Of course the character-portrayal is there; the establishment of Macbeth's character in so few lines at the beginning is a model of economy that any novelist might ponder; but the important thing about him is that as long as he is loyally fighting for his king, he can be described by an admiring fellow-soldier as:

> Nothing afeard of what thyself didst make,
> Strange images of death.

The corpses of enemies legitimately slain in battle do not inspire nervous dread, but the body of one old man who is murdered in the face of 'double trust' turns out to contain a horrifying amount of blood. An Oxford tutor of my acquaintance was once told by an under-graduate that *Macbeth* 'contained nothing to interest a mature mind'. Ludicrous enough; but one can hardly blame the youth if he had always had the play offered to him as a story of blood-and-thunder on a remote Scotch moor.

King Lear is a particularly clear example, as it not only contains the fullest possible statement of the *pietas* theme, but is virtually unintelli-gible on any other basis. The aged despot, proud and opinionated ('He hath ever but slenderly known himself.'), endangers the stability of the social order by wanting to divide England into three parts, and, not content with that, utters a formal renunciation of the bonds that unite him to his daughter:

> Let it be so; thy truth then be thy dower:
> For, by the sacred radiance of the sun,
> The mysteries of Hecate and the night,
> By all the operation of the orbs
> From whom we do exist and cease to be,
> Here I disclaim all my paternal care,
> Propinquity and property of blood,
> And as a stranger to my heart and me

Hold thee from this for ever. The barbarous Scythian,
Or he that makes his generation messes
To gorge his appetite, shall to my bosom
Be as well neighbour'd, pitied, and reliev'd,
As thou my sometime daughter.

After that, the pelican daughters and the symbolic thunderstorms not only may but *must* go into operation, until the natural order has shuddered itself into calm once more—the Shakespearian version of that calm which always returns at the end of a great tragedy.

Once that theme is grasped, the play—like *Macbeth*, like all Shakespeare—seems more logical, less full of frills and inconsistencies: in a word, better art. The repetition of the theme from plot to sub-plot, which once seemed justifiable mainly as a decoration (so that Watts-Dunton, for instance, could say, 'Perhaps from a merely theatrical point of view it complicates the action to excess, though it does not really divide the interest; but the practical effect is enhanced, as that of a thunderstorm by reverberations among the mountains'), is seen as structurally essential: there have to be two suffering parents, who have flouted *pietas* in contrasting ways, and, while one has to go mad in order to understand, the other has to be blinded in order to see.

However, there is no point in spinning out these routine examples; to demonstrate the working of this great principle throughout all Shakespeare's plays is easily done, and, though not criticism, it is an essential preliminary to criticism; one must hope that in the appropriate places—sixth forms, university extension classes, popular handbooks— the work will go quietly forward. For, as I remarked earlier, the elementary business of getting Shakespeare's major concerns into focus is, as yet, by no means complete.

This, unfortunately, applies to detail as much as to outline. If the broad lines of Shakespeare's designs are still not clear to so many of those who love him, neither are the concrete details of his procedure. His use of language, for example, both as regards the individual word (the unit of meaning, the versification, the elaborated structure of such units) is still in need of elementary explanation. One gathers this need, not so much from the remarks one sees or reads made about Shakespeare himself, as from literary generalizations at large. Joyce's puns, for example, would never have seemed as miraculous as they evidently do, had his admirers grasped the simple fact that Shakespeare had anticipated the entire method, though without proffering it so

obtrusively. This side of Shakespeare's mind earned him the disapproval
of the Age of Reason ('a quibble is to him the fatal Cleopatra', &c.);
but, since that disapproval died down, it seems to have been quietly
forgotten that Shakespeare used puns on a scale not attempted again
till the twentieth century, and for the most impeccably *avant-garde*
motives. It looks as if the pioneering work done by Mr. Empson and
others, plus the admirable presentation for the general reader in such a
book as Miss Mahood's *Shakespeare's Word-Play*, is still not enough.
This is a pity, for there is a good deal in the literature of his own time
that encourages the modern playgoer to enjoy and appreciate Shakespeare's habit of throwing in a pun whenever the dramatic tension
mounts more than ordinarily high.

> I'll gild the faces of the grooms withal;
> For it must seem their guilt.

The meeting of double, or multiple, significance in one word seems to
attract Shakespeare as the means of tying a knot round the bundle of
themes and statements he is handling. Here, as elsewhere, his effort is
to unite, to fuse, to present with lightning simultaneity.

I believe that whatever other movements may be traced on the chart
of Shakespeare's development, this one remains steady. All his life, he
voyaged towards a greater and greater inclusiveness. His early work,
like that of many artists, is compartmented; he seems concerned, for
the first ten years of his career, with showing how many already existing *genres* he can successfully tackle. When, in these early days, he
writes a tragedy, it is an unrelieved storm of blood and tears; when he
writes comedy, it is a pretty straight exercise in one or other of the
standard comic modes. This is all very sympathetic; he is learning his
trade; faced with two traditions of comic writing, he sets himself to
produce specimens, and concocts the *Comedy of Errors* out of the
materials of Latin comedy, *The Two Gentlemen of Verona* from those of
romantic comedy as written by, say, Peele, and (for already the impulse
to *fuse* is at work) *Love's Labour's Lost* as an example of how to blend
material from either source. But if we let our minds range from one
end of Shakespeare's working life to the other, we find him still engaged, though now with far greater placidity and strength, in the task
of making a new whole out of already proven components; taking the
new fashion for loosely-constructed 'romances' as practised by Beaumont and Fletcher, he turns them into something new in English
literature: structures of meaning that we cannot help calling 'symbolic',

M

though the symbols are not reducible; works in which we feel the pressure of a shadowy allegory, as we feel it in Conrad's novels, deepening and thickening our sense of the 'meaning' that is coming over to us, without being able, except in extremely cumbrous ways, to expound it.

Inclusiveness in argument, inclusiveness in symbolic structure, inclusiveness within the individual word: this was the quest of which Shakespeare never tired. The later plays, even when they were passing through a period of incomprehension and neglect, were at any rate recognized as miracles of versification. (*Cymbeline* was Tennyson's favourite play, and it is obvious that the technical fascination for the Laureate must have been immense.) Not that one would sacrifice the lyrical, uncomplicated movement of the early verse; *Richard II* alone would be enough to establish Shakespeare as a great poet if he had written nothing else: those springing, unclogged lines, full of open syllables, which balance so delicately that they can at any moment veer towards the weighty or the staccato—it is for Shakespeare a necessary starting-point, but for any other poet it might well be the crown of a lifetime's effort.

> Now mark me how I will undo myself:
> I give this heavy weight from off my head,
> And this unwieldy sceptre from my hand,
> The pride of kingly sway from out my heart;
> With mine own tears I wash away my balm,
> With mine own hands I give away my crown,
> With mine own tongue deny my sacred state,
> With mine own breath release all duteous rites:
> All pomp and majesty I do forswear;
> My manors, rents, revenues, I forego;
> My acts, decrees, and statutes I deny:
> God pardon all oaths that are broke to me!
> God keep all vows unbroke are made to thee!
> Make me, that nothing have, with nothing griev'd,
> And thou with all pleas'd, that hast all achiev'd!

As Shakespeare went on, he integrated his poetry more and more closely with drama, running the rhythms of naturalistic speech contrapuntally across those of decasyllabic verse; but that, the familiar formulation, is only half the story. The complicating, contrapuntally involving process was done as much in the interests of beauty as of dramatic realism; the aim was not merely to get the verse to sound 'lifelike', but to endow it with a more supple life of its own, a more fastidious lyrical movement:

> With fairest flowers
> While summer lasts and I live here, Fidele,
> I'll sweeten thy sad grave; ᵗhou shalt not lack
> The flower that's like thy face, pale primrose, nor
> The azur'd hare-bell, like thy veins, no, nor
> The leaf of eglantine, whom not to slander,
> Out-sweeten'd not thy breath: the ruddock would,
> With charitable bill, —O bill! sore-shaming
> Those rich-left heirs, that let their fathers lie
> Without a monument,—bring thee all this;
> Yea, and furr'd moss besides, when flowers are none,
> To winter-ground thy corse.

A comparison is in order here. Not many years separate *Julius Caesar* from *Coriolanus*, but in the intervening period Shakespeare's stylistic preoccupations had shifted considerably. Here are two speeches devoted to unsympathetic description of a triumphal progress; in each case, the speaker is a tribune.

> Wherefore rejoice? What conquest brings he home?
> What tributaries follow him to Rome
> To grace in captive bonds his chariot wheels?
> You blocks, you stones, you worse than senseless things!
> O you hard hearts, you cruel men of Rome,
> Knew you not Pompey? Many a time and oft
> Have you climb'd up to walls and battlements,
> To towers and windows, yea, to chimney-tops,
> Your infants in your arms, and there have sat
> The livelong day, with patient expectation,
> To see great Pompey pass the streets of Rome:
> And when you saw his chariot but appear,
> Have you not made a universal shout,
> That Tiber trembled underneath her banks,
> To hear the replication of your sounds
> Made in her concave shores?
> And do you now put on your best attire?
> And do you now cull out a holiday?
> And do you now strew flowers in his way,
> That comes in triumph over Pompey's blood?

All tongues speak of him, and the bleared sights
Are spectacled to see him: your prattling nurse
Into a rapture lets her baby cry
While she chats him: the kitchen malkin pins
Her richest lockram 'bout her reechy neck,
Clambering the walls to eye him: stalls, bulks, windows,
Are smother'd up, leads fill'd, and ridges hors'd
With variable complexions, all agreeing
In earnestness to see him: seld-shown flamens
Do press among the popular throngs, and puff
To win a vulgar station: our veil'd dames
Commit the war of white and damask in
Their nicely-gawded cheeks to the wanton spoil
Of Phoebus' burning kisses: such a pother
As if that whatsoever god who leads him
Were slily crept into his human powers,
And gave him graceful posture.

The increase in dramatic immediacy and concreteness is immediately
apparent in the second passage. Admittedly the comparison is not quite
a straight one; in the first extract, Marullus is rebuking the gaping
crowd, and he does so in dignified and lofty rhetorical accents; in the
second, Brutus is hissing and spitting his rage and disappointment to
his fellow-official. Naturally his accents have more of the actual tang,
the taste and texture, of bitterness and contempt than would be proper
in the mouth of Marullus.

> the kitchen malkin pins
> Her richest lockram 'bout her reechy neck . . .
> . . . press among the popular throngs, and puff . . .

The lines are made up of sounds that would convey angry contempt to
a hearer who knew no English. Nevertheless, the difference is a real one;
Shakespeare has, in the intervening period, moved into his mature
manner of kinesthetic unification. The wonderful word 'horsed' contains within itself the dense, physical sensation of overcrowding, as well
as the implied judgment of the incensed observer (the people are
carrying on like animals); one remembers the agonized disgust of
Leontes:

> Is whispering nothing?
> Is leaning cheek to cheek? is meeting noses?
> Kissing with inside lip? stopping the career
> Of laughter with a sigh?—a note infallible
> Of breaking honesty,—horsing foot on foot?

And if 'horsed' carries a strong suggestion of the non-human, there is a similar force in the way various parts of the human body are picked out to stand for the whole, in Marullus's contemptuous description of the crowd. The Romans who jostle so eagerly for a chance to look at Coriolanus, their hero and nine days' wonder, are people; but to Marullus, in his present mood, they are simply so many gaping eyes, prattling tongues, and pushing limbs. The suggestion is reinforced by what might otherwise seem extraneous detail—the 'reechy neck' of the unwashed servant-girl, the cheeks of the 'veil'd dames'; the way the normally aloof 'flamens' (i.e. priests) 'puff' to get a point of vantage; all these isolated physical activities rob their performers of humanity. The speech makes an interesting contrast to Menenius's fable of the belly and the members in the opening scene; where Menenius was adjuring the crowd to remember their status as men (i.e. as co-ordinating and co-operating animals), Marullus is implicitly denying them this status.

This essay will have to break off, rather than end. The theme is one that could be documented through volume after volume, and it is a job that could be done by anybody, Elizabethan scholar or novice, who had read Shakespeare attentively. All that is necessary is to have one's attention focused in the right places. The mountains of misplaced ingenuity which humanity has heaped up round Shakespeare's work is, very obviously, a tribute to his genius; but it seems to have curiously little to do with him. (Masterpiece though it is, who can avoid the impression that Bradley's *Shakespearean Tragedy* is not really 'about' Shakespeare at all?) Perhaps a more rational criticism will, in time, put an end to the state of affairs in which it is felt legitimate to remark that Shakespeare, though very well in his way, was not as clever as Kant; and will help to make it clear that one of Shakespeare's achievements was to demonstrate just how strong, how wide-ranging, how subtly adjusted, the intelligence of a great poet has to be.

12

MEDICINE AND SURGERY IN THE 1955 SEASON'S PLAYS

by HENRY YELLOWLEES

WHEN I was occupied with the preparation of this lecture some weeks ago, a friend rather startled me by asking what the object of the lecture really was. I realized, on thinking the matter over, that it certainly was not to attempt to teach you anything about medicine or surgery. That would be an absurd and impossible task and I should not use Shakespeare as a vehicle even if I were making the attempt.

The real object of this lecture and, I suppose, of all the lectures in the course, is simply to look together at the art of Shakespeare—each speaker from his particular angle—so that we may have the pleasure of discovering various beauties and points of interest, great or small, which had not occurred to us before, or which we had not fully appreciated or understood.

Apart from the intellectual pleasure that this gives, it is also of the greatest practical benefit to those whose business it is to introduce others, particularly boys and girls, to the study of Shakespeare.

Yes, but who am I to have an angle at all—let alone one from which anything new or interesting might be seen? Last year I readily admitted to you that I am very far indeed from being a profound, expert, or scholarly student of Shakespeare, and I strongly suspect that the professional critics would be justified in calling me a 'Philistine'. My equipment for lecturing about Shakespeare is slight indeed compared with that of my distinguished fellow-lecturers. I read Shakespeare (omitting all 'explanatory' notes!) for the sheer joy it gives me, I possess a distinctly adhesive verbal memory, and I have a long practical experience of psychological medicine. That's all there is to it.

Fortunately, for me at least, I think that, even with such a limited equipment, a speaker can occasionally shed new light on some word or phrase in a play, not because he is cleverer than his hearers but because his particular occupation or experiences enable him to appreciate the meaning of some reference or some point of detail more fully than his neighbour. That is where my special training and experience in psychological medicine comes in, and that is why I am going to begin this talk with a short discussion of the wonderful psychological process known as Projection, which is at the very root of both appreciation and censure—indeed, of all criticism, apart from the passing of purely intellectual judgments.

We can only see what is in us to see. You cannot understand conduct which is completely foreign to your own nature, and you are therefore little concerned either to praise or blame it. King Arthur's heart, you may remember, was 'too wholly true to dream untruth' in Guinevere. Sexual infidelity being, as we are told, completely alien to his nature, he was incapable of even suspecting it in others.

I once knew a small but highly intelligent boy who one morning had just mastered the first seven letters of the alphabet. Later that day, on seeing the word BANK in large gilt capitals over its door, he shouted out: 'Look! Stupid! It should be A—B.' The letters N and K meant nothing to him, nor had he any idea that letters could be combined and arranged in various ways and, indeed, existed for that purpose. But he did know that B comes after A and not before it, and he was quick to criticize and resent any tampering with the scheme of things on which he had become an authority.

A young child will greet a picture of some bearded personage such as King Lear or the Prophet Elijah with a gleeful shout of 'Daddy!', should his father be similarly afflicted, and will completely ignore a multitude of striking dissimilarities. A similar result can be achieved if such vanities as a kilt or a top hat can be made the basis of the experiment.

You cannot criticize a piece of music unless you have, as we say, music in you. You cannot appreciate a picture unless you are at heart, although not necessarily in performance, an artist.

This ability to see only what is in us to see is but one of the varieties of projection. Instances of it in all its forms abound, of course, in Shakespeare, and I have made this little excursion into psychology at the very start because we shall be coming across examples of it before the lecture is over.

The approach to Shakespeare from the viewpoint of medical psychology is one of truly fascinating interest. Last year I discussed some general psychiatric disorders and psychological principles, and illustrated them from the behaviour of many of his characters. My more modest aim today is merely to mention and discuss quite simply, but not, I hope, too superficially, a few of the points in this season's plays which, because of their medico-psychological interest appeal particularly to me as a psychiatrist.

I inserted the word 'Surgery' in the title of this address because, without it, I should not have been able to refer to that remarkable, blood-stained melodrama *Titus Andronicus*. As I insisted last year, I am the very reverse of an authority on theatrical or dramatic art, but I do understand just a little about poetry and psychology. I can find no trace of either in *Titus Andronicus*, although I notice with interest that Masefield says it contains three lines of poetry and, of course, there is plenty of psychology, of a sort, behind wholesale and indiscriminate lust, murder, mutilation, rape, premature burial, poisoning, torture and so forth.

I am told that the piece makes good theatre, and I wish I could have seen it before giving this talk. I hope to do so to-morrow, and feel that if my ignorant private views on the play can ever be changed, it will be by the great artists who will appear in it. I will confess to you that I am eager to see how even they can escape getting a laugh of the wrong sort in the very last two lines of the play. About half the original cast have died violent deaths, and a distinct majority of the dwindling band of survivors should, on the most lenient view, be serving life-sentences in prison. Undeterred, however, by this, they order further torture, fling another corpse to the wild beasts, and then move off . . . 'to order well the state'—as they naïvely remark. The wildest performances of our 'planners' are milk and water compared with the blood and iron policy of this criminal gang.[1]

The 'surgery' of the play is, of course, nothing but butchery, and very rough and ready butchery at that. To suggest that Lavinia could conceivably have recovered from amputation of the tongue and both hands, performed in Roman times, without anaesthetics, by the amateur surgeons who had just finished raping their patient after murdering her husband, is the crowning medical absurdity of this fantastic and disgusting business. Throughout the play, the characters make a positive hobby of cutting off each other's heads and hands, and sending them to and fro by messenger.

[1] The lines in question were 'cut' at the performance I witnessed.

There is also, I am almost sure, someone who cut off his own hand for some obscure purpose, but I lost the place and couldn't bring myself to go through the play again in search of him. But if anyone really imagines that it is possible to cut off one's own hand with a sword, in hot blood or cold, let him come to me after the lecture and I shall gladly supervise his efforts. Bring your own swords.

Now that we are done with that highly spiced *hors-d'œuvre*, let us deal with the other one of the five plays which, although it does contain a medical practitioner, is of no great medical interest, namely *The Merry Wives*. Dr. Caius is no doubt duly qualified but, clearly, he is a graduate of a French university and thus as 'a damned foreigner' starts off on the wrong foot in the mind of every true Englishman. From a medical point of view he is not one of Shakespeare's happiest creations. I can find no mention in the play of his undertaking any medical activity whatever, and his professional repute rests entirely on the testimonial to his prowess given in rather crude and outspoken terms by mine host of The Garter Inn.

The testimonial is not altogether free from the suspicion of being in the nature of a *quid pro quo*. Dr. Caius had—or professed to have—an excellent practice in Windsor, presumably at the Court, as we learn from him that his patients included, 'Earls, Knights, Lords and Gentlemen'. In return for mine host's help to him in the matter of Anne Page, plus, no doubt, flattering references to his skill as opportunity offered, the doctor undertook to recommend the Garter Inn to his exalted patients and their relatives. The medical ethics of this proceeding are questionable, to say the least.

Dr. Caius shouts his way through the play in a state of noisy, querulous bad temper, for which it is often hard to find any reason. Nobody likes him very much, really. Page calls him 'the renowned French physician' but says in a delightful phrase that he is at odds with his own gravity and patience. Shallow says that he never heard of a man 'so wide of his own respect', while the good but choleric Sir Hugh Evans first disparages his medical knowledge and then calls him a cowardly knave.

And so to the medical aspect of that—to me—singularly unpleasant and bitter comedy, *All's Well That Ends Well*. In my salad days I accepted the view that Bertram was a loathsome mixture of snob and cad, whose treatment of the fair and virtuous Helena was truly contemptible. I hold it still, but I have come to realize that he was in some ways sinned against as much as sinning, and that Helena, in spite of the many beautiful and pathetic things she says, is really an obnoxious young woman who merits, if ever woman did, the classical title of 'designing minx'.

For years I have mistrusted her, but it was only when rereading the play with this lecture in mind that I realized how thoroughly she is 'on the make' from start to finish, and how very well able she is to look after her own interests. She is the centre and focus of all the medical interest of the play; she is the perfectly drawn representative of the un-qualified practitioner, the Quack. And yet it is all so quietly and gently done that Coleridge, for example, spoke of Helena as 'Shakespeare's loveliest creation'.

Well, it's a matter for the experts. I may be quite wrong but I don't think Shakespeare's truly loveliest creation would have opened a dis-cussion on the keeping and losing of virginity with such a half-bred bit of riff-raff as Parolles. But I must mind my own business and discuss Helena as Queen of Quacks.

The story is quite typical in every single detail. To begin with, Helena uses every means in her power to thrust herself on the king's notice. Perhaps she might be forgiven for that, but she admits very frankly that her chief motive in getting permission to treat the king is to use him to entrap Bertram into marrying her. All this is perilously near what would be regarded, even in these degenerate days, as 'infamous conduct in a professional respect'.

The medicine is, of course, a secret remedy, kept in the family. She cashes in, so to speak, on her father's reputation. Further, the remedy appears to be a cure-all. The king is suffering from fistula—a disease which cannot be radically and permanently cured by medicine alone—but that does not disconcert Helena. Falling back, like all quacks, on a process of suggestion—to which fistula is not amenable—she guaran-tees a complete cure in forty-eight hours, and offers to stake her reputa-tion and her life on the success of her treatment. Needless to say, the case is one which 'has baffled all the doctors'. The king holds out for quite a time. He will not catch at straws when all the doctors have given him up and when, as he puts it, 'the congregated college have concluded' that he hasn't a hope. But he agrees in the end, reasoning that a harmless and painless forty-eight-hour treatment on which a prepossessing young woman bets her life is perhaps worth trying.

Nowadays the quacks don't bet their life: they say 'money back if not satisfied'. Helena puts the thing in more melodramatic fashion: 'If my magic doesn't work, kill me!' but in essence it's the very same thing; the central principle of quackery: no cure no pay. The king yields, and Helena turns to the business side of the contract with almost indecent haste:

HELENA: . . . Not helping, death's my fee;
      But, if I help, what do you promise me?
KING: Make thy demand.
HELENA: But will you make it even?
KING: Ay, by my sceptre, and my hopes of heaven.

Then comes her absurd request, cunningly phrased in general terms, although Bertram alone is in her mind from the start. Bertram, the aristocrat, who has addressed her once only in the play so far, with an off-hand formula of farewell and a patronizing instruction to attend to her duties as his mother's lady's maid. I've often thought, by the way, that Helena must have been an ancestress, in the direct line, of Uriah Heep.

The king, now up to the neck in it, keeps his bargain after the two-day cure. I don't know what his legal authority may have been in relation to the young lordlings about the Court, but I know that his dealings with Bertram in this matter are as devoid of moral right as they are of common sense.

The Mikado, you will remember, punished the advertising quack by decreeing that all his teeth should be extracted by terrified amateurs. But Shakespeare devised a much worse fate for his advertising quack, Helena; he married her to Bertram.

And now for the medicine and surgery in *Twelfth Night*, that loveliest and sunniest of plays, of which Masefield has written: 'It will stand as an example of perfect art till a greater than Shakespeare set a better example further on.'

No doctor appears in *Twelfth Night*. There is but one solitary reference to a member of my profession, one Dick Surgeon, who, I imagine, was probably only the local barber. On one occasion, at least, his services were urgently required: 'For the love of God, a surgeon! Send one presently to Sir Toby,' and the only thing we are told about him then is that he was reported as having been dead drunk since before eight o'clock in the morning. On hearing this news, Sir Toby, of all people, says: 'I hate a drunken rogue.'

We have all laughed many a time at this classical example of Satan reproving sin, but I wonder to how many of us it has occurred that in all probability Sir Toby was speaking in complete sincerity without any attempt at humbug or humour, and that he seriously believed that he was expressing his real feelings.

We are back at projection, in one of its most important and interesting forms. We can only see what is in us to see, and if what is in us is too painful or humiliating for us to realize and accept, we ignore it, turn away from it, and see and criticize it as it is reflected in the conduct of others. We cannot deny its existence, but we hurl it away into our environment.

But the environment acts like the wall against which we throw a tennis ball, and we may expect difficulty in dealing with the rebound. 'A bad workman blames his tools.' Of course he does. He cannot accept the fact of his own incompetence, so fastens the accusation on his tools.

It is the muddle-headed man who complains that none of his colleagues is capable of presenting a clear statement; it is the man whose own level of conduct and degree of adjustment are questionable, who talks most incessantly about cads and snobs and bounders and people who don't know how to behave. It is the man who dare not face the fact of his own dishonesty, who casts the truth away from him, and receives back the suspicion that others are conspiring to deceive and swindle him.

Projection, you will notice, offers to the individual the fascinating occupation of condemning his own unacknowledged faults and tendencies as they appear in other people, thus becoming more royalist than the king, instead of saying: 'There, but for the grace of God, go I.' It is difficult to realize that a man can force himself to be blissfully unconscious of what is painfully obvious to everyone else, but so it is, and this type of projection, as it happens, is particularly well seen in alcoholic patients. I myself have had at least four or five alcoholic patients who assured me in all sincerity that their wretched and ruined homes were entirely due to the alcoholic habits of their wives! You will realize how interestingly this practice of projecting unrecognized aspects of ourselves into our judgments is related to such occupations as those of the professional dramatic critic. I cannot help adding that, though it is far from a complete analogy, the legend of Perseus and Medusa has features which inevitably suggest themselves in this connection. The originator of the fable that Perseus cut off the head of Medusa with averted eyes while he looked at its reflection in the mirror of Athene's shield, must have been a natural psychologist of no mean order.

But to return to *Twelfth Night*. Although my profession does not appear to advantage in it, we have as compensation the antics of a band of amateurs, whose enthusiasm and *joie de vivre* would adorn any medical students' rag.

They are engaged in organizing an elaborate practical joke which results in the wrongful detention of an alleged lunatic. 'Wrongful detention' is, of course, a trumpet call which rouses all true Britons to write to the papers or their M.P., but they don't worry much about it in the cloud-cuckoo land of Illyria. The practical jokers are well up in the kind of psychiatric treatment in vogue at the time, and let fall much interesting information concerning it, but they do not regard Malvolio as insane and are merely concerned to bring him into a notable contempt, so we need not regard their methods as altogether typical of contemporary medical thought.

One of the suggested aids to diagnosis is urine-analysis: a well-known and common procedure even then, and one to which Shakespeare often refers. 'Carry his water to the wise-woman,' says Sir Toby. I don't know how she conducted her analysis or what were her qualifications for the job, but her title reminds me of a young man much interested in clairvoyance and the occult, and with a totally inadequate knowledge of the French language, whom I met in France in the 1914–18 war. He came upon a very solid and respectable little house in the village, with a neat brass plate on the door bearing the word *sagefemme*. Concluding that this must be the abode of some elderly giver of sage counsel—a soothsayer of no mean order—he knocked and entered, in happy ignorance that *sagefemme* is the French for mid-wife!

Malvolio was not mad: he has, indeed, been called, I think with justice, the one wise man in the play, but he was much nearer insanity than his persecutors imagined, or than any Shakespearian critics have, to my knowledge, suggested.

Malvolio suffered from that mysterious disorder of personality technically known as the paranoid temperament, the result of his over-staying his leave in a dream world of his own in which all enemies are routed, all difficulties overcome, and all goals attained, without any effort on the part of the dreamer. This, of course, involves a divorce from reality and a turning of the day-dreamer's attention inwards upon his own fancies, instead of outwards upon healthy human contacts. He thus becomes, as Malvolio did, 'sick of self-love', and 'contemplation' —of his own excellences—'makes a rare turkey-cock of him'.

We must remember, of course, that Malvolio was in this condition long before the incident of the faked letter. He was in it, for that matter, long before the beginning of the play, and I don't suppose he became really insane till long after its close. Perhaps he never became insane at all. It all depends on whether the trick played on him made his hatred of, and contempt for, his fellow men more implacable than ever, or whether, by some happy chance, it jerked him back out of dreamland by bringing him to a realization of the virtues of forgiveness and goodwill, and restoring his sense of humour.

I cannot help fearing that he went from bad to worse. He shut himself off from reality and human intercourse by a fence of his own construction, and to break that fence down again is an almost impossibly hard task as a rule. You cannot read the play without realizing that Malvolio is aloof from everyone else in it. From beginning to end he is separated from all the others by an invisible barrier, of which we are almost painfully conscious, which he does all in his power to strengthen by word and action. 'I am not of your element.' And, of course, his sense of humour, if it ever existed, is completely dead. Not a laugh from him in the entire play. Not one single bit of 'off the record' informality or friendliness. Smiles, yes, to order and by request, and what a pitiable performance his smiling was! His facial contortions were such that Maria could 'hardly keep from throwing things at him', and there was no more humour or humanity in his smile than there was blood in Sir Andrew's liver.

I have always thought that Barrie's John Shand in *What Every Woman Knows* has a good deal in common with Malvolio. He, too, is a man of much ability, but, like Malvolio, he takes himself so seriously that he can never be really human; he, too, is unable to forget his own importance and his ambitions, to relax and to be at ease. You may remember that, happier than Malvolio, Shand finds psychological salvation at the very end of Barrie's play, by achieving for the first time a laugh—at himself.

There are two classical methods of avoiding painful reality. We can avoid the presence of an unwelcome intruder either by throwing him out or by running away ourselves.

The first method corresponds, psychologically, to Projection, which I have briefly outlined and illustrated, while the second is the retreat into Fantasy of which Malvolio is a perfect example.

It is the simpler, pleasanter, and less harmful of the two methods, and most of us are prone to take occasional holidays in the land where dreams come true, with good rather than bad results, provided always that we have been careful to arrange for the return journey to the workaday world. The penalty for overstaying one's leave is a severe one: the dream world becomes more real than the real world, and the dreamer, like Malvolio, becomes completely cut off from effective contact with human life. But most of us have the sense to take a return ticket for a limited period, and we pay the price—temporary divorce from reality—with a smile. After all, one cannot expect to get into fairyland for nothing. Some of us find it easier than others; children in arms, I believe, are admitted free, and those under twelve pay half-price.

Now we come to *Macbeth*, which is fuller by far of medical interest than the other four plays at which we have been glancing together. The play takes us into my native country, and the medicine in it takes us into the very heart of my own specialty.

Two doctors appear in the *dramatis personae* of *Macbeth*. They are referred to as 'an English doctor' and 'a Scotch doctor' and, of the two, I am glad to inform you that the latter is by a long way the more efficient, interesting and hard-working. I don't know if such a thing has ever happened in real life, or if Shakespeare just invented it as a compliment to King James I. Anyhow, the English doctor has such a small part that he has completely vanished from this season's production! 'Enter a doctor' says the stage direction, clearly to relieve the tension after the long interview between Malcolm and Macduff. The doctor is asked if the king is going to put in an appearance. He replies in a speech of thirty-four words about the old practice of touching for the king's evil. Malcolm says politely, 'I thank you, Doctor.' Exit doctor, and we hear no more of him.

The Scotch doctor appears to be a man of much more robust fibre. He is seen in two remarkable interviews: one with the nurse in charge of his patient, and one with his patient's husband.

The patient is Lady Macbeth, who is having a series of what are known as hysterical fugues. The psychological principle involved, put as simply as possible, is this. Some people, when they undergo an emotional experience which is completely unendurable, can obtain relief from it—at a price—by turning away from it and banishing it entirely from their conscious mind. Its memory sinks into their unconscious mind and the price they pay for this respite is that the buried memory constantly seeks elbow-room and opportunity to express itself in consciousness in one of many roundabout, disguised forms; disguised so that consciousness will not recognize it for what it is and be faced with the intolerable idea once again. That is what is called psychological repression.

The intolerable idea may manifest itself as an obsession or an hysterical symptom such as paralysis of a limb or loss of voice, by dreams or, as in this case, by a sleep-walking fugue, in which the conscious mind is in abeyance, while the unconscious takes the stage and relives the intolerable scene. Probably it would not have been relived in this case so accurately without medical help, but Shakespeare certainly got the principle of the thing perfectly.

The medical science of his day, however, had not taken the one step further which might have saved Lady Macbeth. Nowadays she could have been made to relive that terrible scene in complete detail by a competent psychiatrist with the assistance of certain drugs or, possibly, hypnotism. If, thereafter, the physician had gone over the material with her in her waking state, and thus broken the repression, there would have been a terrible emotional reaction but Lady Macbeth would have recovered. Perhaps, therefore, it is just as well that this form of treatment, which is called abreaction, was unknown in her time.

But let us get back to the Scotch doctor who, I should say, is dignified by the title of 'a doctor of physic'. His scene with the 'waiting gentlewoman' whom we should nowadays call the night nurse, is a medical delight. The doctor begins by casting doubt on the nurse's powers of observation, but when she gives him a detailed account of her patient's behaviour he accepts it, summarizes it intelligently and asks for further details. These the nurse promptly refuses to give, a proceeding which would be frowned upon by any hospital matron that I have ever had anything to do with. The doctor is quite nice about it and tells her that it is the proper thing to do to confide in him, but again she refuses because she has no witnesses and quite obviously fears that she will be disbelieved. As the doctor had begun by telling her that he could perceive no truth in her report, I don't know that I blame her very much. Anyhow, a painful professional bickering is avoided by the entrance of Lady Macbeth.

The best thing the doctor does at this stage is to produce his notebook and make a written record of the case. Apart from that he almost plays second fiddle to the nurse and, finally, he is so staggered by what he hears that he confesses frankly 'this disease is beyond my practice'. I can't remember when I heard a doctor saying that last. Then comes the line 'more needs she the divine than the physician', a phrase which I take to be not a reference to pastoral psychotherapy, of which we hear so much nowadays, but to the moral aspect of the crime the patient has committed. She needs forgiveness rather than psychotherapy, he says, though in those days psychotherapy, as we understand it, was only guessed at. I should say that she needed forgiveness *as well as* psychotherapy. They are two quite distinct things and it is a sad pity that many of the public are so prone to slovenly thinking and to seeking for magic that they fail to realize the fact.

The doctor pulls himself together at the end of the scene and orders continuous observation, the only safe rule if you are dealing with a suicidal patient. He then leaves, confessing frankly that the whole thing has been too much for him and that he dare not say what he thinks. I wish every modern psychiatrist had to learn the whole scene by heart before being allowed to practise.

It is a commonplace in psychiatry that patients' relatives are infinitely more trouble than the patients themselves. I feel sure that the doctor must have been looking forward with but little relish to his interview with Macbeth. For my own part I would rather interview a dozen night nurses, however touchy and austere, than the angry husband of an acutely neurotic patient. I speak from long practical experience of such patients, and such nurses.

By the time the doctor comes to make his report, Macbeth is in such a state of mind that anything the doctor said would have been the trigger to set off an outburst of rage. It would have made no difference if the doctor had merely told him that Mary had a little lamb; he would have flown into a fury just the same.

I must digress for a moment to tell you that I have just come across an extremely interesting essay which, no doubt, many of you know. It was written by a Thomas Whately, who was an Under-Secretary of State and died in 1772. In his essay, which is well worthy of study, he compares and contrasts with great skill and insight, Macbeth and Richard III, pointing out that there are no two characters in Shakespeare who are placed in such parallel circumstances and who yet differ so much in disposition.

They are both kings by usurpation and murder: they both lose their thrones by death in battle, and there are very many parallel situations

N

in the two plays but, through them all Macbeth is the introspective, self-tortured, reluctant villain, while Richard is the clear-headed, whole-hearted, cynical, extraverted one. His cool, crisp, practical orders before the battle of Bosworth are a wonderful contrast to Macbeth's excited outpourings, eloquent indeed, but increasingly disjointed and frenzied, till they merge into the courage of despair.

The unfortunate doctor finds himself standing by, during a fierce and confused conference between Macbeth and his attendants. His report is suddenly demanded, and his non-committal reply, suggesting very tactfully that the patient is really a mental case, prompts the famous speech about ministering to a mind diseased. This speech is a wonderful forecast of modern psychological treatment, written 300 years before Freud, but all I have to say about it just now is simply that the 'mind diseased' about which he is talking is not his wife's, but his own. There is nothing more common among patients' relatives than the attempt, under cover of inquiries about the patient, to obtain information and advice for themselves. The doctor realizes this and very neatly keeps the matter on the general level, saying: 'Therein the patient must minister to himself.' He was too honest to say 'herself' when he knew perfectly well that it was not his wife Macbeth had in mind, and he had too much regard for his own expectation of life to say: 'Therein *you* must minister to *yourself*.'

Next we have the typical laugh-it-off reaction of the man who is terrified in his heart. How often have I observed it in patients' relatives, and with what amazing accuracy and insight has Shakespeare depicted it! First, physic is to go to the dogs. Then, with a strained facetiousness, Macbeth invites the doctor to treat the sick country. Note the reference here, as in *Twelfth Night*, to urine-analysis. Rambling on again in forced, unnatural jocularity, he suggests some good strong purgative to get rid of the English invaders. Finally he asks, with sudden suspicion, how much the doctor knows, makes a last arrogant boast to keep up his courage, and storms out. Who can blame the doctor for his quiet aside with which the scene ends? He does not pretend to be a hero, but his frank acknowledgment that if he could only get out of this he wouldn't come back for any money, at least does some credit to both his profession and his nationality.

Well, there it is. I have run over several scenes and passages in these plays, and I have sandwiched in among them three or four little excursions in everyday language into elementary medical psychology. Whether you have regarded these as the interesting middle bit of the sandwich or as the unpleasant powder with jam round it, I cannot say.

I have tried to avoid reference to the more obvious and hackneyed psychological questions which arise in these plays, and to confine myself to smaller points which are, perhaps, less well-known. I assure you, however, than even from these few plays, I could have selected at least half-a-dozen characters, in addition to those I have discussed, any one of whom would have made an adequate text for a full and interesting medico-psychological lecture: Sir Toby, the chronic alcoholic; Parolles, the spiv; Sir Andrew, the high-grade defective; Olivia, the frustrated, maladjusted spinster; about half the cast of *Titus Andronicus* as sadistic psychopaths; Shallow, the senile, and many others.

Shakespeare's characters—especially his minor ones—are what one might call lightning sketches, drawn from life, rather than profound psychological studies, because he is writing a play, not preparing an essay.

He gives them just a few words—the merest touch here and there. But these touches are so wonderfully and inevitably just right that the characters leap into life and we cannot help filling in the picture for ourselves.

So comes about Shakespeare's greatest miracle: that we regard people who never existed outside his imagination as real and living acquaintances of our own, whom we should know at once, if we met them on leaving this hall.

As I have been speaking, that miracle has once more been at work, on me, at least. I can see Sir Toby at the door of 'The Dirty Duck', hoping to find someone who will stand him a drink. Dogberry and Juliet's nurse are inside it, exchanging verbose reminiscence and pointless anecdote. In the garden, there, Benedick and Mercutio are keeping a party of ladies in fits of laughter—I can see Beatrice, Viola and Rosalind among them—and there, coming down the street, is dear old Peter Quince with a worried look on his face, carrying an enormous basket of stage properties.

If we have got far enough away from the professional critics today to share these feelings and fancies together, I am very glad.

INDEX